Beyond Cairo

Palgrave Macmillan Series in Global Public Diplomacy

At no time in history has public diplomacy played a more significant role in world affairs and international relations. As a result, global interest in public diplomacy has escalated, creating a substantial academic and professional audience for new works in the field.

This series examines theory and practice in public diplomacy from a global perspective, looking closely at public diplomacy concepts, policies, and practices in various regions of the world. The purpose is to enhance understanding of the importance of public diplomacy, to advance public diplomacy thinking, and to contribute to improved public diplomacy practices.

The editors welcome submissions from scholars and practitioners representing a range of disciplines and fields (including diplomacy, international relations, international communications, public relations, political science, global media, marketing/advertising) and offering diverse perspectives. In keeping with its global focus, the series encourages non-U.S.-centric works and comparative studies.

Toward a New Public Diplomacy: Redirecting U.S. Foreign Policy
Edited by Philip Seib

Soft Power in China: Public Diplomacy through Communication
Edited by Jian Wang

Public Diplomacy and Soft Power in East Asia
Edited by Sook Jong Lee and Jan Melissen

The Practice of Public Diplomacy: Confronting Challenges Abroad
Edited by William A. Rugh

The Decline and Fall of the United States Information Agency: American Public Diplomacy, 1989–2001
Nicholas J. Cull

Beyond Cairo: US Engagement with the Muslim World
Darrell Ezell

Beyond Cairo

US Engagement with the Muslim World

Darrell Ezell

Northwest State Community College

First published in 2012 by
PALGRAVE MACMILLAN®
in the United States—a division of St. Martin's Press LLC,
175 Fifth Avenue, New York, NY 10010.

Where this book is distributed in the UK, Europe and the rest of the world,
this is by Palgrave Macmillan, a division of Macmillan Publishers Limited,
registered in England, company number 785998, of Houndmills,
Basingstoke, Hampshire RG21 6XS.

Palgrave Macmillan is the global academic imprint of the above companies
and has companies and representatives throughout the world.

Palgrave® and Macmillan® are registered trademarks in the United States,
the United Kingdom, Europe and other countries.

ISBN: 978–0–230–34094–7

Library of Congress Cataloging-in-Publication Data

Ezell, Darrell, 1979–
    Beyond Cairo : US engagement with the Muslim world / Darrell Ezell.
        p. cm.—(Global public diplomacy)
    ISBN 978–0–230–34094–7 (hardback)
        1. United States—Relations—Islamic countries.
    2. Islamic countries—Relations—United States.
    3. Diplomatic and consular service, American. I. Title.

JZ1480.A55E84 2012
327.73017'67—dc23   2012022288

A catalogue record of the book is available from the British Library.

Design by Newgen Imaging Systems (P) Ltd., Chennai, India.

First edition: December 2012

10 9 8 7 6 5 4 3 2 1

Transferred to Digital Printing in 2013

To my dearest mother, Mattie

CONTENTS

TABLES

ACKNOWLEDGMENTS

This book project grew out of my doctoral research question that surveys the role the US Department of State must consider when engaging religion-based societies. With the dedication and support of advisers, friends, family, and conversations with wanderers spanning the globe, this question has materialized into a meaningful body of work committed to improving US–Muslim world relations.

I greatly appreciate my colleagues in the Department of Political Science and the International Studies Program at Louisiana State University for their dedicated support. Special thanks are given to Dean Gaines Foster, Leonard Ray, and James R. Stoner for providing me the opportunity to exercise my academic prowess, which includes teaching courses in international politics and global public diplomacy while completing this book. In this regard, I am grateful for the brilliance of Palgrave Macmillan's Global Public Diplomacy books series editors, Philip Seib and Kathy Fitzpatrick and for considering this manuscript as significant. Working with my editorial director, Farideh Koohi-Kamali, editorial assistant, Sarah Nathan, and production associate, Ciara Vincent, has been a rewarding professional experience.

My initial survey on improving US–Muslim relations encountered slight resistance in parts of the United States in 2004. I am, however, indebted to Scott Lucas and David Cheetham at the University of Birmingham in England who jointly supervised my doctoral studies. Additional thanks are due to Josef Boehle and Giles Scott-Smith for their honest critique and examination of my doctoral dissertation. Further thanks are offered to the Department of American and Canadian Studies, The Center for US Foreign Policy in Birmingham, and the Department of Theology and Religion for granting me an opportunity to conduct joint interdisciplinary studies in religion and diplomacy. I am grateful for the Nali Dinshaw Foundation for granting a scholarship to advance my studies on interfaith relations, and the University of Birmingham's Roberts Funding Scheme for aiding my research in EU studies in 2006 as well as providing further bursary assistance to conduct two field research projects in the United States.

I am deeply appreciative of the US Department of State for granting me an opportunity to work in 2007 with the Office of Peacekeeping, Sanctions, and Counter-terrorism that resulted in expanding my familiarity with US public diplomacy. Special thanks are owed to Ambassador Harry K. Thomas and James Dandridge for their mentorship, and to Dennis Hankins, Anne O' Leary, Col. Lawrence Mrozinski, Kathy Davis, and Wes Moore for their steadfast advisement that led to the completion of my postgraduate studies. I also offer deep appreciation to the University of Arkansas Clinton School of Public Service and The William J. Clinton Foundation for providing the space to allow me to conduct my practicum. Designing the "Post-secular Communicative Framework" would not have been possible without James L. "Skip" Rutherford and the counsel of Michael R. Hemphill with his cutting-edge views on social constructionism. Matt Weiner (The Interfaith Center of New York) and Kimberly Bo Bo (Interfaith Worker Justice), thank you for granting me the opportunity to practice interfaith dialogue at the grassroots level in New York and Chicago as a tool to resolve religious conflicts as a graduate student studying political theology at Union Theological Seminary.

This book would not be possible without the instruction of several experts and scholars who offered comments and encouragement on this manuscript over the last two years, particularly Akbar Ahmed, Lee Williams II, Charles Mercieca, Noor Gillani, Col. James R. Johnson, Col. James O. Heyward, Rev. Patrick and Sheri Clayborn, E. G. McIntosh, Douglas Turner, and Leadership Huntsville/Madison County. Appreciation is also extended to my dearest family and friends for their prayers and unceasing support. Thank you for your encouragement through the joy and pain when my internal light was dim— Harvey L. Robinson, Walter B. Harris, Katara Jackson, Carlos Cardenas, Steven and Dixie Berrios, Raymond Nomel, Kenneth Flowers, Juliane Honisch, Roderick Grice, Darla Price, and Montraze Slater.

My deepest thanks are owed to my mother, Mattie Ezell, for her unfailing support. Without your love, I would never have envisioned that I might achieve any goal that I put my mind to.

Introduction

The Muslim world, 58 countries and territories with significant Muslim publics, is one of the most rapidly expanding demographics that will command the attention of public diplomacy practitioners in the foreseeable future. The challenge for Western nations in recent years has included balancing their global interests against the disdain projected by a relatively small clan of extremists. Among several lessons the last decade has taught us, it is evident that a communication problem exists between the United States and Muslim world that neither the *Obama effect* nor upgrading public diplomacy programs can solve, apparently. After September 11, 2001, both US foreign policy and American public diplomacy reflected a narrow reading of the Muslim world as a homogenous society acceptable to traditional secular communication. As the battle to win the hearts and minds of global Islamic communities intensified, global public diplomacy practitioners and ambassadors informed the US Department of State that its antiquated public diplomacy apparatus was misguided.[1] Their shared perspectives implied that only more direct measures operating from the bottom up could ensure a positive outcome.

Against this backdrop, the American public's choice to elect Illinois's Senator Barack Hussein Obama as the 44th president of the United States of America in 2008 represented an unparalleled period in American history, pointing toward a new political era in Washington. From the outset, both Obama loyalists and critics alike pondered on whether a one-term senator turned US president was capable of balancing a polarized nation, while delivering on political promises to the international community. Amid a global economic crisis creating an inhospitable environment to fulfill the colossal task of restoring America's ailing economy, efforts to balance increasing US national security concerns throughout the Middle East, and addressing the Pentagon's military objectives on the battlefield in South Asia have both obstructed opportunities to restore relations based on mutual trust with Muslim majority audiences. Shortsighted goals coupled with symbolic gestures pursued under the Bush and Obama administrations frame Washington's post-9/11 public diplomacy strategy to reach Muslim audiences.

Looking back at the months prior to 9/11, the State Department had implemented a shortsighted public diplomacy campaign to win the *hearts and minds* of global Islamic communities by upgrading academic programs, increasing foreign aid to Middle East allies, and depleting US political and military capital in Afghanistan and Iraq. More than a decade later, perceptions of America continue to decline, suggesting both a failure of foreign policy and a breakdown of public diplomacy. The once enthusiastic commitment to restore trust with Muslims has dwindled considerably since Obama's "A New Beginning" address in Cairo, Egypt. This book draws on the attempt by a US president to use his leverage as the leader of the world's dominant state to motivate 1.5 billions Muslims to quell tension and help in reducing America's increasing trust deficit. The central argument of this book proposes that the White House and State Department move beyond relying on symbols, as demonstrated in Cairo, to consider a more practicable and realistic response that reaches the core of global Islamic communities.

Beyond Cairo

On June 4, 2009, Obama embarked on the groundbreaking mission to improve America's standing with the Muslim world, delivering the watershed address, "A New Beginning" at Cairo University. The US president's visit marked the administration's first major attempt at "extending a hand to the Muslim world,"[2] amid tensions surrounding a potentially nuclear Iran. Just a year later the Arab world would become engulfed in subsequent uprisings. Despite being criticized for promoting a new way forward, Obama appointed Farah A. Pandith as US Special Representative to Muslim Communities and Special Envoy Rashad Hussain to the Organization of Islamic Cooperation. In addition, several discontinued academic/cultural exchanges and public diplomacy programs targeting Muslim women and youth were reinstated, special envoy visits to Muslim majority countries were launched, and State Department officials extended Bush era engagement measures that overlapped one-way public diplomacy and nation-branding practices, while maintaining a narrow outreach agenda limited primarily to Arab audiences. Considering the Obama administration's innovative measures, why then are confidence levels in American leadership and efforts to fulfill promises made at Cairo dwindling? Is it feasible we assume that one-way communication tools are sufficient to engage religion-based societies that generally practice two-way communication as a primary communicative action?

In answering the question of whether Washington's political promise to engage the Muslim world was foiled by inexpert critical judgment, this book explores the origin of Washington's political apprehensiveness toward religion in the public sphere, and the impact of neoconservative special interests to guide American foreign policy and its communication apparatus after 9/11. Did US neoconservative special interests groups purposely derail forward-thinking efforts to engage global Islamic communities? Has the misconception that America is a Christian nation eroded the reassurance of the concept of religious pluralism as offered under the Establishment Clause? These and other essential questions are surveyed in parallel with the concepts explored in *Beyond Cairo*, which establish the most significant moment under Barack Obama's 2009–2012 term, when an American president publicly introduced measures to engage the Muslim world—though many overlooked the need to build long-term relations with nonelite Muslims at the grassroots level.

The conceptual structure of *Beyond Cairo* addresses the notion that short-term symbolic gestures are effective in winning hearts and minds. From a philosophical position, the concept of moving beyond Cairo proposes that the White House and State Department not rest upon the laurels acquired from Obama's "New Beginning Address." Therefore, *Beyond Cairo* insinuates that US government officials in particular:

- Acknowledge that US policymaking has entered the postsecular era (a period of an unprecedented worldwide resurgence in religious activity confronting international relations) necessitating that state actors become cognizant of religious aspirations as they set out to restore trust with Muslim majority audiences;
- Evaluate the State Department's unsuccessful secular communication approaches that often overlook implementing trained experts to carry out two-way engagement at the grassroots level;
- Give consideration to expanding US-Muslim outreach beyond its narrow fixation on the Arab world, thereby including broad

US-Muslim engagement opportunities in African and South East Asian countries where religion-based conflict and sectarian strife are salient; and

• Overcome preconceived myths in the US political sphere about the religion of Islam and of Muslims at home and abroad as provoked by conservative special interests in Washington.

Maintaining a Sustained Effort

Despite shifting America's foreign interest in 2011 to the Asia-Pacific region, which includes increasing America's military presence in northern Australia to deter a rising China and an unstable North Korea, key political decisions and security concerns guarantee that US-Muslim outreach must remain at the front and center as a major national security priority over the next decade or more. Meeting with Afghan president, Hamid Karzai on May 2, 2012, Obama signed an agreement on future cooperation to keep US troops in Afghanistan until 2024 (despite a 2014 drawdown). This single measure is capable of inciting tension that is likely to span the next three US presidential administrations.

From America's relations with the Jewish state of Israel to its transcontinental energy partnership with Saudi Arabia, both the US government and key private sector industries for nearly a century have destabilized the Middle East region, placing new demands on the role of public diplomacy in connecting with Muslim audiences. The spread of Islamist teaching in madrassas in Pakistan, the undetermined direction of the Arab Spring (with the rise of new political actors such as the Muslim Brotherhood in Egypt), and interestingly, the frequent collapse of Middle East peace talks indicate that stronger measures that function from the bottom up are required. If this is the case, then attention at the grassroots level of the nonelite base should serve as focus of the State Department's central public diplomacy in the coming decade.

These and other security measures such as civil strife and increasing death tolls in religion-based countries due to intractable conflict reinforce the argument on why sustained public diplomacy measures with the Muslim world are significant to maintaining US national security. Just over the last few years, new media tools and investigative reporting have shed light on internal events taking place in Afghanistan, which were successful at unsettling the emotions of Muslims while enraging insurgents. This was highlighted by the murders and decapitation of Afghan civilians by a four-man US soldier "Kill Team" in the spring of 2010, videos of American soldiers urinating on the corpses of dead Taliban fighters in January 2012, the desecration of the Quran at Bagram Air Field Military Base that led to over 40 retaliatory deaths in February 2012, the mass murder of 16 innocent civilians in Kandahar province by US Army Staff Sergeant Robert Bales in March 2012, and controversial photos uncovered by the *Los Angeles Times* in April 2012 depicting US paratroopers posing with the remains of suicide bombers. Both the Quran burning and Kandahar massacre are irreconcilable incidents, which send the message to global Islamic communities that neither the United States nor its military forces respect the religious infrastructure of the Afghan people, which infuriates some people, while making others more vulnerable to the Taliban's and al-Qaeda's ideology regarding the West. Arguably, these incendiary developments are a direct result of Washington's haphazard efforts to deliver successful results, which often means dealing with failures in intelligence and launching counterinsurgency operations at an accelerated rate that are rooted in a *success-over-understanding* posture. This form of activity centers especially on discounting key human rights and socioreligious elements that are instrumental to religion-based societies.

This book argues that the key alternative for Washington at this juncture is ensuring all measures to sustain efforts that work toward repairing the US–Muslim world trust deficit. This must include prescribing a shift in the mentality of: (i) how state actors approach religious issues in international relations, (ii) consideration toward the value of both secular and sacred actors engaged in the dialogical setting, and (iii) implementing expertise to restore relations from the bottom up. Making sense of these measures, Phillip M. Taylor reminds us, "You can't fight a war against an idea, at least not with tanks and bombs and missiles. That is why the West is losing the propaganda war and why it will continue to lose it, and indeed make it harder to win...It needs to recognize that if it continues to be waged with hard power it will not be the 'Long War' but the 'Forever War.'"[3]

Making the Case

Beyond Cairo explores a set of new challenges confronting the formation of the relationship between state and nonstate actors, in the context of the State Department's post-9/11 collapse of public diplomacy with the Muslim world. This new postsecular era invites new challenges that traditional state-to-state actor diplomacy is incapable of handling. The case is made here that restoring US-Muslim world engagement begins with revitalizing the mindset of US state actors, in an era demanding competence in religio-cultural understanding and awareness of a society's social terrain. America's awkward relationship with religion in the public sphere is the reason behind its disastrously ineffective strategy to reach out to Muslims, whether by keeping them at arm's length via one-way communication, or by relying on short-term symbolic gestures.

This book will focus on the role of US public diplomacy as considered and pursued after 9/11 in three parts. Part 1: "Demystifying the Communication Game" explores a set of immediate challenges that over the last decade or more have disrupted US-Muslim world communicative relations. Whether relying on state-centric approaches or on fear manufactured by neoconservative special interest groups, I argue that a reassessment of Washington's narrow political mindset is essential to promote broad measures that include a "new public diplomacy" that helps to cultivate relations between state/nonstate actors. Chapter One makes the argument that rather than the US Department of State setting out to establish trust or applying consistent two-way communication opportunities that function from the bottom up, its post-9/11 public diplomacy response relied on antiquated one-way communication tools that led to an increased trust deficit with the Muslim world. Chapter Two debunks the communication game by exploring the role of fear manufactured by conservative forces and the influence of American Judeo-Christian special interests groups as two divisive forces injurious to US policy on Muslim world outreach. Chapter Three sharpens this analysis by focusing on the evolving "new public diplomacy" argument that introduces both broad and innovative measures to enrich state and nonstate actor engagement. The general argument here is that a new way of thinking rooted in tolerance and dedicated to pursuing dialogue-based public diplomacy is the practicable way forward with predominantly religious audiences.

Part 2: "Crusading US National Security" explores the influence and impact of conservative-led religious and academic theories that shaped US policymakers attitudes and the American public diplomacy environment between 2001 and 2008. Here we will survey how the State Department engaged the Muslim world through communication and why a "neocon" led agenda disrupted the establishment of long-term sustainable efforts. Chapter Four explores several dimensions of post-9/11 public diplomacy, thereby moving beyond "what" precisely contributed to distorting the engagement process to "how" exactly neoconservative-led interests derailed efforts to build trust. Chapter Five evaluates how this influence coupled by the absence of a dialogue-based public diplomacy approach hampered outreach efforts during the Bush era. Attention is given in this chapter to the epic failure of Charlotte Beers and Karen P. Hughes and their executive-level efforts to overlap nation branding and public diplomacy measures to sell America's values to Muslim audiences. Chapter Six provides an analysis of the Obama Doctrine on US Muslim Outreach, a set of formal policies and positions employed between 2009 and 2011. This chapter defends the position that a commitment to restore trust with the Muslim world requires dialogue-based public diplomacy measures that set out to convene state and nonstate actors in a dialogical setting at the grassroots level.

By accomplishing this task, Part 3: "Reshaping the Communicative Context" will establish a new path to engaging Muslim audiences by proposing a new framework to carry out a shift in diplomatic mentality, communication strategy, and representation. Considerable emphasis is given in this last section to the dialogical function of effective state/nonstate actor engagement and postsecular communication as a tool to enrich dialogical opportunities. It is against the backdrop of the Arab Spring that the case is made in chapter seven that Washington was blindsided because a communication structure capable of getting feedback from the grassroots perspectives was nonexistent. This chapter proposes that both the White House and State Department take into consideration seasoned proposals prescribing the establishment of a new corps of specialists adept in religion and culture to pursue dialogue-based engagement with key nonstate actors in the Muslim world. Chapter Eight facilitates this measure by introducing an efficient postsecular communication approach to enrich dialogical opportunities between state and nonstate actors that reach beyond short-term measures and symbolic gestures.

Postsecular communication will be explored through an examination of two prominent communication theories (The Theory of Communicative Action and Coordinated Management of Meaning). Postsecular communication is the art of embracing a new mindset to craft two-way communication opportunities that acknowledge the impact of religion and citizens' views about geopolitics by fostering cooperative engagement between the sacred and the secular. When both intersect, they provide a foundation to commence effective postsecular communication training. While working within this new framework, members of this new corps will be able to engage across sacred-secular lines freely from the bottom up. In such a framework, a new corps of actors will be able to employ traditional diplomatic approaches while practicing a new public diplomacy approach that incorporates state/ nonstate actor aspirations.

This book will serve as a companion for policymakers and practitioners in their quest to comprehend the intricacies of the communication problem between Washington and the Muslim world and recent limitations in pursuing a new way forward. In addition to its contribution to the US policymaking community, this book offers a set of cross-cultural recommendations for global nongovernmental bodies and private sector establishments in their endeavor to engage religion-based demographics as the Muslim world. As the relationship between the private and public becomes an increasingly important topic in global affairs, the cross-cultural analyst will benefit by drawing upon this study as a case, to conclude that religion-based societies warrant direct two-way engagement in order to establish effectual relations.

PART 1

Demystifying the Communication Game

CHAPTER ONE

Engaging the Muslim World

The future of American public diplomacy is an important and increasingly popular topic of inquiry as anti-Americanism dominates parts of the Arab and larger Muslim world. Debate between American think tanks pursuing private foreign policy agendas and contemporary public diplomacy practitioners in search of a new way forward offers an appropriate starting point to assess a new set of challenges confronting Washington's most vital communication apparatus. While American public diplomacy experienced relative success during the Cold War era, a turning point, months prior to and after 9/11, illustrated that an outmoded one-way transmission model of communication coupled with contemporary nation-branding approaches was no match when selling America to a value-defined, religion-based, and socially constructed Arab world. During this period, a paradox emerged with America's post-9/11 communication efforts, which moved counter to the foundational goals of public diplomacy. This chapter argues that rather than establishing trust or applying long-term two-way communication opportunities with global Islamic communities, America's post-9/11 public diplomacy response centered on short-term one-sided messaging leading to a wider trust deficit with the Muslim world. Therefore, three principal components contributed to the paradox and failure of post-9/11 public diplomacy: (i) the promotion of adverse foreign policies to target key audiences in the Arab world against the backdrop of a chaotic history of US-Mid East foreign relations, (ii) relying on short-term messaging that overlapped public diplomacy with nation branding, and (iii) discounting the role of both religion and culture when analyzing the social terrain of target audiences in the Muslim world. As several post-9/11 public diplomacy attempts failed at connecting with Arab audiences, a renewal in strategy and representation are required in a new global era where nonstate actors are increasingly vital in setting the international agenda.

New Realities

According to the dominant theoretical approach in analyzing international relations, political realism proposes that states are the most important actors in the international system. It claims that the state exists in a dangerous and anarchic world, where the pursuit of national interests is accompanied by the desire of the states to acquire power at any cost. Since signing the Peace of Westphalia in 1648—ending the Thirty Years' War that led to the creation of the modern nation-state—political realism has become influential in Western political thought, dominating the interest of states and state actors in the Westphalian system for nearly four centuries.

The premise of traditional realism is accentuated in the three S's, or what is considered its widely held beliefs: *statism, survival,* and *self-help.* *Statism* asserts that nation-states are the main actors and preserving state sovereignty is a principal trait in statecraft. This belief is held in high regard in the realist tradition, considering the conviction that nation-states are born out of war and are destined to place national and security interests over morality and ideology. "For realists, ideologies do not matter much, nor do religions or other cultural factors with which states may justify their actions."[1] Furthering this perspective, noted political realist Hans Morgenthau maintains in the "Six Principles of Political Realism" that "For realism, theory consists in ascertaining facts and giving them meaning through reason."[2] In this tradition, both the subjects of religion and ideology are regarded as nonsecular elements that are largely incomprehensible if approached through intellectual deductive reasoning. This state-centric approach in international relations produces a critical reading of legitimacy, thereby discounting the religious and cultural perspectives held by nonstate actors are unjustifiable, creating a new set of challenges in this post–Cold War era.

The second principle, *survival,* asserts that the state must ensure its interests, which generally result from the accumulation of power within the international system, whether acquired through peaceful or violent means. According to political realists, power is regarded as a precondition for a state to achieve its supreme national interests to become the dominant state within the international system. Survival and the preservation of state sovereignty rest upon the third principle, *self-help.* The basis of this tenet contends that the state must rely solely on itself for survival, therefore, pursuing national interests may prove detrimental within an international system perceived as anarchic.

As the three S's underscore, the widely held realist tradition, political realism, as an influential global worldview, is confronted in this global era by a set of new realities that crystallize the fact that states and state actors are no longer the principal agents shaping the international agenda. Liberal secular Western nations today are having to readjust to this reality that is forcing state actors within the United States and Britain to acknowledge the liberal or idealist perspective in international relations that *true survival* and *peaceful coexistence* between states no longer hinges on power politics or trumpeting military power. Peaceful coexistence and true survival between states in this era rely more on effective diplomatic communication between actors. In addition to the first reality, the second acknowledges that the realist tradition is challenged on the basis of its worldview that discounts morality and ideology as nonlegitimate matters in world politics. An emerging new reality confronting the realist worldview is shaped in part by the fact that moral and cultural ideals are moving center stage, creating intrastate clashes between state and nonstate actors linked to worldwide religious movements. This is marked in the new global era by the proliferation of nonstate actors or *new players* and their presence in setting the international agenda. Hence, the ongoing shift toward a new reality and proliferation of *new players* is of particular interest to traditional diplomacy and especially the practice of contemporary public diplomacy.

Traditional diplomacy—the practice of nation-state negotiation or *negociation continuelle*—is conducted by state actors on behalf of governments so that they might achieve their national interests. G. R. Berridge informs us that, "Diplomacy is an essentially political activity and, a well resourced, and skillful, and major ingredient of power. Its chief purpose is to enable states to secure their objects of their foreign policies without resort to force, propaganda, or law. It follows that diplomacy consists of communication between officials designed to promote foreign policy either by formal agreement or tacit adjustment."[3] Since the end of the Cold War, it is evident that many US state actors are forced to adjust from their traditional state-centric posture to reconsider the perspectives and ideals of the *new players*. This includes moving away from discounting the aspirations and perspectives, especially those of nonelites living in traditional societies that are socially constructed, culturally diverse, and religion-based, as they are throughout the Muslim world.

Communication theorist, R. S. Zaharna, captures this perspective in the study, *Battle to Bridges*. She highlights that in this new global era there are generally four different types of nonstate actors that include: *transnational corporations* who exchange more than a trillion dollars a day in international markets; *nongovernmental organizations* that increased from 176 in 1909 to an estimated 62,036 in 2008; *international media outlets* that are privately owned and are driven by a 24/7 news cycle; and *prominent individuals* and *private actors* as, for example, celebrities like UN Goodwill Ambassadors.[4] While these particular *new players* are gaining prominence, it is the emergence of nonelite players living in religion-based societies who are linked to transnational movements that present unparallel challenges to nation-states and state actors. Such actors are significant to the discussion in this study. For this reason, we look to Jan Melissen's description of the current adjustment underway in the field of diplomacy. He writes:

> Diplomacy in a traditionalist view is depicted as a game where the roles and responsibilities of actors in international relations are clearly delineated. This picture no longer resembles the much more fuzzy world of postmodern transnational relations—a world, for that matter, in which most actors are not nearly as much in control as they would like to be. Moreover, the interlocutors of today's foreign service officers are not necessarily their counterparts, but a wide variety of people that are either involved in diplomatic activity or are on the receiving end of international politics.[5]

Melissen's description of the present sea change transpiring in international politics is led by a demand for transnational cooperation that emerges when states and state actors adjust their traditional posture to accept the presence of new players, thereby, providing a new opportunity to ensure peaceful coexistence within the international system. "Such openness and multi-level cooperation calls for the active pursuit of more collaborative diplomatic relations with various types of actors."[6] This adjustment is of particular interest to the practice of American public diplomacy. Hence, if this adjustment is required by states and nonstate actors to ensure peaceful coexistence in this new era, it is of equal importance that we assess how either consideration toward or discounting of this shift may impact the practice of US state-nonstate actor engagement.

The Role of Public Diplomacy

As is the case with most fields of study that are shaped by international events and critical periods in history, global public diplomacy is currently evolving in both concept and practice. Unlike most terms in the field of political science, public diplomacy lacks what some practitioners may regard as a universally accepted definition that contextualizes both concept and practice. For this reason, the term *propaganda* is often applied interchangeably with public diplomacy, though both have what some will agree are two different meanings.

Generally defined as the dissemination of deceptive or misleading information, for centuries the practice of propaganda (with origins reaching far back to the Catholic Church's 1622 declaration against Protestants, *Sacra Congregatio de Propaganda Fide*) has maintained a disturbing undertone yielding references to *manipulation* and *deception*. Fullerton and Kendrick denote in their study that "propaganda is neutrally defined as a systemic form of persuasion which attempts to influence the emotions, attitudes, opinions, and action of specific target audiences for ideological, political or commercial purposes through the controlled transmission of one-sided messages (which may or may not be factual) via mass and direct media channels."[7] Propaganda as a communicative action seeks to benefit the "propagandist" or the nation disseminating propaganda, rather than building two-way channels with foreign audiences.

Thus, the principal difference between propaganda and public diplomacy hinges primarily on the intention of both the message and the messenger. Where propaganda is generally concerned with one-sided communication, in contrast, public diplomacy is a communicative process concerned with building two-way communication between states and foreign audiences with the purpose of influencing public opinion. Coined by former US Foreign Service officer and dean of the Fletcher School of Law and Diplomacy in 1965, Edmund Gullion contends that public diplomacy "encompasses dimensions of international relations beyond traditional diplomacy; the cultivation by governments of public opinion in other countries; the interaction of private groups and interests in one country with another; the reporting of foreign affairs and its impact on policy communication between those whose job is communicating, as diplomats and foreign correspondents; and the process of intercultural communication."[8]

In recent years, as the new and expanding field evolves, so does its definition. According to the USC Center on Public Diplomacy at the Annenberg School:

> In the past few decades, *public diplomacy* has been widely seen as the transparent means by which a sovereign country communicates

with publics in other countries aimed at informing and influencing audiences overseas for the purpose of promoting the national interest and advancing its foreign policy goals. In this traditional view, public diplomacy is seen as an integral part of state-to-state diplomacy, by which is meant the conduct of official relations, typically in private, between official representatives (leaders and diplomats) representing sovereign states. In this sense, public diplomacy includes such activities as educational exchange programs for scholars and students; visitor programs; language training; cultural events and exchanges; and radio and television broadcasting. Such activities usually focused on improving the "sending" country's image or reputation as a way to shape the wider policy environment in the "receiving" country.[9]

This description can be summarized as three foundational elements of global public diplomacy that generally include: (i) gathering perspectives held by foreign audiences, (ii) assessing those perspectives which includes developing programs (or exchanges) to aid in competing with negative perceptions held within a foreign audience, and (iii) applying two-way communicative engagement with foreign audiences to strengthen foreign relations. Shedding light on this perspective with regard to American public diplomacy, Ambassador William Rugh says:

Public diplomacy can be defined as informing, engaging, and influencing foreign publics in support of a country's national interests. Public diplomacy professionals work towards these ends in several ways. First, they help explain to foreign audiences the rationale for the policies of the administration in office, as well as the American public's support for these policies. Second, they help these audiences understand American society and culture. Third, they provide policymakers with information about and analysis of, foreign public opinion about U.S. interests.[10]

Emerging into the two-way process that is present today, Gyorgy Szondi takes the position that American public diplomacy was shaped particularly by the Cold War and is divided into three different stages. The first extends over a period of four decades, when American ideals were projected throughout Eastern Europe between the 1940s and early 1990s. The second began with the collapse of the Berlin Wall, when American public diplomacy entered a dormant period resulting from budgetary cuts, and the Clinton administration merging the United States Information Agency (USIA) public diplomacy apparatus into the US Department of State. The second stage, however, was marked by the attack of the World Trade Center and what is regarded as post-9/11 public diplomacy. The third stage (or post-9/11 era) is defined, to a large extent, by the missteps and current adjustments underway toward the presence of new influential nonstate actors shaping the aspirations and perspectives of audiences in parts of the Muslim world.[11]

As covered later in this chapter, several months prior to and after 9/11 the State Department had concurred with other vital US agencies that America suffered from an explicit image problem induced by both an American history of inconsistent foreign policies in the Middle East, and by post-9/11 military activities in Afghanistan and Iraq. Thus, to a large extent, American public diplomacy throughout this third stage has focused primarily on projecting a message that works in conjunction with the US military agenda to combat terror and the spread of anti-Americanism. Entangled in a battle to win hearts and minds, Philip Seib suggests that too many American public diplomacy ventures in this third phase are "rooted in cold war-era thinking and are most noteworthy for their lack of imagination. Not surprisingly, they are not accomplishing what needs to be done."[12]

Holding to nostalgic approaches that were vital to the USIA in its dissemination of propaganda to combat the spread of Communism and efforts to conduct outreach behind the Iron Curtain, key State Department actors prior to and after 9/11 suffered from a lack of coherence on why two-way communication and relationship-based strategies were necessary to promote transnational cooperation. The emphasis under George W. Bush's administration included applying a short-term communication approach that moved parallel with Washington's military and intelligence objectives.

> Against this emotional backdrop, getting America's message out became Washington's goal, while the Arab and Islamic world became Washington's primary target audience. Not only were the hijackers from this area, but it was also where many believed the U.S. image was most distorted. The two-prong goal of U.S. public diplomacy entailed promoting U.S. values, while trying to marginalize and isolate the terrorists' messages...They repeatedly voiced concerns that the war on terrorism appeared to be a war of civilizations pitting the West against Islam.[13]

Despite the well-funded and robust one-way communication efforts to engage the Arab and Muslim worlds by the State Department after 9/11, public diplomacy practitioners are comprehending that a set of broad and holistic strategies that seek to accommodate a new set of players in international relations is imperative to ensure US national security. Regarded as the "new public diplomacy," its conception and practice stands in distinction to traditional public diplomacy, which is essentially state-centric and vaguely recognizes the vital importance of engagement with nonstate actors.

> This view aims to capture the emerging trends in international relations where a range of non-state actors with some standing in world politics—supranational organizations, sub-national actors, non-governmental organizations, and (in the view of some) even private companies—communicate and engage meaningfully with foreign publics and thereby develop and promote public diplomacy policies and practices of their own...As a result, a new public diplomacy is seen as taking place in a system of mutually beneficial relations that is no longer state-centric but composed of multiple actors and networks, operating in a fluid global environment of new issues and contexts.[14]

While several studies investigate why post-9/11 American public diplomacy failed, here we will assess this failure in the context of the current sea change in international politics linked to new demands presented by a new era ridden by polarization. In doing so, we will comprehend how a narrow post-9/11 American public diplomacy campaign failed in its attempt in building relations with the Muslim world. As the foundational elements of public diplomacy focus on promoting broad opportunities that are inclusive, it is evident why failure occurred, and how post-9/11 public diplomacy is regarded as paradoxical, due especially to: (i) America's adverse foreign policy in the Arab and larger Muslim world, (ii) the State Department's application of one-sided messaging attempts that overlapped public diplomacy with nation branding, and (iii) discounting the role of religion and culture when analyzing the social terrain of Muslim majority nations.

Adverse Foreign Policymaking

Washington's foreign policy goals over the last decade revolved around securing America's energy interest and the spread of democracy within

Muslim majority countries in an effort to curb global terrorism. In meeting these demands, a clear reality stands that the United States, in its dealings with Arab nations, for more than half a century, has never held consistent foreign relations with Muslim audiences. Recalling America's energy interest and the demand for "Islamic oil" in the Arab world, Juan Cole writes:

> Among the major drivers of Islamic Anxiety is the dependence of the United State and its major allies on petroleum and gas produced in the Persian Gulf. As the twenty-first century unfolds, and as oil producers with shallow reserves exhaust them, and as those producers with growing economies export less and less, the world will increasingly depend on Islamic oil. The United States' status as a global superpower was built on the basis of cheap energy, including coal, petroleum, and natural gas. Petroleum underpins America's entire transportation system, and hence [its] way of life.[15]

Over the last decade, the concentration of American foreign policy to curb Islamic anxiety—*that leads to terrorism and asymmetrical warfare*—was led by the Bush administration's commitment to promoting democratization. Committed to the democratic peace thesis, the Bush White House and State Department built its argument on their right to enter Iraq upon the conception that liberal democratic states generally show restraint in their relationship with other democracies and they should stand together against authoritarian states—though several limitations to this argument exist. Esposito reminds us that, "It is against this backdrop that the United States desires stable, secular democracies in the Muslim countries it views as supporting terrorism, with the successful creation of such democracies being the ultimate measure of victory in the 'war on terrorism.'"[16]

Both America's energy interests and its agenda on democratization throughout the Arab world contributed to a historical process of adverse foreign policymaking that undermined post-9/11 public diplomacy efforts. Ensuring Washington's foreign policy agenda required leading a Western-led military campaign in two predominantly Muslim countries, while employing one-sided public diplomacy initiatives to pacify global Islamic communities. These one-sided transmission models of communication moved from Washington to the Muslim world as the aspirations and perspective of nonelites fell upon deaf ears. In American foreign policy, Melissen points out that the aims of public diplomacy are not achievable

> if they are believed to be inconsistent with a country's foreign policy or military actions. US policies towards the Middle East or its military presence in Iraq, for instance, undermine the credibility of public diplomacy... Another lesson from the US experience is that sound policies may be of enormous support to public diplomacy, but that money and muscle are no guarantee for success. The availability of unparalleled financial and media resources does not prevent small non-state actors, even terrorists, from being more successful in their dealing with critical international audiences.[17]

However, in recent years several debates and public enquiries have surfaced on the failure of US-Arab and larger Muslim world public diplomacy efforts. Though misreading the social and religious terrain of Muslim majority countries and the application of one-sided messaging severely crippled the State Department's public diplomacy efforts, its principal failure is linked to Washington's well-established and adverse foreign policy in the Arab world.

For example, over the last half-century, Washington's commitment to the Jewish state raises suspicions throughout the Arab world about whether the United States is a trusted partner in the international system. As expressed in public opinions taken from Arab audiences, findings reveal that suspicion toward America is linked to Washington's affiliation with a loose coalition of individuals, conservative special interest groups, and think tanks dedicated to steering American foreign policy in a pro-Israel direction. Regarding the American public sentiment, Noam Chomsky contends,

> A large majority of Americans oppose U.S. government policy and support the international consensus on a two-state settlement—in recent polls, it's called the "Saudi Plan," referring to the position of the Arab League, supported by virtually the entire world apart from the United States and Israel. Furthermore, a large majority think that the United States should deny aid to either of the contending parties—Israel and the Palestine—if they do not negotiate in good faith toward this element. This is one of a great many illustrations of a huge gap between public opinion and public policy on critical issues.[18]

Thus, two general arguments surround Washington's unwavering support for Israel. The first argument that Israel is a strategic asset is often presented by US state actors, alluding to America's strong bilateral relationship with the Jewish state that serves the strategic purpose of disrupting pan-Arab nationalism and ensuring that transnational corporations meet their energy interest in the region. This is substantiated by America's increasing financial support to Israel. Presently, Israel is the largest cumulative recipient of US foreign assistance of nearly $3 billion in annual grants.

Outlined in the September 2010 CRS Report for Congress, Jeremy Shark points to Israel's strategic asset status.

> For decades, the United States and Israel have maintained strong bilateral relations based on a number of factors, including strong domestic U.S. support for Israel; shared strategic goals in the Middle East (concern over Iran, Syria, Islamic extremism); shared democratic values; and historic ties dating from U.S. support for the creation of Israel in 1948. U.S. foreign aid has been a major component in cementing and reinforcing these ties.[19]

The second argument implies that America's support for the Jewish state is underpinned by a moral rationale. This position is taken, for example, by conservative academics like Bernard Lewis who declare that US-Israeli bilateral relations must be located in a moral context, denoting the current resurgence of political Islam as a piercing threat to Israel and the United States and the West's Judeo-Christian values. The controversial Mearsheimer and Walt study argues that America's moral support for Israel rests on several contentious arguments. These include:

> Specifically, Israel is said to deserve generous and nearly unconditional U.S. support because it is weak and surrounded by enemies dedicated to destroying it; it is a democracy, which is a morally preferable form of government; the Jewish people have suffered greatly from past crimes; Israel's conduct has been morally superior to its adversaries' behaviour, especially compared to the Palestinians; the Palestinians rejected the generous peace offer that Israel made at Camp David in July 2000 and opted for violence instead; and its is clear from the Bible that Israel's creation is God's will. Taken together, these arguments underpin the more general claim that Israel is the one country in the Middle East that shares

American values and therefore enjoys broad support among the American people.[20]

Claims that the Jewish state is either a strategic asset or America's moral responsibility are impressed upon by both Washington and a loose coalition of state actors with motives, either to disrupt the spread of pan-Arab nationalism, or to promote a narrow agenda that ensures US national security and transnational energy interests are met at the expense of regional instability. Influential nongovernmental special interest groups instrumental in steering America's foreign policy agenda include, for example, the American Israel Public Affairs Committee with ties to the US Congress, Pastor John Hagee's Christians United for Israel, the Conference of Presidents of Major American Jewish Organizations with links to Oval Office, and the Anti-Defamation League. According to Mearsheimer and Walt, several US-based think tanks are instrumental in penetrating both the American academy and foreign policy circles in a direction favorable to conservative Judeo-Christian interests. These include: the American Enterprise Institute, the Hudson Institute, the Heritage Foundation, Washington Institute for Near East Policy, and the Brooking Institute's Saban Center for Middle East Policy.[21]

Looking further at the chaotic historical process of US Middle East foreign policy in the Arab region, we learn that it is this half-century relationship that indubitably contributed to the decline in America's image among Arab audiences. While US foreign policy in the Middle East gains many economic, diplomatic, and military successes, it succeeds at the expense of complicating relations with global Islamic communities. While key leaders in the Middle East may readily embrace America's presence in the region (through foreign aid or military assistance) nonelites often regard American military presence and its political influence in the region as irksome. Some fear that this arrangement has the potential to contribute to the spread of an American hegemony throughout the Arab world. This challenge to the American approach interacts with an uneven US foreign policy, based particularly upon bilateral relationships with Israel and Saudi Arabia, two regional pillars presenting different agendas inciting regional conflict and anti-Americanism.[22]

Since building relations with the Kingdom of Saudi Arabia and recognizing the State of Israel in 1948, the United States got involved itself in a growing catastrophe. Both its foreign policy and strategic interests in the Middle East translated themselves into what is interpreted as an awkward form of communication by both US allies and foes alike throughout the Muslim world. Indicators of this communication problem are twofold, linked specifically to: (i) Muslims' dismay about an American history of inconsistent foreign policymaking in the Middle East, which includes its unbreakable bond with Israel and America's oil interests; and (ii) Positions held by US officials, neoconservatives, and academics toward the role of political Islam and Islamic extremism projected at America and its allies.[23] The context for the growing skepticism of Muslims toward the US government includes: Resistance toward modernization introduced by interaction with Western nations like the United States, the prospects of spreading America's growing political and ideological influence in Islamic society, and America's ardent support for the state of Israel as a "strategic asset" in the Middle East.[24] Each concern is shaped out of an acute awareness by Muslims that the United States since World War II has become a dominant power in the Middle East and that its foreign policy is essentially crafted remote from the many aspirations and perspectives of nonelite Muslims in the region.

Since 1933, when King Abdel Aziz granted American oil companies entrance into the kingdom of Saudi Arabia, the US government has built a relationship to fulfill its oil interest (and after 1945) to establish a geopolitical position against the Soviet Union to combat the spread of Communism.[25] In achieving its contemporary goals, the United States has to deal with a set of issues that may complicate or support its current foreign policy approach: security in the postwar Gulf region, the Saudi position on the Arab-Israeli conflict, arms transfers to Saudi Arabia, Saudi external aid programs, bilateral trade relationships and oil production, and Saudi policies involving human rights and democracy.[26] While the United States may have played on both sides of the US foreign policy table with Israel and Arab allies to fulfill its self-interest, grievances of many Muslims in the region have been fueled by the US's relationship with the Jewish state (especially since the Six-Day War of 1967). Since this period, US foreign aid has led to Israel's military strength "transforming Israel's armed forces into one of the most technologically sophisticated military in the world."[27] Muslims presenting vocal opposition to the US's foreign aid policy with Israel sees its financial support for the Jewish state as an instrument abetting the Arab-Israeli conflict. For many, this stands as a direct contradiction to the relationship that Washington fosters with Arab nations.

One of the most recent attempts to assess the tension between US foreign policy and its reception by Muslim communities was the US-Muslim Engagement Project (led by former US Secretary of State

Madeline Albright and Richard Armitage) that acknowledges uneven US foreign policy activities and critical events occurring that color Muslim world perceptions of American leadership and American foreign policy.[28] The first, notably, is marked by America's intervention and participation (in 1948) in recognizing a homeland for Jewish settlers in Palestine, openly leading to wide suspicion of the United States among key Arab nation-states. By 1953, Operation Ajax (the CIA-sponsored coup of Mohammad Mossadegh to install Shah Mohammed Reza Pahlavi in Iran) caused tension among religious leaders in Iran and set the stage for political Islam to emerge two decades later. Ending Eisenhower's first term, in 1957, the Suez Crisis would make the United States an unlikely superpower in the region when it brokered a peaceful accord between Egypt, France, and Britain in an effort to restore international control of the Suez Canal.

Pro-Israeli Foreign Policymaking

Further, the 1960s saw its share of US-Middle East foreign policy initiatives, beginning with President Kennedy's affirmation in 1961 that America was "committed to Israel's right to exist, while at the same time [assuring America's] access to Arab oil"[29] (especially for America's European allies, which depended on the region for three-quarters of their petroleum). After Kennedy's assassination and Johnson's succession in 1963, mounting tension led to the Six Day War in 1967, where American intervention proved one-sided in settling the discord between Syria, Egypt, Jordan, and Israel. Like the Kennedy and Johnson administrations, by 1972 the Nixon administration was forced to confront the Middle East as well, owing to the counterattack on Israel by the Syrians and Egyptians over the Golan Heights and the Suez Canal.

Upon taking office, President Carter presented a public appeal for a Palestinian homeland, which prompted a backlash by US Jewish lobbyists and pro-Israeli supporters throughout his administration.[30] This challenge continued throughout his presidency, and throughout America's efforts to dispel the tension in the Middle East following the Six Day War, by maintaining stability between Egypt and Israel up to 1977. Beyond doubt, the Iranian Revolution in 1979 and the hostage crisis thereafter became a further tipping point for Carter's presidency and American credibility throughout the Middle East. In reaction to the mounting pressure from American and British interests in the Middle East, by the 1970s, political Islam would take precedence as a religio-political ideology, creating an unmanageable tension in US-Iranian relations.[31]

If the 1980s were given a label, it might read: *the decade when the US made friends out of enemies and enemies out of friends.* This decade saw Washington covertly supporting Islamic factions and governments whom, today, it is forced to confront (for example, the Afghan Mujahedeen [later becoming the Taliban] in the US's proxy war against the Soviets) as it sought to contain Communism. During this period, the Reagan administration took centre stage in carrying out its implicit foreign policy objectives to contain Communism in Central and South Asia, even if it meant funding the militant Mujahedeen and openly regarding the faction as "freedom fighters."[32] The events that occurred during the Reagan administration would include Israel's withdrawal from the Sinai in 1982, the same year as its invasion of Lebanon; the failure of the Middle East peace process in the early 1980s; the rise of Hezbollah in 1983; and, the unforgettable the Iran-Contra Affair. By the time George H. W. Bush took office in 1989, Iraq's invasion of Kuwait and America's Gulf War military intervention in Iraq contributed to generating negative perceptions held by Iraqis toward the United States. Al-Marashi and Durlacher suggest:

> Iraqi perceptions of the US were [affected] by certain events that were shared by other Arabs who hold critical views of American foreign policy. The first factor is American support for Israel, which became US policy after the 1967 Arab-Israeli war and continues to the present. Iraqis seem to express almost equal hostility towards Israel and the US support for this country. The second factor that formed Iraqi perceptions of the US was the 1991 Gulf war. Regardless of whether or not the Iraqi masses agreed with Hussein's decision to invade Kuwait, most Iraqis hoped for a negotiated settlement to avoid war, and they formed critical opinions of the US when it did launch a war which devastated their nation yet kept their dictator intact. Lastly, whether Iraqis supported the Hussein regime or not, they universally suffered under UN imposed sanctions. During this period, many Iraqis blamed America for perpetuating these sanctions that hurt the Iraqi people.[33]

Arguably, the 1990s would become the most hostile decade of the twentieth century for the United States, and one in which its solid relations with some Muslim countries, their dictators and Islamic fundamentalist factions such as the Taliban and Iraq's Saddam Hussein, became tenuous.[34] During this period, Muslim extremist movements were not as successful as earlier in toppling governments in such countries as Algeria, Uzbekistan, and Chechnya. With many of these countries perturbed by American dominance in Muslim majority nations, Muslim extremist groups began shifting their strategic interests and attacks toward the United States and other Western countries.

> Al-Qaeda affiliates were involved in attacks on the World Trade Center in 1993, US embassies in East Africa in 1998, and the USS Cole in 2000. Their core justification for attacking the US was to free the Muslim world—particularly the Arab lands that house Islam's sacred sites—from what they saw as Western domination. Pushing the West out of Muslim lands was to be the first step toward overthrowing the governments they saw as illegitimate, and establishing true Islamic states.[35]

By the 1990s, the Clinton administration showed some promise in its landmark success with the Oslo Accords (a tenuous accord signed between Israel's Yitzak Rabin and Yasser Arafat, Chairman of the Palestinian Liberation Movement). The legacy of Camp David II in July 2000, where a settlement between the United States, Ehud Barak, and Yasser Arafat was broached, established a workable framework for George W. Bush's administration.

Reacting to Adverse Foreign Policy

However, since the US-led invasion of Afghanistan (October 7, 2001), maintaining the US's favorable and credible standing throughout the Muslim world has proven to be a difficult task. In a Pew Forum sub-study on anti-Americanism and favorable opinions of US perceptions (polling 17,000 people from 15 different nations) US favorability not only slipped in the five Muslim countries polled, but severely declined.[36] US favorability among the general population of the five Muslim countries polled indicated that ratings had plummeted to: Indonesia 30 percent, Egypt 30 percent, Pakistan 27 percent, Jordan 15 percent, and Turkey 12 percent. As an indicator, each country's rating consistently fell below 50 percent since polling began in 2002. Strangely, each Muslim majority nation polled since 2001 had maintained something of a diplomatic relationship with Washington since the attacks of 9/11 and the entry of Western allied forces into Afghanistan and Iraq. However, if we look closely at these findings, we observe that the general population, as opposed to the government in each country, was growing indifferent to the US political agenda and American leadership in the Muslim world.

According to Pew Forum president Andrew Kohut, in his 2007 testimony on Foreign Affairs—US House of Representatives, presented to the Subcommittee on International Organizations, Human Rights, and Oversight (March 2007), findings of polls stretching back to 2002 revealed that in:[37]

- December 2002—America's image slips, although goodwill towards the United States remains.
- June 2003—US image plunges, in the wake of the Iraq War.
- March 2004—No improvement in US image, some worsening in Europe.
- June 2005—US image improves slightly, although still negative in most places; anti-Americanism is becoming increasingly entrenched.
- June 2006—Little progress—in fact, some backsliding, even though the public of the world concurred with the Americans on many global problems.

A rapid sense of global distrust of America's unilateral foreign policies surfaced between 2001 and 2002 as the cause of this continuing decline by 2007 in a similar study entitled "America's Image Slips, But Allies Share US Concern Over Iran, and Hamas" (2007).[38] In its polling of ten predominantly Muslim countries, each openly expressed their discontent with the United States. The 2007 report stated that:

> Not only is there worldwide support for a withdrawal of US troops from Iraq, but there also is considerable opposition to US and NATO operations in Afghanistan... In nearly every predominantly Muslim country, overwhelming majorities want US and NATO troops withdrawn from Afghanistan as soon as possible. In addition, global support for the US-led war on terrorism ebbs ever lower.[39]

Confounding variables linked to this decline in US favorability were associated with additional polled reactions to American leadership throughout the Muslim world. These views were expressed further in the overwhelmingly unfavorable ratings as registered in ten Muslim majority nations.

Comparing the findings taken from the 2006 study with those of 2007, it is identified that US favorability continued to fall a degree in four out of five Muslim countries. For example, the 2007 study reveals that Indonesian perceptions of the United States had fallen from 30 percent to 29 percent; Egypt 30 percent to 21 percent; Pakistan 27 percent to 15 percent; and Turkey 12 percent to 9 percent. An uneventful 5 percent spike from 15 percent to 20 percent showed in Jordan, but countries with close ties to Washington such as Pakistan, Kuwait, Lebanon, and Morocco each contributed favorability figures below 50 percent.

Both domestic political tension coupled by expectations led by state-centrist views held by US state actors has contributed to drawing President Barack Obama away from his 2008 campaign and inauguration promise to restore trust with the Muslim world. Saving face, a piecemeal approach has been implemented, which seems to be relying on the previous administration's ordeal to apply one-way communication symbols to spark the interest of nonelite Muslims. Unfortunately, this poorly scripted attempt is indubitably worsening America's standing and thus widening an already increasing trust deficit. Findings reveal that President Obama quickly lost the confidence of the Muslim world soon after taking office. Thus, if looking back at the *Pew Forum's Global Attitudes Poll 2007* (table 1.1), its results during the Bush era strikingly resembles *Gallup's Muslim World Facts Project's Poll* (May 2010) (table 1.2). While approval of American leadership and US foreign policy slightly increased upon President Obama taking office, a dip occurred soon after due to unfulfilled promises linked to Obama's "New Beginning" address at Cairo, reluctance about closing Guantanamo Bay prison facility, US drone surveillance along the Pakistani border, and Washington's lack of opposition toward the expansion of Israeli settlements, which undermines US-Middle East peace talks.

It is critical that we understand that America's image problem did not begin after September 11, 2001. This problem is long-standing and is rooted in more than a half-century of Washington's ascendancy in the Middle East after World War II. Based on fulfilling the American foreign interest, US policymakers often overlook the perspectives and aspirations of nonelites living within Muslim majority countries. This in turn has provided additional motivation by nonelites to form unfavorable opinions of US foreign policy and American leadership.

Table 1.1 Global Unease with Major World Powers and
Leaders (The Pew Global Attitude Project, 2007)[40]

Nation	Favorable	Unfavorable
Kuwait	46	46
Lebanon	47	52
Indonesia	29	66
Malaysia	27	69
Egypt	21	78
Jordan	20	78
Morocco	15	56
Pakistan	15	68
Palestinian Ter.	13	86
Turkey	9	83

Table 1.2 Some Arab Countries Make U-turn on U.S. Leadership in
2010 (Gallup Center for Muslim Studies, 2010)[41]

Nation	2008	2009	2009	2010
Mauritania	44	56	78	69
Iraq	35	(not recorded)	33	30
Algeria	25	47	43	25
Lebanon	25	22	30	25
Palestinian Ter.	13	7	20	16
Egypt	6	25	37	19

Misreading the Social Terrain

A reliance by US state actors on both the state-centric and rational
actor models contributed to a misreading of the social terrain of the
Muslim world. Thus, identifying the Muslim world as a monolithic
mass served a purpose of convenience after 9/11, at the expense of
limiting Washington's scope and discounting both the significance of
culture and religion and their multidimensional roles in Islamic society.
In this respect, limiting such roles in analysis discounted the opportunity of state actors to apply relationship-based strategies to connect
with Arab audiences that operate via two-way communication. R. S.
Zaharna writes:

> The focus on getting [the State Department's] message out [was]
> a one-way communication approach that requires very little par-
> ticipation from the audience beyond the Arab and Muslim public

accepting the American message. Nothing in the Arab or Islamic world suggests that this public subscribes to a one-way, transmission model of communication. The culture and society are built around relationships. Relationship-building strategies tend to be more long-term, but they are more in tune with the culture of the people in the Arab and Muslim world.[42]

By relying primarily on traditional state-centric approaches, US state actors were more keen after 9/11 to discount the role of religion and socioreligious influences in Islamic society. Therefore, it is only appropriate that Washington calibrates its lens and recognizes that a more precise form of communication is essential to engage what this study regards Muslim communities as *socially constructed traditional societies*.

According to the Center for Strategic and International Studies' report, "Mixed Blessings: U.S. Government Engagement with Religion in Conflict-Prone Settings," Danan and Hunt contend that three obstacles often contribute to the US government's narrow vision and misreading of Muslim majority nations leading to its indirect engagement with religion and religious communities.[43] The first relates to the misreading by key officials of the US Establishment Clause and the parameters identified within it: "Congress shall make no law respecting an establishment of religion, or prohibiting the free exercise thereof." Misinterpreting this significant clause contributes to creating a US government culture apprehensive toward engaging religious issues. The second obstacle is linked to the US government's contemporary framework for "approaching" religious issues, which has often led to frequent misreading. For example, this narrow vision after 9/11 translated itself into a tone, thereby declaring the violent aspects associated with the religion of Islam as the problem, consequently creating an insular US Department of State culture skeptical of both US-Muslim relations and direct engagement with global Islamic communities. The final, but most important, obstacle identified acknowledges the typical stance taken by US policymakers to reduce the concept of religion to a nonsubstantive topic or an issue related to international religious freedom. If and when the topic of religion is broached, it is often regarded as nonsubstantive or approached nonchalantly as a "broad cultural [issue] rather than religion specifically."[44] Stripping away the theological significance reduces these new religious movements to basic cultural issues, which are often discounted or pushed to the fringes.

While Danan and Hunt present a clear-cut approach, the problem lies with Washington's reliance on a "one-size" state-centric fits all solution. Without critical analysis on emerging religious issues confronting the international agenda, key State Department actors are prone to accept that one-way transmission models of communication are suitable to engage socially constructed traditional societies that comprise the Muslim world. This study disagrees with the perception that the Muslim world is a monolithic mass that holds a set of predetermined set of convictions; its composition as a multidimensional society where both traditional religious and cultural values contextualize its identity as a social world is socially constructed by a series of adverse interactions with the West.

Engaging the Socially Constructed Society

In contrast to Europe's historical industrial societies of the nineteenth and twentieth centuries that were driven by secular ideals, science, and technology, traditional societies comprising a large demographic of the Muslim world differ along the lines that widely accepted traditional religious and cultural value systems serve as the interconnective force that shapes the social reality of nonelites and nonstate actors living within this society. Peter Berger and Thomas Luckmann contend in the seminal study, *The Social Construction of Reality* implying that all knowledge as held by members of a group is constructed through group interaction within a social system. Within this system, the memorization of rules, customs, mores, and traditions form over a period of time, leading to a set of constructed norms. Thus, such knowledge as learned by actors within the society becomes a part of the social ethos or principal fabric that composes the group's social world. According to Berger and Luckmann, our interaction within the world is shaped directly from the interaction of members or groups from different social worlds.

Such behavior is congruent with traditional societies that are found in most predominantly Muslim countries, where religion and cultural values construct the communicative actions of actors living within the society. Arab societies in particular are relationship based and are overwhelmingly comprised of nonstate actor network bases that relay messaging between nonelites and state actors. In addition to this constructed communicative action and due to its uneven relationship with Western nations, global Islamic communities have assigned a specific meaning to their interaction with the West. Where trust is lost, for Arab audiences, only a two-way communicative engagement system is likely to restore relations. Through critical analysis of the social and religious terrain, public diplomacy practitioners will comprehend that communication strategies that work at keeping engagement with these societies at arm's length are prone to increasing the deficit. A difference in expectations emerges between the group or actors it grants access to, in that members of the traditional society expects their aspirations and perspectives be considered during the decision-making process. When their aspirations and perspective are taken for granted, a moral difference in opinion emerges.

W. Barnett Pearce and Stephen Littlejohn take this point further in *Moral Conflict: When Social Worlds Collide*, acknowledging that "Moral difference exists when groups have incommensurate moral orders... Groups that differ morally in how they view knowledge, and values. Moral differences may tend to be expressed on surface issues such as abortion, sexual orientation, and school curriculum, but the differences that lie deep in the moral order are rarely expressed directly." Identifying the framework of the moral order, Pearce and Littlejohn posit,

> It is the theory by which a group understands its experience and makes judgments about proper and improper actions. It is the basis of what most people think of as common sense. A moral order thus provides a tradition of truth and propriety... any action that threatens the concept of order within the tradition will be seen as an abomination, and what is a perfectly acceptable act within one tradition can be an abomination in another.[45]

Disregarding the aspirations and perspectives of nonelites within traditional societies yields the potential for highly volatile clashes between groups. This has been expressed in recent years with visible intractable conflicts in South Asia and the Middle East with nonstate actors making political claims opposing the United States' presence in Afghanistan and Iraq or, for example, President Obama's wavering stand on the settlement construction in East Jerusalem.

Given this structure in the context of most Muslim majority nations, it is clear that specific sets of assumptions exist, which comprise a moral order by which a specific group "understands its experience and makes judgments about proper and improper actions"; it is based upon the social experiences and laws that emerge out of this group's religious traditions.[46] As in many Muslim majority countries, the practice and principles of the Islamic faith determine what is politically and socially appropriate and inappropriate. This is the case in countries where political Islam is widespread, as in Iran, Saudi Arabia, Pakistan, Yemen, and Sudan. There, religion within the *ummah* is interconnected and centralized, spanning every level of society and binding communal, social, political, communicative, and economic activities together. Akbar Ahmed acknowledges the potency of the *ummah* when moral difference occurs:

> The concept of the *ummah*, a community or brotherhood, may be intangible and even amorphous but it is powerful. It allows ideas to be carried across national borders and can generate emotions wherever Muslims live. It is the notion of the *ummah* that triggers a response when Muslims see or hear scenes of other Muslim being denied their rights or being brutally suppressed when voicing them.[47]

Presently, a set of new realities exist that require US state actors to immediately reassess the impact of US foreign policy, the State Department's new culture to sell America to value-defined societies, and how state-centrism contributes to a narrow view toward traditional societies that undermines the role of religion and culture in America's efforts to engage the Muslim world. A pro-Israeli foreign policy agenda has not only led to a decrease in American popularity throughout the Arab world, but it weakens Washington's credibility within the region, while increasing the US-Muslim world trust deficit. Furthermore, discounting the application of relationship-based communication strategies after 9/11 derailed a decade of US-Muslim engagement at the expense of state actors exercising short-term one-way transmission models of communication and nation branding to restore America's ailing image.

Based on this survey, it is critical that key US Department of State officials take into account the recommendation that both improving America's image and increasing US favorability is an interconnective task requiring that Washington implement two-way communication that builds strategic relations with nonelites from the bottom up. This requires a holistic approach that: (i) acknowledges a shift is pertinent in US-Mid East policy which presently drives anti-Americanism, and (ii) applies a new public diplomacy far removed from antiquated Cold War communication approaches. Chapter Two examines the role of fear manufactured by conservative American political and academic forces and the appropriate role US policymakers should consider when engaging postsecular issues in this new era.

CHAPTER TWO

Calculating the Cost of Manufactured Fear

Fear manufactured by exclusive worldviews in the Western world leads to distorted readings on new religious movements in the Muslim world, contributing to both narrow US domestic as well as foreign policymaking. For nearly four decades, US policymakers on occasion have compromised the US Establishment Clause to accommodate Judeo-Christian interest groups at the expense of advancing US foreign interests. Such actions are reflected in policies that set out to keep Muslim audiences at arm's length, as was the case with post-9/11 American public diplomacy. This chapter goes a step further by calculating the cost of fear and an American history of political compromise driven by Judeo-Christian interests as two distinct impediments that are injurious to US policy and its aspiration to engage global Islamic communities in a postsecular era. Moving beyond "otherness" and trepidation toward Muslims is essential in order that US policymakers exercise religious tolerance, leading to a new public diplomacy with Muslim audiences.

A New Era of Postsecularism

Since the collapse of the Soviet Union in the late twentieth century, American foreign policy shifted from containing Communism to spreading US primacy throughout parts of the Arab and Muslim world, with an emphasis on securing Western energy interests. Washington has not registered that the United States has entered a postsecular era—*a*

period where the presence of religion in global politics is unprecedented. This
period is marked by what German social theorist Jürgen Habermas
regards as a time where "religion is holding its own in an increasingly
secular environment and that society must assume that religious fel-
lowships will continue to exist for the foreseeable future."[1] Among the
new challenges confronting state-nonstate actor engagement are a set
of preconceived notions formed by state actors within liberal secular
societies about non-Western societies and their religious systems. As
this chapter will indicate, a new type of frustration is growing, linked
particularly to the inability of Western state actors to practice religious
tolerance or to accommodate emerging perspectives held by nonstate
actors in the Muslim world.

The highly regarded *secularization thesis,* held by nineteenth- and
twentieth-century sociologists and philosophers, puts forward the view
that a rise in science, technology, and urbanization would engender a
decline in the practice and importance of religion in society. Assertions
by C. Wright Mills that "in due course, the sacred shall disappear alto-
gether except, possibly in the private realm," and the allied beliefs held
by seminal thinkers like Emile Durkheim, Herbert Spencer, Auguste
Comte, Max Weber, Karl Marx, and Sigmund Freud "that religion
would gradually fade in importance and cease to be significant with the
advent of industrial society,"[2] were an exaggerated misreading of the
impact that secularization would soon have on the practice of religion
the world over. By the mid-twentieth century, the secularization thesis
fell on deaf ears due, to a large extent, to the new reality that science
and technology contributed to new sophisticated wars, underpinned by
competing religious and cultural ideals. What was apparent, but less
often explored by Western scholars, were the socioreligious realities that
had existed for centuries in non-Western societies. While the concept
of secularism did not exist in non-Western countries, both religion and
traditional practices have been intertwined with the political, economic,
and social infrastructure of most Asian and African societies. Thus, in
these societies, the global public practice of religion has yet to enter a
period of retreat, or show signs of decline due to Europe's industrial
progress.

The decline or disappearance of religion from public space is regarded
as "secularization," a term that has taken on numerous meanings.[3] Max
Weber acknowledged secularization as "disenchantment" with religion, suggesting, "The fate of our time is characterized by rationalization and intellectualization and, above all, by disenchantment of the
world."[4] The world, as Weber observed, was destined to become more

dependent on material progress, reason, and science, and less on the mystical or archaic traditions of religion. Other theorists, like Emile Durkheim, saw secularization taking its course along two time scales: "First, over a wide historical spectrum, in which secularization has been in progress for millennia. Second, in more recent times, in which there has been an acceleration of the process due to particular circumstances in Western society."[5] Taking a psychoanalytical position—unlike other social theorists during his era—Sigmund Freud accepted neither urbanization nor modernization as being responsible for the decline of religion, but rather, suggested that it was the instinctual urge of human wishes relating to religion that contributed to its decline. Freud regarded the mystical urge of religion as the *future of an illusion*, an event that tore humans away from doing what was best for society.[6] The social theories of Durkheim and Weber, in particular, emerge out of a period of social transition in Western society, which interpreted the decline in traditional practices and archaic mystical beliefs as a loss, brought about by urbanization and an absence of religion's influence on the political realm.

Defining Postsecularism

Regarding the increasing influence of religion in the global sphere, let us turn our attention here to the new descriptive term of this age, "postsecularism." This term is often applied to affluent societies of Europe or to countries like Canada, Australia, and New Zealand, where the public practice of Western Christianity in particular has declined tremendously since World War II. The Norris and Inglehart survey indicates that the United States, Italy, and Ireland are the most religious countries in the Western world. In juxtaposition, France, Denmark, and Great Britain are regarded as less religious among the Western nations.[7] In an effort to escape from the constraints of religion in Europe during the seventeenth and eighteenth centuries, the social process of Western society, as it moved from a narrow sacred position to a broader secular body, outlines in clear terms William H. Swatos's argument that secularization is, as this study agrees, "the process by which societies in the experience of 'modernisation' have created competing institutions for doing better."[8] This position highlights the fact that the only continent that has ventured far in distancing society from religion, both in practice and in its trust in sacred frameworks, is Europe, and not the United States—*since there has yet to be a dramatic decline in religious practices and beliefs in America.*[9]

The term "postsecularism" also yields a more concrete meaning that aids our discussion at this point. Comprehending a fresh new term like postsecularism (as with the term and practice of public diplomacy) can be a challenging experience, considering the limited literature that exists on this subject. Hence, to avoid mislabeling it, it is imperative that we turn to assess the rationale behind the term as presented in the Jacobsens's study. Douglas and Rhonda Jacobsen acknowledge:

> Putting a "post-" in front of a word often signals a complex redef-inition of the subject under discussion, but that is not what we have in mind. What we mean by the term *postsecular* is the simple fact that secularization as a theory about the future of human soci-ety seems increasingly out of touch with realities on the ground. To speak, as we do, about the emergence of a *postsecular* age is not a veiled attempt to foster and encourage religion's resurgence. Nor is it a claim that more religion is better for the world than less... Postsecular is used merely as a descriptive term. If secular-ization means that the world is getting a little less religious every day, then we live in a postsecular world.[10]

Nonetheless, acknowledgement of the present global condition and how both state and nonstate actors should inevitably respond to this new condition is a critical component in studies that deal with post-secular issues. When intersecting this position with Habermas's notes on a postsecular society, we arrive at a practical twofold theoreti-cal description that: (i) postsecularism calls into question the highly regarded secularization thesis in this new era, and (ii) it contends that a shift in political and communicative consciousness is imperative when positioning sacred and secular actors together in discourse to promote peaceful coexistence within the global public sphere. If we were to expand this description, it is clear that postsecularists generally adhere to three alternative perspectives :

1. Recognizing that the widely held secularization thesis is chal-lenged by an unexpected worldwide resurgence of religious activity.
2. Acknowledging that multilateral relations are essential between state and nonstate actors (local networks and religious leadership) to promote transnational cooperation and sophisticated levels of tolerance within society; and

3. Asserting that new forms of communication and consciousness are required to advance engagement between sacred and secular members within the international system. While secular engagement approaches often govern state-actor relations, nonsecular complementary learning approaches are imperative to enrich the relationship between state/nonstate actors.

Considering that a decline in Judeo-Christian religious practices is not underway in the United States, there is frustration between US state actors and nonstate actors throughout the Arab and Muslim world. It is essential that both ardent defenders of secularism and postsecularism acknowledge that the secularization thesis should not be swept under the mat and this merely deserves adjusting. According to Norris and Inglehart, three conclusive trends make this case: first, the public of virtually all advanced industrial societies are moving toward more secular orientations; second, demographic trends in poorer societies show that the world as a whole now has more people with traditional religious views than ever before; and third, the divide between the sacred and the secular societies around the globe have important consequences for world politics—thereby raising the question of the role of religion in the international agenda.[11]

If we are to focus on the principles of liberal secularism, which seek to extinguish the sacred from secular space, one might assume that America's historical link to the Western secular tradition provides an answer on why Washington set out to engage the Muslim world at arm's length prior to and after 9/11. By evaluating the contributions of Western secularism to the American political and social system, we might dispel the myth that secularism is the single factor contributing to an American political apprehension toward religion and the interests of religious groups (especially, in this case, the religion of Islam and global Islamic communities). For example, Washington has publicly accommodated the aspirations and perspectives of conservative Judeo-Christian special interest groups in their quest to promote biased social and political agendas—both within the United States and abroad. In unfolding America's relationship with Western secularism, we gather that space has existed for some time within America's liberal secular political framework to promote religious tolerance and accommodate a broad perspective on publicly engaging religion. As determined later, it might very well be the case that a narrow reading of the religion of Islam and Muslims—as argued by Edward Said in *Orientalism*—has tainted US policymakers' views about the Muslim world.

Sketching the Secular Tradition

George J. Holyoake acknowledges, in the study *The Principle of Secularism*, that "Secularism is a series of principles intended for the guidance of those who find Theology indefinite, or inadequate, or deem it unreliable. It replaces theology, which mainly regards life as a sinful necessity, as a scene of tribulation through which we pass to a better world. Secularism rejoices in this life and regards it as the sphere of those duties which educate men to fitness for any future and better life, should such transpire."[12] Holyoake's view of religion implies that, before the nineteenth century, broader issues contributed to Western societies' uneven relationship with religion. The religious wars of the seventeenth century, tyranny by rulers, and "Enlightenment" endeavors by man to elevate reason over divine right are three of the greatest social influences in encouraging the growth of secularism. In both European and American societies during the eighteenth century, there was the fear that the first two influences would lead the new nation-state to steer clear of religion in public affairs. At a deeper level, memories of early seventeenth-century disputes between the European church and political institutions contributed to a well-established fear by state actors that translated into political apprehension toward religious institutions.

Determined not to return to an era where the European public sphere is again dominated by authoritative religious institutions, enlightened French, Dutch, and English nation-states emerged, to some degree, out of this indirect counterresponse taken in the seventeenth century toward Christian religious bodies and European powers. From the horrors of the Thirty Years' War rose insurmountable tragedy, religious division, and the formation of a new religio-political framework with the strategic aim of combating religion-based conflict between newly formed European states. In an effort to curb religious wars and interchurch hostilities, two treaties were signed in 1648 (the Treaties of Osnabrück and Münster; recognized later as the Peace of Westphalia), ending both the Thirty Years' War in Germany and the Eighty Years' War fought between the Netherlands and Spain.[13] By signing and implementing the Peace of Westphalia, Western powers pushed back religious tension, bringing peace to the vast lands of the Holy Roman Empire (which included modern Germany, Belgium and Luxembourg, Austria, the Czech Republic, Slovenia and parts of Poland and of northern Italy). The establishment of the Westphalian system led to the formation of the modern nation-state, the conceptualization of state sovereignty, and the political ideal of religious tolerance.[14] This treaty

ratified the existing territorial divisions and required many rulers—
Catholic, Lutheran, and Calvinist—to tolerate worship by denominations other than the established one, on the basis of the conditions
prevailing in each state in 1624.[15]

Clashes of sectarian violence on the European continent throughout the sixteenth and seventeenth centuries were not a distant recol-
lection in countries like France, where widespread skepticism among
the French intelligentsia about religion's influence became rampant.
Skepticism about French leadership and religion is present in the work
of leading *philosophes* like Voltaire, who acknowledged that the public
apprehensiveness about religion and its rule was linked to "the evils
[that] Christianity had perpetrated through wars of religion, burning
heretics, executing so-called 'witches' as well as restrictions imposed by
the Vatican and Jesuit communities."[16] *Philosophes* and Encyclopedists
Diderot and Baron d' Holbach echoed similar sentiments, not-
ing absolutism and divine right as forces restricting freethinking.[17]
Demonstrating the possibilities of religious tolerance while endorsing secularity and free speech, we might cite non-French despots like
Catherine the Great of Russia and Frederick the Great of Prussia, two
enlightened rulers who set an example of advancing the social stability
of their countries by endorsing rationality and freethinking. Immanuel
Kant, in 1784, utilized Fredrick's enlightened vision when answering
Rev. Johann Löllher's enquiry *What is Enlightenment?* by exclaiming:

> Enlightenment is man's emergence from his self-imposed imma-
> turity. Immaturity is the inability to use one's understanding with-
> out guidance from another. This immaturity is self-imposed when
> its cause lies not in lack of understanding, but in lack of resolve
> and courage to use it without guidance from another. *Sapire Aude!*
> [dare to know] "Have courage to use your own understanding!"—
> that is the motto of the Enlightenment.[18]

Kant's belief in man's ability to evolve apart from religious authority
highlighted what later became a growing phenomenon in the West.
This point is exemplified in the decline of Judeo-Christian practices
after the eighteenth century in Europe. Joachim Whaley contends
that the "Enlightenment saw the decline of religious belief and the
secularisation of European society. [It] promoted rationalism; new science undermined the basis of traditional belief; Christianity was edged
out of the central position it occupied in Western society by the rise
of a new 'paganism.'"[19] Freethinking as the new paganism developed

into the central pillar that ensured that Western society remained far removed from religious authority and the confines of princely rule. "By the 1780s, at least among the upper classes, dogmatic religion seemed to give way among both Catholics and Protestants—and even among practising Jews—to a generalised and tolerant benevolence uninterested in the ancient ideal of asceticism or in doctrinal precision."[20]

Establishing Religious Tolerance in the New Republic

Both European and American societies were influenced by Enlightenment secularization, but, unlike what we see in Europe, the United States has wavered in its commitment to secularity by allowing Judeo-Christian forces to influence American political decision making, despite implementing the US Establishment Clause.[21] Just like their enlightened contemporaries in Europe, the framers of the US Constitution considered it fruitful to establish a new republic, where religious tolerance within a secular context could exist in the absence of divine absolutes. Strengthening this vision, pre-Enlightenment philosophies found in Locke's *Letters on Tolerance* and Hobbes' proposals for a commonwealth of civil law were incorporated into the American constitution.[22]

Framers of the American republic, like their European counterparts, were suspicious of religion and the influence that it could potentially have on the political infrastructure in the new colonies. However, many of the founding fathers valued the philosophical perspectives of religious tolerance as written in Montesquieu's *The Spirit of the Laws*.[23] In *Religion in Public Life: Must Faith Be Privatized?* Roger Trigg points out that the "lingering distrust of the Church of England, coupled with denominational rivalry, led the Founders to be determined that the federal government should pursue a policy of neutrality concerning denominations."[24] James Madison, writing in *The Federalist Papers* on the need to safeguard the Union against domestic terrorism, emphasized the ills that corroded European society throughout the seventeenth century. Madison insisted that historical events should not, in any way, plague the new republic.[25] Further, in 1779, with the support of fellow statesmen, Thomas Jefferson made this case against state-supported religion in the Virginia Act for Establishing Religious Freedom (passed in 1786). This pre-Constitutional act served as a clause supporting religious tolerance, giving freedom to all Virginians to practice the religious denomination of their choice. This act prevented the state of Virginia from establishing its own state religion and from taxing the dissenters of the Anglican Church.

According to Montesquieu's and Locke's vision, Madison and Jefferson encouraged the spread of religious tolerance throughout the American colonies, focusing on four points: (i) oppression from domestic and foreign rulers; (ii) ensuring that the new government could not establish a national religion comparable to the "Church of England"; (iii) protecting the many religious sects of the colonies; and (iv) ensuring that religious tolerance was implemented within the new republic.[26] What is of central importance to our discussion is the way in which the Virginia case aided in constructing a plan to promote sacred-secular relations between state actors and nonelites in the new republic. Though established to combat against the ills that once threatened European society, the concept and practice of religious tolerance were implemented, neither to discourage state actors from engaging religious institutions, nor to support ignorance of religious concerns in the public sphere. This tool was implemented to ensure balance and fair association between state actors and religious institutions. Thus, Madison's efforts were implemented in Article I of the US Constitution (passed December 15, 1791) and are identified as part of the First Amendment's Establishment Clause, which makes it clear that:

> Congress shall make no law respecting an establishment of religion, or prohibiting the free exercise thereof[27]

As the architect of the Establishment Clause, Madison's vision for the Virginia Act: (a) ensured that the US federal government did not establish a national church (or religion); and (b) guaranteed that the many religious denominations in the colonies were free from discrimination and were able to freely practice their chosen religion. However, out of Madison's and Jefferson's good political intentions, two disturbing crosscurrents have surfaced over the last half-century and are present in this era: first, secularist aims to protect freethinking and rationalism in America often move in contradiction by pushing non–Judeo-Christian religious voices to the fringe; and second, in demonstrating an exceptionalist posture that allows special interests as Judeo-Christian groups to superimpose their moral and policy agenda on state actors, ultimately damaging prospective US relations with traditional societies in the non-Western world.

Commandeering the US Establishment Clause

Since the latter part of the twentieth century, American Christian Evangelicals have politicized their moral beliefs in the public sphere to

influence US domestic and foreign policy. America's religious entangle-
ments in this political sphere runs deep with its imbalanced relations with
Judeo-Christian special interests groups that share a twofold agenda that
includes shaping US domestic policy in favor of political moralism, and
steering US foreign policy in a pro-Israel direction. This shift in policy
interest would take shape during the mid-twentieth century, when fragments of the Christian revivalist movement of the early 1900s merged
into the highly regarded New Christian Right (NCR), an assembly of
Christian political action and lobbying organizations. By the 1970s, its
views were revived by well-funded Religious Right organizations with
close links to the Republican Party such as the Christian Voice, The
Religious Roundtable, and the National Conservative Political Action
Committee. Effecting the socioreligious change that this conservative
Christian movement envisioned required projecting their moral vision
of America on the US political establishment and its leadership in order
to rescue the United States from decay.

Christian revivalism assumed a new prominence in US public life
during the late twentieth century through the electronic church via
televangelism and its *moral campaign,* which included direct mailers to
its 20 million supporters—representing a substantial conservative voting bloc. Antisecularist and Christian fundamental hardliners like Jerry
Falwell, Paul Wyerich, and James Robinson, televangelists including Pat Robinson and Charles Stanley, and prophetic preachers with
financial interests like James Bakker were to secure prominence in the
movement. Their moral campaign essentially carried out the spread
of an apocalyptic gospel in order to influence liberal-secular political
decision making. The movement met its agenda by 1979, maturing
into the widely recognized umbrella organization, the Moral Majority,
raising substantial capital through James Robison's "moral report card"
campaign, which focused on the domestic and foreign interest of particular US politicians.[28] The project "rated the votes of national lawmakers against [Evangelical Christian] standards of what constituted a
'moral' or 'immoral' vote on a key public issue."[29] During this period,
the Moral Majority targeted key congressional officials with agendas to
deter the passing of legislation that it considered unchristian. According
to Erling Jorstad in *The Politics of Moralism,* many of the Moral Majority's
projects were interrelated crises influenced by secularity in society and
particularly,

> the results of the 1973 Supreme Court decision on abortion,
> demands by homosexuals for civil rights, the Supreme Court's

prohibition of religious exercises in public schools, the Equal Rights Amendment, the accessibility of pornography, and, in a different realm, the alleged decline of American prestige and power abroad due to a weakening military posture compared to increasing Soviet might.[30]

As part of this movement, an apocalyptic culture war was soon waged against the US political establishment, with Christian fundamentalism dictating the direction of US domestic and foreign policy. This narrow partisan vision, however, lost momentum and failed to attract many to "the politics of doomsday," forcing what would become the NCR to restructure itself. By the mid-1970s, its views were revived by more Christian action committees, such as the Christian Voice, the Religious Roundtable, and the National Conservative Political Action Committee (together with other smaller organizations) with ties to the Republican Party. NCR recognized that, to effect sociopolitical change, it could not concentrate on raising mass enthusiasm for its concerns and to shape its characteristic moral vision, it had to put pressure of its own on the US political establishment and its leaders.

The Moral Majority

Arguably, between 1976 and 1980, US policymakers failed to uphold the US Establishment Clause, thereby compromising its secularity to the Christian Right in exchange for access to its growing evangelical voting bloc. Even Jimmy Carter's public religious conversion in 1976 as a "born again" Christian was a narrow political appeal for Democrats to secure the vote of evangelicals. Taking for granted the Religious Right's commitment to win the White House and US Congress in 1980, Democrats in Washington were manipulated by a well-funded grassroots religious movement that projected its narrow partisan politics of moralism, thereby toppling the principles of religious pluralism and religious tolerance that shape the American political system.

Washington compromised the US Establishment Clause, thereby conceding its political power to conservative Judeo-Christian special interest groups and lobbies in two distinct ways: US policymakers exchanged secular public space for evangelical votes, which ended in Washington and the US Establishment Clause being commandeered by the Moral Majority; and due to this arrangement, lawmakers surrendered their secular decision-making power to offset the accusation of being unmoral.

First off, during this period, Washington never maintained its commitment to the US Establishment Clause. It gave preferential treatment to the Moral Majority while overlooking efforts to pursue an equitable engagement or dialogue within a tolerant context. The Religious Right was never confronted with the boundaries outlined in the Constitution on the influence that religious expression might exert on secular political decision making. But how could Washington accuse them of overstepping their ground when political capital was involved? In an effort to win the "hearts and minds" of the evangelical bloc, Washington allowed the Moral Majority to publicly take a stand on social issues relating to affirmative action: prohibition on school prayers, secular curriculums in public schools, abortion and the Equal Rights amendment even if it might cost some Democrats their seats. According to the Right, these were concrete issues that US elected officials had a "moral" responsibility to correct.[31] Falwell and others implied that "Salvation was to be found not only at the altar, but at the ballot box. [Thus, the argument ran], with the right man, highly moral men, in public office, America could yet be redeemed to continue its God-given destiny."[32] Meeting this agenda meant imposing a conservative religious belief system and ideology on public lawmakers.

Second, US lawmakers surrendered their secular decision making power to appease a growing American evangelical voting bloc. Spreading a *politics of moralism* became the driving force behind the movement. The Moral Majority seized control of America's public space during this period by challenging the moral nature of America, US political officials, and the notion of traditional morality as enshrined in the US Constitution. Though the founding fathers may have doubted whether the decisions of one group, man, idea, or society enjoyed "an absolute significance" with regard to right and wrong, the Moral Majority thought otherwise:

> Scriptures yield only one answer to each question. Those persons who accept that view of authority are the people qualified to decide what action is right and what is wrong, what is moral and what is immoral... They can measure in quantifiable terms (such as voting report cards) the degree of morality of a person, in this case a public lawmaker, by choosing a select number of public issues and controversies on which the lawmaker must vote. Since those who speak with absolute authority have the moral answers

they turn morality into moralism because they state they have the answers; those who disagree with them may not necessarily be "immoral" but they are not "moral."[33]

Being cast as immoral by an entire political voting bloc was essentially a scare tactic that put unforeseen pressure on US lawmakers to acquiesce to the Christian Right's far-reaching hand in US politics and its public discounting of traditional morality, as set out by the founders. This pressure marked the onset of a phase in contemporary history leading to US state actors conceding political privileges to Christian-led special interests groups and lobbies in Washington. Robert Billings elaborated on this issue with his "Family Issues Voting Index," which provided a set of key social issues and policies voted on or to be voted by liberal lawmakers.

Targeting officials in the Senate and the House, the index expressed extreme opposition to sex education in public schools and Patricia M. Wald's confirmation for US judgeship, while it would go on to advocate school prayer and a Bible reading amendment in the Senate.[34] In the House, the index expressed further opposition to "a bill establishing a programme to curb domestic violence (and provide aid to its victims) and to the Child Health Assurance Act of 1979—while favouring a bill to balance the budget for fiscal 1980."[35] These legislative issues became a yardstick for deciding whether various members of Congress were moral or not, and if they deserved to remain in office. As Jorstad observed, "The moral report card campaign allowed for no explanation by lawmakers, who now stood rated as…moral or immoral."[36] Therefore, the religious and nonreligious voices could not convene to consolidate opposition, for state actors under pressure were either concerned with restoring their public image or anxiously aligning themselves with the Moral Majority to maintain their political appeal. This especially applied to liberal Democratic senators such as George McGovern of South Dakota, Frank Church of Idaho, John Culver of Iowa, Alan Cranston of California, Birch Bayh of Indiana, and Gaylord Nelson of Wisconsin, who were targeted by the Moral Majority.[37] In the case of the Moral Majority, it is clear that severe political pressures from conservative Judeo–Christian special interests had a bearing on US policymaking moving state actors from their commitment to religious tolerance.

Presently, we have reached a postsecular era where a worldwide resurgence of religion in the global public sphere dictates that US policymakers pursue a path of fair play and tolerance. In our review of Western secularism and the creation of the new American republic, it is clear that a substantial space exists within America's liberal secular framework for competing religious views and balanced sacred-secular engagement, as ensured by the US Establishment Clause. But, as trepidation about global Islamic engagement increases, it is imperative that we go a step further to examine how US academics and policymakers manufacture and estimate this fear in an effort to discourage a long-term sustainable engagement with global Islamic societies.

A Narrow Political Mentality

For centuries, a preoccupation led by global insecurity and fear manufactured by an exceptionalist worldview toward non-Western societies that comprise parts of the Muslim world has transpired in developing the narrow political mentality held by American policymakers. The term *manufactured fear* is used in this chapter to bring meaning to the agitation held by those that influence key state actors that originates from a deep-seated phobia of Muslims, which seeks to lessen the value of Islamic society by advancing a Western worldview in exchange. This new type of fear provided both the context and political mindset for the promotion of a set of highly regarded preconceived perceptions held by confrontationalist thinkers like Bernard Lewis and Samuel P. Huntington about the religion of Islam and Muslims.[38] Considering Lewis's and Huntington's close proximity to the White House and Washington think tanks, both their personal views and academic recommendations would have steered US foreign policymaking in an exceptionalist direction, thereby distorting prospective engagement efforts. As Lawrence Pintak acknowledges in the study *Reflections in a Bloodshot Lens,* traditional Western "worldview exclusivism" runs parallel with American exceptionalism, and as its predecessor, it aids in "othering" non-Western societies. At first glance, it might appear that American exceptionalism as projected during the Bush era was a new occurrence, but it derived, in part, from fragments associated with classical Orientalism.

Sketching the Influence of Classical Orientalism

The thirteenth- and fourteenth-century European-led Crusades serve as a reference point in Western history of an era that later introduced a set of narrowly preconceived assumptions by the West about Islamic society and Muslims. The first real attempt by Western scholars to depict the Orient (Islamo-Arab world) through literature and art came during the eighteenth century, a period leading to heightened Western colonialism and conquest of the Asian continent. This period has been regarded by anti-Orientalists as an era of Western misinterpretation of Islamic society as an exotic, dark, and savage-ridden world aching for Western enlightenment. The academic field and social practice dedicated to this unapologetic misreading of the Orient is regarded as "Orientalism." In the classic text bearing the same name, leading anti-Orientalist Edward Said explains:

> Orientalism is a style of thought based upon an ontological and epistemological distinction made between "the Orient" and (most of the time) "the Occident." Thus a very large mass of writers, among whom are poets, novelists, philosophers, political theorists, economists, and imperial administrators, have accepted the basic distinction between East and West as the starting point for elaborate theories, epics, novels, social descriptions, and political accounts concerning the Orient, its people, customs, "mind," destiny, and so on.[39]

Establishing an antithesis to the narrow depiction of the Orient by the Occident, Orientalist Egyptian philosopher, Anouer Abdel-Malek and Palestinian historian A. A. Tibawi led a counter crusade in postcolonial studies dispelling a set of preconceived views that shaped the Western psyche about Islamic society and the religion of Islam. Among the anti-Orientalist perspectives, Said's influence on the subject supports this chapter's argument that a peculiar relationship exists, where the West is dependent to a large degree on the key Muslim majority nations in the Arab/Muslim world. In the contemporary sense, this relates to the West forming strategic relations with these nations in order to reach its energy and national security interests. Said clarifies:

> The Orient is not only adjacent to Europe; it is also the place of Europe's greatest and richest and oldest colonies, the source of its civilizations and languages, its cultural contestant, and one of its deepest and most recurring images of the Other. [Nonetheless], the Orient has helped to define Europe (or the West) as its contrasting image, idea, personality, experience.[40]

However, it is precisely this mentality that provides the foundation for contemporary American exceptionalism and distorted views about the religion of Islam and global Islamic communities within the US political realm after 9/11. Regarding Washington's contemporary view of the Muslim world, this argument is framed in the historical Western response to the "other" by perpetuating this sociopolitical fear in relation to its commitment to conservative Judeo-Christian interests. This notion introduces a sharp contrast that implies that Western society maintains pure knowledge as derived by its Judeo-Christian heritage, establishing a sense of entitlement leading to imperialist policies toward Muslim majority nations, especially in the Arab world. Pintak takes up this point describing the term Western "worldview exclusivism" as

> the dogmatic claim by a particular in-group to possess Truth with a capital "T." In other words, the conviction that God is on *my* side. And where one culture becomes dominant, in either a local or global context that worldview exclusivism can lead to what the experts call the psychological colonization of others. The crusades, the Spanish conquest of the Americas, the British Empire; each marched beneath the banner of God and Truth.[41]

Such notions of pure knowledge held under the banner of American exclusivism guided both US foreign policy and diplomatic strategy with global Islamic communities months prior to and after 9/11. Drawing on Said's position, Pintak continues,

> By framing "Islam" as a monolithic entity, Said wrote, "[l]ocal and concrete circumstances are thus obliterated." Any discussion or examination of Islam becomes "a one-sided activity that obscures what *we* do, and highlights instead what Muslim and Arabs by their very failed nature *are*." As a result, he argued, the label "Islam" distorted and idealized Western perceptions of the region and its people. Central to this approach was what Foucault, who heavily influenced Said, called the "truth games" played by those in positions of power, giving them the ability to dictate what is truth and define the sense of Self among all parties to the game.[42]

By viewing the Muslim world through a distorted lens, US policymakers would adhere to a conservative reading of the world and to their historical attitude that America is a distinctly Christian nation with a set of universal values. Hence, America's Judeo-Christian heritage facilitates this distortion in its intersection with contemporary American exceptionalist views. In particular, early colonial settler and Puritan, Reverend John Winthorp, among others, set the stage for contemporary American exceptionalists, proclaiming that the New England colonies have a divine covenant with God to lead the world's nations in the sermon, *A Model of Christian Charity,* writing in 1630:

> We shall find that the God of Israel is among us, when ten of us shall be able to resist a thousand of our enemies; when He shall make us a praise and glory that men shall say of succeeding plantations, "may the Lord make it like that of New England." For we must consider that we shall be as a city upon a hill. The eyes of all people are upon us. So that if we shall deal falsely with our God in this work we have undertaken, and so cause Him to withdraw His present help from us, we shall be made a story and a by-word through the world. We shall open the mouths of enemies to speak evil of the ways of God, and all professors for God's sake. We shall shame the faces of many of God's worthy servants, and cause their prayers to be turned into curses upon us till we be consumed out of the good land whither we are going.[43]

Today, American exceptionalism as a sociopolitical worldview is challenged on two levels. First, exceptionalists in the political arena often cling publicly to a preconceived notion that they bear a clear understanding of individuals living in a distant land without directly engaging the core of their society. This occurred on several levels after 9/11, with Bush's God-Talk and one-way engagement with keeping Muslim majorities at arm's length through consumer marketing approaches. And second, exceptionalists in both the private and political arenas are apt to believe that America shares a messianic role among Western nations to implement its value system in these distant lands. Insecurity that fuels this dangerous *messianic consciousness* led US state actors after 9/11 to view the Muslim world through a distorted lens that provided a false story about the religion of Islam and about Muslims in order that Washington might secure its energy and security interests by invoking a *religio-cultural dichotomy.*

Extending a Tradition

While there are scholars who may contend that classical Orientalism has all but vanished from the Western academy, Tobias Hübinette in the essay, "Orientalism Past and Present: An Introduction to a Post-colonial Critique" introduces a convincing set of positions that fragments of classical Orientalism can be regarded as *post-Orientalism* in the geopolitical sphere of security politics, and as so called *re-Orientalism* as an indigenized form of nationalism and fundamentalism in Asia are present today.[44] In addressing the influence of a new set of fears being calculated toward the Muslim world, it is vital that we acknowledge how conservative academic views by *confrontationalist* thinkers and competing mindsets by Islamists challenge US engagement with key nonstate actors in the Muslim world.

Fawaz A. Gerges points out in *America and Political Islam* that two strands of expert opinions shaped US foreign policymaking after 9/11. These two strands are regarded as the *accommodationalist* and *confrontationalist* perspectives. Accommodationists like Graham Fuller, John Esposito, and Ian Lesser put forward the view that the contemporary clash between the Muslim world and the United States, which are fueled particularly by religious extremists, are shaped largely by US foreign policy and a narrow political mindset projected by US state actors toward the Middle East, producing political disenfranchisement and social inequality.[45] For the accommodationalists, distinct US policies that reflect an imperialist tone are held as key instigators behind anti-Americanism and the decrease in favorable perceptions held by nonstate actors in the Muslim world toward America. On the contrary, confrontationalists view the current tension between the Muslim world and the United States through the distorted lens that the religion of Islam is America's archenemy, and that America's Judeo-Christian values are presently under attack.

While the spread of confrontationlist ideals did not start with the Bush administration, it was given an academic grounding both in discourse and in theory in the purported application by Bernard Lewis, Samuel P. Huntington, Gilles Kepel, and Daniel Pipes. The collective argument of confrontationalists declares that liberal democracy is not compatible with Islamic fundamentalism, or the religion of Islam itself.[46] For this reason, in order that liberal secular policymaking may be effective through the Muslim world, both Islamic society and the religion of Islam itself must reform, in order that Western democracy might be effective in the Muslim world. The meat of the confrontationalist argument, however, centers on its reading of the religion of Islam, or more appropriately, its narrow reading of Islamic fundamentalism as a perspective and practice that American society must essentially fear. According to Daniel Pipes, Islamic fundamentalism, is "a militant, atavistic force driven by hatred of Western political thought, harking back to age-old grievances against Christendom."[47] In the words of Mortimer Zuckerman, "[America is] in the front line of a struggle that goes back hundreds of years, the principal obstacle to the extremists' desire to drive nefarious Western values into the sea, just as they once did with the Crusaders."[48]

While Huntington's study, *The Clash of Civilization and the Remaking of World Order*, gained commercial appeal after 9/11, it was in fact the confrontationalists' inspired "identity politics" of Princeton University historian Bernard Lewis which had a tremendous influence on post-9/11 Bush era foreign policy. As a close advisor to the White House, Lewis's narrow reading on the Middle East and the religion of Islam suggests that on the face of it, aspects of Islam are inherently troubling to Western democracy and its "Judeo-Christian heritage." While Huntington's analysis of the problem would later center on the ideological struggle, Lewis articulates the problem in religious terms. He outlined this position first in *The Atlantic* (September 1990) essay entitled "The Roots of Muslim Rage," indicating that the anger of Islamists derives from hidden tension within Islamic society over secularism, as opposed to an open rejection of a history of inconsistent American foreign policies. Lewis maintains, American foreign policy, in itself, neither creates the atmosphere, nor supplies the fuel to incite "Muslim Rage."[49]

Thus, Lewis suggests, it is the selfish reaction of Muslims to America's relationship with Israel and America's extended relations with Europe that foments anti-Americanism. While Lewis may be partly correct that Washington's commitment to recognize Israel's existence and its strategic relationship with the Jewish state raises several red flags throughout the Islamic world, just like Huntington and Pipes, he is reluctant to examine the modus operandi of US-Israeli relations in parallel to Washington's association with pro-American autocratic leaders in Muslim majority countries as Syria, Egypt and Libya (prior to the Arab Spring). He contends:

> If we turn from the general to the specific, there is no lack of individual policies and actions, pursued and taken by individual Western governments, that have aroused the passionate anger of Middle Eastern and other Islamic peoples. Yet all too often, when these policies are abandoned and the problems resolved, there is only a local and temporary alleviation. The French have left Algeria, the British have left Egypt, the Western oil companies

have left their oil wells, the westernising Shah has left Iran—yet the generalised resentment [of fundamentalists] in particular against the West remains and grows and is not appeased. Clearly something deeper is involved than these specific grievances, numerous and important as they may be—something deeper that turns every disagreement into a problem and makes every problem insoluble.[50]

Shifting the blame, Lewis implies that a reform to the religion of Islam, rather than a shift in US foreign policymaking and its view of Islam will ensure peaceful coexistence between the West and Muslim world. Elaborating on this point, he writes:

Ultimately, the struggle of the fundamentalists is against two enemies, secularism and modernism. The war against secularism is conscious and explicit, and there is by now a whole literature denouncing secularism as an evil neo-pagan force in the modern world and attributing it variously to the Jews, the West, and the United States...[Hence] It should by now be clear that we are facing a mood and a movement far transcending the level of issues and policies and the governments that pursue them...This is no less than a clash of civilizations—the perhaps irrational but surely historic reaction of an ancient rival against our Judeo-Christian heritage, our secular present, and the worldwide expansion of both.[51]

This tension emerged out of an ongoing debate on both sides between American exceptionalists and Islamists after 9/11. Both professed that their exclusive worldviews should be held as the universal truth. Huntington takes up this argument up in his 1993 *Foreign Affairs* article, insisting that the real struggle between Islam and the West is not over political or economic interests, but that it is a clash of civilizations:

[T]he fundamental source of conflict in this new world will not be primarily ideological or primarily economic. The great divisions among humankind and the dominating source of conflict will be cultural. Nation states will remain the most powerful actors in world affairs, but the principal conflicts of global politics will occur between nations and groups of different civilizations. The clash of civilizations will dominate global politics. Civilization identity will be increasingly important in the future, and the world will be shaped in large measure by the interactions among seven or eight major civilizations. These include Western, Confucian, Japanese, Islamic, Hindu, Slavic-Orthodox, Latin American and possibly African civilization. The most important conflicts of the future will occur along the cultural fault lines separating these civilizations from one another.[52]

Pakistani scholar Fuad Naeem of Duke University reacts with disapproval toward the confrontationalists who propose that if the religion of Islam and Islamic society are to flourish and be respected as a political-religious system by the West, reform is essential.[53] Naeem attacks the confrontationlist recommendation by asking *"Why should Islam reform itself in order to meet Western standards?"* He notes:

Islam's traditional understanding of itself as a message of salvation that affirms the primacy of God, and seeks to awaken men and women to their true spiritual nature and make possible the actualisation of their God-given possibilities, stands in stark contrast to an anthropocentric, rationalistic, and materialistic framework which relegates the sacred to the private sphere—the very framework that determines much of modern Western civilisation. This is why Islam does not need to be reformed or modernised; it already contains within itself the principles necessary for renewal from within. These principles provide the discernment to both integrate truth wherever it is found and to reject falsehood decisively.[54]

While Naeem's study adopts a traditional Islamic perspective, he, along with Maulana Ashraf 'Ali Thanwi, maintains that if reform is necessary within the religion of Islam, such adjustment should be directed at restoring the intellectual, moral, and truth-related facets of Islam to Islamic society, and less on reforming Islam's core principles and social ideals to appease the West.[55]

Re-Orientalism as Islamist Revival

Tobias Hübinette maintains that re-Orientalism is a reflection of classical Orientalism's perception of Muslims in a negative (or barbaric light) and is expressed through fundamentalist and nationalist strands of Islam in Muslim majority nations. The argument presented in his essay is that,

> [Classical] Orientalism has also survived as re-orientalism in the forms of [Islamic] fundamentalism and nationalism in the newly independent former colonies of Asia. It is possible to view fundamentalism, especially its Islamic version, as a form of indigenized orientalism whereby the orientalized re-orientalize[s] himself in a manner which can be summed up as: "Yes, we orientals are really religious minded, despotic and cruel by nature."[56]

Youssef Choueiri indicates that this growing Islamic revivalist (or Islamist) mentality is not a new response directed toward a pro-Western alliance, but a conventional response to regain what Islamic society sees as a loss of identity, values, traditional customs, and religious authenticity, due in part to the West pursuing its interests in the Muslim world.[57] Thus, the response to Westernization and Western secular influence has been unfavorable and linked to historical agitation since the onset of Western colonial influences in the Middle East.[58] Western influence, coupled by the Catholic Church's endorsement of the colonization of the Arab world, nineteenth- and twentieth-century American and European oil interests, and present US foreign policy in the Middle East region contribute to a rise in revivalist movements, put Islamic societies on the defensive to secure their land and maintain their traditional customs in juxtaposition to the spread of Western values. It is imperative that we understand the nuances of the Islamists' argument to comprehend why conservative political and religious sources in America often "other" the religion of Islam as a violent and vitriolic religion. Thus, this particular debate has created a strain within Islamic society between rising Islamic modernists and traditional religious leadership in Islamic societies.

Noah Feldman affirms that the standard view of scholars and experts in and outside the Muslim world that the "classical Islamic state had failed" was misguided.[59] Standing on opposite sides are two differing positions relating to the motivation behind Islamic fundamentalism, each linked to a different interpretation of Islamic law and the way in which it should be implemented, both within society and among those living outside of the Islamic state. This distinction is made in connection with the idea of *Islamist Sharia* and *Islamic Sharia* and the quest of both to assure justice within the *umma* and between Muslims and the rest of the world. Feldman explains, "Islam, according to this view, is the thing that makes Islamism into a distinctive approach to the reform of government and society. It is the engine meant to restore Muslim societies to world prominence and power. When called upon to define the Islamic character of the state as they envision it, Islamists typically say that what makes the state Islamic is that it is governed through Islamic law and Islamic values."[60] This point is particularly important to US-Muslim world engagement, in that we may comprehend the true intention of the extremist strand or re-Oreintalist mentality linked to Islamic fundamentalist ideology regarding the West.

J. G. Jansen suggests that this strand and mindset, in a real sense, becomes its own religion within itself, with its own religious imagination, religious dream, and theology, calling forth nonstate actors to embrace a religio-political ideology of social emancipation. In both the imaginative and religious dream world of Islamic fundamentalism, the principal concern, as expressed in the Iranian revolution of 1979, is to oppose (or unravel, by any means available) the present political system, which is tainted by Western political and social ideals by basing one's actions on an ideology rooted in religious ideals. Its aim, in consequence, is to pointlessly replace this system by a subversive one that is, as Jansen argues, "[an] imitation of the secular regimes... The different fundamentalist movements and the very power which the governments they oppose exercise: total power, complete power, supreme power, over anyone or anything that even contemplates resisting them."[61]

Furthermore, this type of Islamic fundamentalism is a brand of "identity politics," in that it functions as a collective belief and practice. Thus, it thrives among a small minority practicing Islam who interpret the Arab and larger Muslim world's decline in values as a reference point of its moral decay. Mary Kaldor argues:

> The new identity politics is about the claim to power on the basis of labels—in so far as there are ideas about political or social change, they tend to relate to an idealised nostalgic representation of the past. It is often claimed that the new war of identity politics is more a throwback to the past, a resurgence of ancient hatred kept under control by colonialism and/or the Cold War. While it is true that the narratives of identity politics depend on memory and tradition, it is also the case that these are "reinvented" in the context of the failure or the corrosion of other sources of political legitimacy—the discrediting of socialism or the nation-building rhetoric of the first generation of post-colonial leaders.[62]

Comprehending in clear terms this identity politics and what exactly the United States is up against, Akbar Ahmed puts forward in, *Islam Under Siege,* that the rise in this brand and practice of Islamic fundamentalism by state leaders and nonstate actors emerges from a breakdown in Islamic society and the social cohesion of Islamic society (*asabiyya*).[63] Acknowledging that the fabric of Islamic society was damaged due to concurring political development from the mid-twentieth century onward, Akbar informs us:

> The creation of Pakistan and Israel, the revolution in Iran, the civil wars in Algeria, Afghanistan, and parts of Central Asia displaced and killed millions, split communities, and shattered families. A disproportionately high percentage of the refugees of the world—the truly dispossessed of our time—are from Muslim lands. Refugee camps are notoriously breeding grounds of anger and despair. The young are consumed with a rage that derives from the memory of a home robbed. They have seen little but injustice and indifference in their lives.[64]

The *asabiyya,* which provides a central interconnected support system of social cohesion within Islamic society, according to Ahmed, has succumbed to dishonor and fragmentation under Western secular influence. He asserts, "The dangerously ambiguous notion of honour—and the ever-more dangerous ideas of the loss of honour—propel men to violence. Simply put, global developments have robbed many people of honour, [whereas] rapid global changes are shaking the structures of traditional societies."[65] In an effort to regain this loss of property and value, *hyper-asabiyya,* described by Khaldun as exaggerated tribal and religious loyalties, resulted in extreme cohesion and contributed to a new type of global war.

The new type of war we see emerging in this postsecular era is defined on the basis of regaining honor and lost values and traditions, while spreading a universal truth by exceptionalists and Islamists alike. This is pervasive in the new global jihadist movement of the twenty-first century as led by Osama bin Laden and al-Qaeda's newly assumed leader, Ayman al-Zawahiri and noted figures like Abu Yahya al-Libi, Mustafa Abu Yazid, Saif al-Adel, Abu Musab al-Zarqawi, and Khalid Sheikh Mohammed.

While it is conceivable that the influence of Western secularism provides the principal answer on why US policymakers harbor political apprehensions about religious engagement, this chapter explains that fear manufactured and calculated by conservative forces in America contributes to diverting engagement oppor-tunities. American and Western interests along a historical time line as well were instrumental in infuriating nonelites and nonstate actors throughout the Muslim world. Thus, the new reality confronting this subject is that neither fear manufactured by an exclusive worldview, nor a narrow mindset is productive in this postsecular era to restore US-Muslim relations. As the secularization the-sis is not an accurate reflection of this period, it is imperative that Washington acknowledge that religious movements will continue to contribute to setting the international agenda, which requires that US policymakers move toward the center, away from conservative religious influences to publicly promote and actu-ally practice tolerance and mutual understanding, as set forth by the founders of America's republic.

It is unveiled at this early stage that nefarious forces linked to a Western his-tory of imperialism contributed to the production of a "worldview exclusivism" that leads to a narrow political mindset for engaging global Islamic communities. A capacity of religious tolerance is required in this postsecular era by exercising a "new public diplomacy." The next chapter takes a look at several compelling arguments that further explain the tension present between religion and the dis-cipline of international relations. These perspectives are taken into account as we survey the "new public diplomacy argument," and the relevance of direct two-way engagement between state and nonstate actors that requires players to move beyond a narrow posture to embrace a new way of thinking.

CHAPTER THREE

The New Public Diplomacy Argument

As competing religious and political views converge in the global public sphere, American public diplomacy should consider promoting a more strategic communicative posture that cuts against discounting the aspirations and perspectives of key nonstate actors living in global Islamic communities. Though the practice of traditional diplomacy is essential to statecraft, a bold new form of public diplomacy—broad in scope that incorporates the aspirations of both state and nonstate actors in the dialogical setting—is critical to building sustainable relations with the core of Islamic society. Presently, former US policymakers, public diplomacy practitioners, and academics are embracing a new movement that supports the introduction of bold new approaches to foster creative and long-term collaborative engagement opportunities. This movement's collective argument stresses that the "new public diplomacy" will not displace traditional state-to-state diplomacy, but seeks to expand the role of public diplomacy by engaging nonstate actors to build mutually beneficial relations that move beyond traditional state-centric procedures. This chapter defends this thesis by first appraising the reticence of state actors about acknowledging religious voices, while drawing attention to the imperative of employing a dialogue-based public diplomacy to effectively engage Muslim majority audiences.

Responding to Religion in International Relations

Recent discussions on updating American public diplomacy practices from its narrow state-centric model to reflecting the changing nature brought about by new players and global communication are making headway among practitioners and policymakers. Arguments on the importance of building collaborative relations between state and nonstate actors over the last decade have ranged from incorporating enhanced web 2.0 social networking tools into public diplomacy discourse practices to collective recommendations on advancing soft power (i.e., the ability to shape the preferences of foreign audiences without implementing physical force).[1] As the tectonic plates of global politics shift, ushering in a proliferation of nonstate actors who are setting the international agenda, global public diplomacy is tasked with moving beyond its traditional one-way message transmission posture to one that enters into new corridors to connect with religious voices that are often pushed to the fringe or discounted as nonsubstantive in international relations. If we are to fully comprehend the new public diplomacy argument, it is imperative that we begin by surveying several compelling arguments that further explain the tension present between religion and the discipline of international relations.

As addressed above, realism is a widely accepted political theory that liberal secular states rely upon during traditional track one state-to-state interaction. In recent years, modern realism has successfully stymied prospective healthy state-nonstate actor relations due the adverse attention it brings to the debate on sacred-secular engagement. Relying on traditional state-centric models to engage global Islamic communities in order to disseminate Western values underpins the current context and actions applied by the White House and State Department. While looking into the core principles of realism, we gather why exactly Western state actors oftentimes are reluctant to shift from the realist perspective to comprehend, for example, theo-political motivation behind new religious movements developing in parts of the Arab and Muslim world. Generally, in the case of the US government, analysis related to religious movements in the Muslim world and the religion of Islam itself is carried out within 16 separate agencies that comprise the United State Intelligence Community or within the Department of Defense to enrich US military strategy, as in the case of the US Army's Human Terrain System that utilizes the social science expertise of anthropologists and political scientists. Further, realism as a political philosophy works within a narrow construct which defines the state and state actor relations in terms of power and secularity, thus impeding the formation of a relationship needed between state and nonstate actors.

Noted pioneer, Hans Morgenthau, justifies the separation of religious concerns in the secular political arena in *Politics among Nations: The Struggle for Power and Peace,*

> Realism maintains that universal moral principles cannot be applied to the actions of states in their abstract universal formulation, but

they must be filtered through the concrete circumstances of time and place...Political realism refuses to identify the moral aspirations of a particular nation with the moral laws that govern the universe. As it distinguishes between truth and opinion, so it distinguishes between truth and idolatry.[2]

In a text that has served as a guide to traditional state-based American diplomacy and the study of international relations, a clear line is drawn by Morgenthau between moral ideals and what modern realism defines as legitimate for state and state actor engagement. He defends this, saying, "[for] realism theory consists in ascertaining facts and giving them meaning through reason. It assumes that the character of a foreign policy [for example] can be ascertained only through the examination of the political acts performed and the foreseeable consequences of these acts...[It] believes that politics, like society in general, is governed by objective laws that have their roots in human nature."[3] While assuming it is possible to segregate the concerns and voices of both religious and political citizens within the global public sphere, Morgenthau fails to identify that we are unable to comprehend some human events by ascertaining the facts solely on the basis of reason or secularity. This is the precise reason why comprehending the development of religio-political activities in a postsecular context is imperative. This means coming to terms with the fact that while secularity is real and will not disappear, the proliferation of new players in emerging transnational religious movements requires fair and balanced attention from the nation-state and state actors. Hence, Morgenthau's scholarship in the field of political science demonstrates the highly exaggerated notion that state-actor communication must inevitably be in liberal-secular terms. Consequently, relying on a traditional Western political framework makes appreciation for state/nonstate actor engagement between sacred-secular players incomprehensible.

Recognizing Religion

Elizabeth S. Hurd makes two important observations regarding the interaction between religion and international relations.[4] She notes that "religious fundamentalism and religious differences have emerged as crucial factors in international conflict, national security and foreign policy," and that "the power of this religious resurgence in world politics does not fit into existing categories of thought in academic international relations."[5] Thus, a systemic underestimating of religion in global politics encourages the tendency of state actors and some public diplomacy practitioners to regard religion as a nonsubstantive element, thereby making it convenient to push non-Western religious voices in particular to the fringes, in order to disseminate Western values in parts of the Arab and Muslim world.[6] In "Theorizing Religious Resurgence", Hurd argues,

> Since the end of the Cold War, most political scientists have seen religion as an inexplicable obstacle on the road to secular democracy or as evidence of cultural and civilizational difference in world politics... [The main assumption] is that religion should be expelled from democratic politics; this is laicism. The objective here is to create a public life in which religious belief, practices and institutions have lost their political significance, fallen below the threshold of political contestation and/or been pushed into the private sphere.[7]

Going along with Hurd's perspective, Monica Toft in "Religion Matters in International Relations," says, "Religion matters a great deal, and its positive and negative influence both within and between states is certain to continue well into the coming decades."[8] Thus, Fox and Sandler remark:

> Religion is rarely included in most major theories of international relations and when it is addressed, it is usually through viewing it as a subcategory of some topic that is considered more important, such as institutions, terrorists, society, or civilisation. This disregard is related to the premise that primordial factors such as ethnicity and religion had no part in modern society or in rational explanations for the way the world works, because international relations is perhaps the most Western-centric of the social science disciplines.[9]

Instead of emphasizing the apparent theoretical and philosophical differences amplified by modern realist theory, Craig Calhoun claims that the state actors in this new era should center their attention on what religion and religious nonstate actors might offer the international agenda, in terms of promoting peace in times of great trouble. He explains:

> Religion appears in liberal theory first and foremost as an occasion for tolerance and neutrality. This orientation is reinforced by both

the classification of religion as essentially a private matter and the view that religion is in some sense a "survival" from an earlier era—not a field of vital growth within modernity... [in as much] as religion, moreover, is a part of the genealogy of public reason itself. To attempt to disengage the idea of public reason (or the reality of the public sphere) from religion is to disconnect it from a tradition that continues to give it life and content.[10]

It is through "citizen participation" that both state and religious non-state actors unconsciously fine-tune their usage of Athenian democracy and ensure that the civic virtues of the state are carried out on their behalf.[11] As Roger Trigg reminds us, "Public debate about the proper basis for society is necessary and the religious voice should be heard in that debate."[12] Hence, it is critical we understand here that religious citizens deserve public acknowledgement, considering that the natural rights of all citizens within the liberal-secular state deserve recognition. The new reality that American public diplomacy faces is one where, if increasing religious voices are continuously pushed to the fringes, contempt toward America's national interests will result, furthering increased clashes in the years ahead. Arguably, the most important factor in reaching the core of a traditional society will require that US state actors move beyond preconceived notions of how sacred and secular citizens should interact within this society. Through Jürgen Habermas's and Gerard Hauser's analyses, we may comprehend that developing a common ground for engagement, coupled by a new mindset, offers a unique method to broaden interaction between state and nonstate actors. So that we may gather how actors might consider engaging with one another, let us look first at the dynamic behind the formation of opinions about religion taking place in both the public and private spheres.

Religion in the Public Sphere

In *A Secular Age*, Charles Taylor illustrates that after Enlightenment, religious voices in the West grew less influential due to a "widening gamut of new positions and ideals (some secular and others religious) that evolved among elite groups in Western society."[13] He regards this shift in influence as the *nova effect*.[14] However, one of the smaller changes to occur during this period was the partitioning of social space into the binary worlds that structure the now separated *public* and *private* spheres. For some time, this division has made defining a common ground for both sacred and secular players all the more difficult, out-side of convincing parties that engagement across sacred-secular lines is of the essence. The private sphere consists of civil society, religious traditions, and citizenry that identifies itself with a sacred or moral identity. On the other hand, the public sphere refers, in broad terms, to the secular-political realm of society.[15] However, Taylor argues that the public spheres in both the United States and Europe "have been alleg-edly emptied of God, or of any reference to ultimate reality."[16] Since Enlightenment, most Western public spaces no longer "refer us to God, but to rationality that aids society in reaching its greatest benefit, with-out solely drawing on moral ideals."[17] Habermas clarifies this point,

> By the end of the eighteenth century society had broken apart into private elements on the one hand and into public on the other. The position of the church changed with the reformation: the link to divine authority which the church represented, that is, reli-gion, became a private matter. So-called religious freedom came to insure what was historically the first area of private autonomy. The church itself continued its existence as one public and legal body among others.[18]

Reticence of the Western secular public sphere during the late eigh-teenth century contributed to this decline, placing an emphasis on free-thinking and public reason—no longer drawing solely on moral ideals. Nearly two centuries later the effects of emptying the public sphere of God, and a reliance on political philosophies that discount religion as nonsubstantive have led to the resurgence of religious activity in and toward Western society due to increasing fear religious actors have of losing their traditional values and moral identity. As Europe's public sphere has been forced to redefine its posture toward the influx of new religious voices, so too did the United States with the sudden influx of Islamic voices penetrating the US political decision making. Habermas's descriptions of both the *bourgeois* and *public sphere models* offer a unique starting point for comprehending the value of opinion forming among a body of nonelites.

For nearly two centuries, the *bourgeois public sphere* served, in European society, as a social prescription for an alternative sphere, where pri-vate citizens could meet in café salons and coffeehouses in newly "enlightened" London, Germany, Paris, and Vienna.[19] The aim in the "bourgeois public sphere" was that of generating widespread public discussions and political debates, while promoting social engagement.[20]

Though many of these European homes of public criticism were not specific political institutions, their widespread reputation throughout the Continent held mass credibility in their ability to unite a diverse citizenry, and to test state laws and policies through public discourse.[21] Habermas informs:

> The bourgeois public sphere may be conceived above all as the sphere [in which] private people come together as a public; they soon claimed the public sphere regulated from above against the public authorities themselves, to engage them in a debate over the general rules governing relations in the basically privatised but publicly relevant sphere of commodity exchange and social labour.[22]

Bringing this concept into the present era, he contends that the same strategies as put forth in the traditional *bourgeois public sphere* are practicable in this era with the contemporary *public sphere model,* which, on the other hand, functions as a "realm [in] our social life in which something approaching public opinion can be formed."[23] Both a progressive mindset and balance discourse setting are appropriate to cultivate collaborative relations and a deeper form of engagement between state and religious nonstate actors. Here Habermas calls for the establishment of a forum within society that is conducive to the cultivation of authentic forms of engagement between actors of both worlds. While some will argue that new social media tools such as Facebook, Twitter, Skype, and the creation of virtual US embassies are productive avenues to promote new media activism and the spread of US national interests in the Muslim world, the reality is that their "constituency is too small and their content too superficial to be heavily relied upon in building and maintaining global friendships."[24] Hence, the fact that is widely embraced by public diplomacy practitioners is the precise reason why the US Department of State must turn the page to embrace a new public diplomacy strategy to build long-term direct relations with target audiences on a mutually beneficial common ground.

While the public sphere has descended from coffeehouses and public discourses in religious institutions to the corridors of cyberspace, moving to a more authentic forum that sets out to physically engage religious nonstate actors is a realistic posture that stands as a representation of American democracy. According to Gerard Hauser,

> Democratic forms rest on opportunities for citizens to discuss issues that concern their interests so that they may influence intelligent

public opinion. Concomitantly, people engaged in every day congress with strangers holding diverse beliefs, traditions, and interests have a comparable need for discursive forums in which they may develop a sense of prevailing opinion and participate in charting its course.[25]

Sustaining "democratic forms" ensures that actors or even sacred-secular citizens may contribute to crafting a progressive agenda. Thus, broadening engagement opportunities that will allow both sacred and secular players to coexist to form collaborative relations serves as the bases of the new public diplomacy argument. This position, nonetheless, is an argument that runs counter to previous state–centric models that aid in defining the national agenda of the modern nation-state, which openly excludes engaging nonstate actors (religious players) to promote peacemaking in the public sphere. In contrast to its predecessor, the new public diplomacy provides a broad context for state actors to exercise complementary relations with religious nonstate actors to promote two-way dialogue-based engagement opportunities to establish genuine relations.

A New Argument for Dialogue-based Public Diplomacy

As realism will remain the dominant theoretical approach to international relations for years to come, a shift toward an international paradigm that places a new emphasis on nonstate actors will serve as a fresh concern for Western nation-states in their attempt to engage traditional societies that comprise parts of the Muslim world. The shift toward this new reality in recent years has been of increasing importance to the field of traditional diplomacy and the contemporary practice of public diplomacy. Global public diplomacy is a vital component to foreign policy, considering the changing dimension of global communication and state–nonstate actor relations in recent years. Moving beyond preconceived notions of non-Western societies is critical in an era largely dependent upon two-way relationship-based engagement. Marked by a new call, communication transmission has shifted in recent years from the traditional *one-to-many* mode, which dominated the Information Age, to a *one-to-one* communicative posture represented by culturally diverse relationships between global networks.[26]

Global public diplomacy is currently redefining itself against the backdrop of the Information Age and today's global communication era, marked by what this chapter regards as the old public diplomacy. This—still in use by several nation-states—as Paul Sharp suggests is, "the process by which direct relations of people in a country are pursued to advance the interests and extend the values of those being represented."[27] Moreover, it draws upon a state-based approach to diplomacy that discounts both religion and nonstate actors as nonsubstantive players in the international system. The old public diplomacy is antiquated, and reliant upon communication models as propaganda and contemporary nation-branding campaigns that largely reflect the one-way tools applied during the Cold War era. Philip Seib reminds us that the old public diplomacy "has drifted farther and farther into self-promoting 'branding' that will win over only the most gullible."[28] The emphasis of the old public diplomacy in this new era remains focused on disseminating "a product" by the state in order to achieve an immediate short-term result.

In this period of postsecularism where religious voices are reasserting their presence in global politics, global public diplomacy is forced to adapt its methodology and conceptual approach to state-nonstate actor relations. As state actors acknowledge these new voices in global politics, their reluctance is apparent and distinctly present in American public diplomacy that openly discounts establishing long-term collaborative relations with religious nonstate actors in order to get the feedback from the aspirations and perspectives of nonelites into the foreign policy discussion. Considering the ineffectiveness of the old public diplomacy to connect with key target audiences, contemporary public diplomacy practitioners and former US policymakers collectively are calling for a *new public diplomacy approach* that is broader in scope and capable of functioning effectively in an era driven by network-based communication and new players.

According to the USC Center on Public Diplomacy at the Annenberg School, the essential argument behind the new public diplomacy is:

As distinct from the "narrow" traditional, state-based conception of public diplomacy described above, recent scholarship has offered a "broader" conception of the field's scope by developing the concept of the new public diplomacy which defines public diplomacy more expansively than an activity unique to sovereign states. This view aims to capture the emerging trends in international relations where a range of non-state actors with some standing in world politics—supranational organization, sub-national actors, non-governmental organization, and (in the view of some) even private companies—communicate and engage meaningfully with foreign publics and thereby develop and promote public diplomacy policies and practices of their own.[29]

Functioning within a broad context, the new public diplomacy is far removed from its state-based cousin. It first recognizes the current shift occurring in the international paradigm in state-nonstate actor relations, while second, demanding that the liberal secular nation-state comes to terms with the increasing role nonstate actors may play in providing analysis and promoting cooperation at the grassroots level. Instead disseminating messages via a one-way transmission model of communication, generally from the top-down, the new public diplomacy offers a broad playing field to cultivate long-term collaborative dialogue-based engagement.

> As a result, a new public diplomacy is seen as taking place in a system of mutually beneficial relations that is no longer state-centric but composed of multiple actors and networks, operating in a fluid global environment of new issues and contexts. This new diplomacy will not in the short term displace traditional state-to-state diplomacy as practiced by foreign ministries, but it will impact the way those ministries do business. More than ever before, foreign ministries and diplomats will need to go beyond bilateral and multilateral diplomacy and to construct and conduct relations with new global actors.[30]

Melissen claims that the new public diplomacy is not a reflection in any way of its cousin. Its aim "requires practitioners and diplomats to adopt a new set of broad skills, techniques, and attitudes than those found in traditional state-based diplomacy."[31] The new public diplomacy is dialogue based and will require diplomats to approach communication differently in order to establish direct relations. It has the ability to transform the position of the diplomat from traditional *messenger* to an *interlocutor* who accepts the task of entering into communication with nonstate actors, who under the old public diplomacy might otherwise have been regarded as a threat to the political realm.

Building international relationships dictates applying bold new approaches and a new social ethic driven by mutual understanding and above all, respect for nonsecular opinion holders. Amelia Arsenault informs us that "the benefits of dialogue are most pronounced when communicative interaction is the goal, not a mean's to an ends."[32] The most evident evolution from the old public diplomacy is the new public diplomacy's commitment to promoting genuine dialogue over symbolic interaction, which hinges on building mutually beneficial state–nonstate actor collaborative relations. Joseph S. Nye adds that this broad new approach "is also about building relationships with civic-society actors in other countries and facilitation networks between nongovernmental parties at home and abroad. In this approach to public diplomacy, government policy is aimed at promoting and participating in, rather than controlling, such cross-border networks."[33]

Thereby, as the old public diplomacy is single-mindedly concerned with reaching foreign audiences to shape opinions and restore favorability, the new public diplomacy realizes that this approach, at best, is perceived as disingenuous, unless actors pursue long-term dialogical engagement. While the contemporary new public diplomacy argument is gaining notoriety, the position that the US Department of State expands its diplomatic infrastructure to engage religious nonstate actors is not a new suggestion. Former US government officials like Madeline Albright, Edward Luttwak, and Ambassador John McDonald are reintroducing this proposal that fits into our new public diplomacy argument. Hence, let us turn our attention here to the role of dialogue-based engagement as a vital tool of the new public diplomacy that provides a broader opportunity for two-way communication— and in the case of US–Muslim relations—adequate space for US diplomats to build genuine dialogue and restore trust with key religious nonstate actors.

Dialogue-based Engagement

Daryl Copeland argues that expanding the scope of US public diplomacy requires reimagining the creative ability of the state actor—in this case the American diplomat—within this new framework. As the tectonic plates of global politics shift, both an adjustment in mindset and approaches taken by diplomats are required to invoke change due to the transforming nature of target audiences and their environments. Copeland suggests here that a shift in mindset and the performance of diplomats are taken together, considering the new terrain and the unpredictable set of new players whom the diplomats will engage. He argues, however, that a new methodology and a doctrine of statecraft, regarded as guerrilla diplomacy, be considered "to improve the performance of foreign ministries, and the efficacy of diplomatic practice."[34] Invoking a commitment to direct two-way communicative engagement, guerrilla diplomacy is defined as a flexible form of interaction that responds "to the marginalization of dialogue, negotiation, and compromise that has come with the militarization of international policy."[35] It is an aggressive approach that complements the new public diplomacy argument in that it makes the clear distinction that diplomatic activity is no longer confined to quiet clubs and quaint meeting rooms, but is in barrios, favelas, and war zones and that American diplomats especially must be trained in a new communication strategy before entering these domains.

Assessing the role of this new public diplomacy in context with engaging Muslim voices, Shaun Riordan reminds us that Western nations should consider altering their public diplomacy message, tools, and actors in order that their governments might successfully engage the "Islamic Street." Consequently, this requires pushing beyond a "worldview exclusivism" that clashes with the social and theological tenets held by those in global Islamic communities. Riordan contends that "successful [public diplomacy] engagement must be built upon a genuine dialogue that accepts that Islam is different and has its own values and historical and cultural traditions; that the West does not have all the answers and that, while maintaining its own values, it accepts that not all of them are universally valid for every one everywhere and that there are many paths to democracy and civil society."[36] Taking this position requires Western nations like the United States to come to grips with the new reality that many different worldviews exist and that in order to make a successful connection with foreign audiences, America must respect the aspirations and perspectives cultivated by the *Islamic Street* (i.e., the grassroots level of global Islamic communities).

While Rirodan's proposal hints at a new way forward in global public diplomacy activity by informing us that genuine dialogue is essential for connecting with nonelite groups in the *Islamic Street*, it however puts at risk ensuring long-term engagement between the United States and Muslim world by implying it is better that Western governments outsource dialogical engagement opportunities to nongovernment organizations and their agents. He argues that Western state actors have neither the credibility nor access to engage Islamic society to promote a modern approach to Islam. He makes the claim that "Neither Western governments nor their agents (namely, diplomats) have either the necessary credibility or access. Their need to maintain good relations with existing Islamic governments and political elites further constrains their freedom of action. More credible agents will need to be found among nongovernmental agents in broader Western civil society."[37]

While NGO credibility outranks the credibility of Western governments, efforts that completely outsource broad two-way engagement approaches with the *Islamic Street* to the NGO sector is flawed and inevitably counterproductive. The following three points should be taken into consideration when making the case of exactly why Western governments and their agents should pursue direct dialogical engagement with the *Islamic Street*.

(i)   By outsourcing dialogue-based engagement to NGOs, Western nations run the risk of losing what little credibility they have with global Islamic communities. Though NGOs stand adjacent to governments and are capable of presenting a formidable critique of its policies, while engaging nonstate actors, what is really required are efforts by both Western nations and nonstate actors with the assistance of NGOs to provide training and resources to enrich the capacity for dialogue that leads to mutually beneficial relations between Western governments and the *Islamic Street*.

(ii) While NGOs may provide both cultural and religious education training to enrich dialogical opportunities, both long-term credibility and respect will be established via consistent interactive engagement between state and religious nonstate actors from the *Islamic Street*.

(iii) Dialogue-based engagement with the *Islamic Street* is an essential activity that takes a shift from focusing primarily on promoting Western values to that of reinforcing the future development of policies that feed back the aspirations and perspectives of Muslims into the foreign policymaking circle.

As it is easy to assume that the waning credibility of the Western nation-state is a valid reason to outsource, the reality is that by outsourcing, Western nations (like the United States) will most likely miss a key opportunity to directly restructure a framework that will lead to the adoption of a new public diplomacy approach. Hence, Marshall and Farr illustrate my point in the essay "Public Diplomacy in an Age of Faith," by looking to American public diplomacy and suggesting its aim in this new era must be to "advance U.S. interests and security by imparting to foreign audiences an understanding and appreciation of America's founding principles, ideals, institutions, and policy."[38] To a great extent, this means exerting "a robust vision of a religious freedom that provides a foundation for liberty, preserves religious integrity, enables religious pluralism, and reconciles the dual authorities of religion and state."[39] Furthermore, challenging the absence of this robust vision, Marshall and Farr recommends that the US Department of State consider several proactive strategies. The most vital one encourages "Reforming Foreign Service Officer training and career options, which includes establishing a religion subspecialty corps."[40] Rather than looking to the NGO sector to restore US relations in religious communities, they acknowledge that promoting a new public diplomacy requires that "U.S. diplomatic posts [are] staffed by individuals who have a deep understanding of the particular religious dynamic and are grounded in the importance of religious liberty and practice in the American order."[41]

For this reason, improving US public diplomacy relations with the Muslim world is not a task that should be performed unaccompanied by a state actor promoting two-way dialogical engagement on the state's behalf. Nye argues that in "communicating with distant audiences, leaders need the ability to communicate one-on-one or in small groups. In some cases, the close communication is more important than public rhetoric. Organisational skill—ability to attract and inspire an effective inner circle of followers—can compensate for rhetorical deficiencies, just as effective public rhetoric can partly compensate for low organisational skills."[42] If US diplomats will be responsible for exercising this engagement, arguably this requires that they adopt a mutually beneficial mindset that is culturally competent and capable of functioning within a multitrack framework.

If we are to consider a new approach to communication and the role of a dialogue-based new public diplomacy, let us then turn our attention here to three leading perspectives by Ambassador John McDonald, Madeline Albright, and Edward Luttwak that demonstrate my earlier position on advancing a dialogue-based approach to public diplomacy accompanied by a competent US state actor. Collectively, these perspectives enrich the contemporary new public diplomacy argument. While the following suggestions are not without limitations, they ensure that successful nation-state engagement with key religious nonstate actors be led by actors who are capable of implementing a communication platform that promotes religio-political cooperation.

Multitrack Dialogical Engagement

Former US Ambassador and cofounder of the Institute for Multitrack Diplomacy (IMTD), John McDonald advocates that the State Department consider incorporating elements of *multitrack diplomacy* into its diplomatic framework when engaging nonstate actors, especially in conflict-prone settings, to promote peace and reconciliation.

The term multi-track diplomacy is based on the original distinction made by Joseph Montville in 1981 between official, governmental actions to resolve conflicts (track one) and unofficial efforts by nongovernmental professionals to resolve conflicts within and between states (track two). Later, Louise Diamond coined the phrase 'multi-track diplomacy', recognizing that to lump all track two activities under one label did not capture the complexity or breadth of unofficial diplomacy.[43]

The *multitrack diplomacy* system is comprised of nine individual tracks that operate on separate levels, but which when integrated, formulate a system that accommodates dialogue-based engagement. Diamond's and McDonald's research findings suggest that when this system's approach is used, actors become more accommodating to the mutual interests of both state and nonstate actors in their pursuit to build relations across sacred-secular lines and in promoting two-way dialogical opportunities.

- Track 1: **Government**—*Peacemaking through traditional diplomacy*
- Track 2: **Nongovernmental/Professional**—*Peacemaking through professional conflict resolution*
- Track 3: **Business**—*Peacemaking through commerce*
- Track 4: **Private Citizens**—*Peacemaking through personal involvement*
- Track 5: **Research, Training, and Education**—*Peacemaking through learning*
- Track 6: **Activism**—*Peacemaking through advocacy*
- Track 7: **Religion**—*Peacemaking through faith in action*
- Track 8: **Funding**—*Peacemaking through providing resources*
- Track 9: **Communication and the Media**—*Peacemaking through information*

IMTD experts Notter and Diamond acknowledge that when building such relations, especially in conflict zones, key actors engaged in the peacemaking process should focus their attention on three specific areas while pursuing dialogue-based engagement. The first area is *bridge building*. This includes building bridges through dialogue and actions that "bring together parties in conflict to create mutual understanding,

rebuild trust, and examine together the root causes, needs and interests that underlie each side's stated positions."[44] Communication practices that build relations from the bottom up are indispensable and
require that American diplomats move beyond their constricted posture to embrace a broad holistic approach to engagement.

The second action is *capacity building*. Actors involved in peacemaking efforts should be cognizant in building relationships that lead to
the development of "[core] skills in conflict resolution and reconciliation within a group of local peace-builders who can then use these
skills within and between their own communities. These skills include
a creative blend of both the local, indigenous, traditional methods of
addressing conflicts and Western-based methods...Capacity building is a key component of the social peace building process, which
is about building a human infrastructure."[45] There is a unique value
here in applying interdisciplinary methods in the dialogical setting. For
example, this means that when pursuing conflict resolution actors must
demonstrate that they are comfortable with incorporating traditional
and intercultural approaches that reflect their target audience. This in
essence will require diplomats to take seriously aspects of interreligious
and intercultural dialogue to reach the core of traditional societies,
where large-scale intrastate conflict is pronounced. Hence, as covered
earlier, several post-9/11 failures are a direct result of key diplomats
proving to be incompetent toward the functionality of communication
in the Arab and Muslim world.

Lastly, there is *institution building*. This position includes ensuring
"efforts to help the local peacebuilders develop sustainable institutions—organizations, alliances, working groups, university programs,
etc.—that can further the work of peace building theory and practice in
the conflict system and the broader region."[46] Though referring to the
work of IMTD, Notter and Diamond are implying that actors should
center their attention on building trust and cooperation that evolves
by constructing dialogue-based opportunities and cross-cultural infrastructures. While there are several postconflict peace-building reform
efforts underway in South Asia and in parts of the Middle East, many
fail due to a lack of trust and confidence within global Islamic communities about American leadership and US foreign policy interests.
Ambassador McDonald agrees with this point, acknowledging that the
USG is overwhelmingly political and bureaucratic as well as deeply
engaged in meeting secular demands rather than the mutual concerns
of nonstate actors at the grassroots level. "The negative potential [of the
USG] is its rigidity, exclusivity, elitism, and potential abuse of power.

Its institutes and thinking are strongly embedded in the state-centric mode of power politics, and is [resistant to] change."[47]

Notter and Diamond make the case that by taking a holistic approach, incorporating bridge building, restoring capacity, and utilizing institutions, will allow actors to apply transformational elements that are often at the disposal of nongovernmental organizations. These elements include working within a network-based setting by promoting cooperation and strategic relationship building through direct interpersonal, intercultural, and in some cases interreligious dialogical engagement.

Promoting Sacred-Secular Fellowship

Former US Secretary of State Madeline Albright makes the claim that since living in a world without religion is highly unlikely, the next best alternative is to engage the dynamics of religion in international affairs through direct two-way communication to better comprehend its mission. She says, "The challenge for policymakers is to harness the unifying potential of faith, while containing its capacity to divide." Hence, "This requires, at a minimum, that we see spiritual matters are a subject worth studying."[48] In pursuing a new well-informed way forward to promote sacred-secular fellowship, the former US Secretary of State, in *Mighty and the Almighty*, points to three areas that encourage: (i) the study of religion, (ii) consideration of religious negotiators, and (iii) establishing a corps of specialists adept in international religious affairs.

Bringing attention to the role of education, Albright proposes that US diplomats and foreign policymakers should critically study religious matters and incorporate their findings into progressive strategies for peacemaking at the US Department of State.[49] This guidance is led by J. Bryan Heir's position held by staunch realists "that you do not have to understand religion in order to understand the world. You need to understand politics, strategy, economics and law, but you do not need to understand religion."[50] Hence, Albright makes the case that a broad posture, which includes learning the theological aspects behind religion, can facilitate in enriching US foreign policymaking. She insists that US diplomats, "should develop the ability to recognize where and how religious beliefs contribute to conflicts and when religious principles might be invoked to ease strife... To lead internationally, American policymakers must learn as much as possible about religion, and then incorporate that knowledge in their strategies."[51] Walter McDougall adds to this perspective in the article, "Religion in Diplomatic History," acknowledging the limitation of state-centrism by making the claim that "very few scholars, much less pundits, theologians, or diplomats, display expertise in both fields. Some have a profound understanding of one or more religious traditions, perhaps also a personal faith, but lack knowledge or experience of the rough and tumble of politics. Others are wise in the ways of statecraft either from analysis or practice, but confess to being out of their depth in spiritual matters."[52]

Second, from comprehending the dynamics of religion to making a critical assessment, Albright advises that the State Department utilize religious negotiators as support personnel to encourage conflict reconciliation in hostile settings. Reflecting on several ethnic and religious conflicts during her tenure, she argues, "When participants in a conflict claim to be people of faith, a negotiator who has the credentials and credibility to do so might wish to call their bluff."[53] Reflecting on the sharp deficit in readily available negotiators in cases where intrastate conflicts took center stage during her tenure, she contends that having available competent state actors to build trust with key religious nonstate actors in the dialogical setting, the state actor might convene parties together by drawing on a "creative blend" of factors when pursing reconciliation. She argues:

> If I were secretary of state today, I would not seek to mediate disputes on the basis of religious principles any more than I would try to negotiate along the more intricate details of a trade agreement or a pact on arms control. In each case, I would ask people more expert than I to begin the process of identifying key issues, exploring the possibilities, and suggesting a course of action. It might be well that my involvement, or the president's, would be necessary to close a deal, but the outlines would be drawn by those who knew every nuance of the issues at hand.[54]

And lastly, as several former US policymakers propose, Albright calls for the State Department to "hire or train a core of specialists in religion to be deployed both in Washington and in key embassies overseas."[55] This recommendation comes as no surprise, considering Albright's familiarity with the contribution of Track 2 NGO peacemaking under the Clinton administration during the 1990s. However, Albright's suggestion was introduced previously by former US military strategist Edward Luttwak in 1994 in the essay "The Missing Dimension," where he writes that, "religion attachés could be assigned to diplomatic missions in those countries where religion has a particular salience, to monitor religious movements and maintain contact with religious leaders, just as labour attachés have long been assigned to deal with local trade unions. Intelligence organizations that already have specialists in many functional areas could usefully add religion specialists as well." He continues, "Certainly one should not perpetuate administratively the misconception that religion with its institutions and leaders is necessarily a marginal factor, or necessarily a diminishing force, or necessarily a purely political (or social, or economic, or ethnic) phenomenon in religious guise."[56] Taking note of Luttwak's guidance and the proactive position this might have on American diplomacy, from a reading of "faith-based diplomacy," Albright adds that such a recommendation is capable of providing the structure for the future development of a religious specialists' corps.[57]

Driving Albright to recommend the creation of a religious specialists corps includes the five characteristics of the "faith-based intermediary," which Johnston and Cox identify as an actor: (a) endowed with an ability to utilize spiritual principles in peacemaking; (b) capable of operating with spiritual authority in times of crisis; (c) being able to respect the essence of other religious traditions; (d) understanding the impact of utilizing spiritual texts to connect with religious audiences at a deeper level; and (e) being recognized as having a spiritual perseverance that is grounded in their own faith tradition.[58] Scott Appleby takes the Johnston-Cox position a step further, suggesting that (in addition to these five characteristics) the faith-based intermediary should also reconsider the use of traditional conflict resolution approaches, which most often overlook vital cultural and religious tenets beneficial to the conflict transformation process.[59] Drawing from Appleby's argument, it appears that this new type of actor must either come from or resonate with the conflict-habituated community. This action allows time and space for the intermediary to listen so that he avoids taking an unreasonable position. In addition, this is what Albright has envisioned of this future corps of specialists on religious matters—corps respectful of multireligious beliefs, capable of engaging religious analysis while promoting sustainable US foreign policy; and individuals who are well prepared to engage religious audiences by utilizing two-way dialogue-based engagement to promote sacred-secular fellowship that functions from the bottom up.

This chapter introduced a new argument comprised of several forward thinking proposals that draw attention to Washington's narrow view toward engaging foreign audiences through the communication apparatus of public diplomacy. Its general argument is that a new mindset based on tolerance and dedicated to

pursuing dialogue-based public diplomacy accompanied by US diplomats work-
ing at the grassroots level is a practicable way forward to promote direct two-way
relations with key religious nonstate actors. As Part 1 makes the case, US
policymakers have openly wrestled with engaging religious voices, whether with
conservative Judeo-Christian special interests at home or against radical Islamic
opinion holders abroad. It has failed in both cases to establish a common ground
to survey the aspirations and perspectives of either group, which requires embrac-
ing a new mindset toward religion in international relations.

Interaction across sacred-secular lines in this current postsecular age requires
both state and nonstate actors to acknowledge the value in both religious and
political opinions that are rapidly intersecting in the global public sphere. Part 1
established that deep-seated challenges exist in Washington toward engaging
traditional religion-based societies; the next chapter will take a step back to com-
prehend how these challenges became manifest through conservative religious and
political ideals in American leadership and public diplomacy during the Bush era
months prior to and after 9/11.

PART 2

Crusading US National Security

CHAPTER FOUR

Distorting the Process

While practitioners and theorists are inclined to argue that an absence of grand strategy or a dependence on Cold War communication approaches resulted in America's post-9/11 public diplomacy failure, there are more concrete reasons for this breakdown. For example, a US president publicly projecting American Judeo-Christian ideals, the Project for a New American Century steering post-9/11 US foreign policy, and an open disregard by US state actors toward nonelite Muslim perspectives held in global Islamic communities, thereby counteracting any positive public diplomacy attempt. This chapter explores numerous dimensions of the post-9/11 engagement process, moving beyond "what" precisely contributed to distorting US-Muslim relations to "how" exactly American leadership and key conservative special interests distorted relations. Ensuring that the Bush administration met its post-9/11 "unilateral" objectives to win America's War on Terror and halt the spread of global Weapons of Mass Destruction (WMD) required that a different political atmosphere be established—driven largely by manufactured fear and a rigid neoconservative agenda. Coupled with US President George W. Bush's "God-Talk", a neocon-led agenda succeeded in promulgating America's political and social arrogance. As this dual agenda failed in winning the War on Terror and attracting global Islamic communities to embrace American values, this chapter makes plain how such attempts created a false sphere of confidence in order to crusade for a staunch US national security agenda, while pacifying yet keeping global Islamic communities at arm's length.

A Neoconservative-led Agenda

In presenting a declaration of war at a joint session of the US Congress on September 20, 2001, newly elected US President George W. Bush posed this stirring question to Americans asking, "Why do *they* hate us?" As a young nation turned superpower after the Cold War, America would again be caught in an ideological struggle, this time between political Islam and a conservative "Western world-view exclusivism" personified by Bush's faith-based values.[1] Providing clarity as to why the *terrorists* hate America, President Bush stated:

> They hate what they see right here in this chamber: a demo-cratically elected government. Their leaders are self-appointed. They hate our freedoms: our freedom of religion, our freedom of speech, our freedom to vote and assemble and disagree with each other. They want to overthrow existing governments in many Muslim countries such as Egypt, Saudi Arabia and Jordan. They want to drive Israel out of the Middle East. They want to drive Christians and Jews out of vast regions of Asia and Africa. These terrorists kill not merely to end lives, but to disrupt and end a way of life. With every atrocity, they hope that America grows fearful, retreating from the world and forsaking our friends. They stand against us because we stand in their way.[2]

Oftentimes conservative leadership in the US assumes that America's liberty stirs rage among radical Muslim opinion-holders (as predicted by Bernard Lewis). However, it is essential to realize that a set of concrete irritants contribute to the insecurity projected by Islamists. Fareed Zakaria agrees that something much greater than American democracy contributes to anti-Americanism. Acknowledging the cowardice of the 9/11 hijackers, Zakaria disputes Bush's claim that American democracy or its freedoms are the substantive reasons that justify why poor and desolate people blow themselves up. Hence, "if envy were the cause of terrorism, Beverly Hills, Fifth Avenue and Mayfair would have become morgues long ago."[3] Reminding us that "There is something stronger at work here than deprivation and jealousy, it is something that can move men to kill but also die." In contrast to America's Cold War nemesis (the Soviet Empire) jockeying for world supremacy—its new enemy is now a radical conservative religious ideology emerging as a powerful force in global politics. Remarking upon this new irritant in his address, Bush specified it as a "fringe form of Islamic extremism that has been rejected by Muslim scholars and the vast majority of Muslim clerics—a fringe movement that perverts the peaceful teaching of Islam."[4]

From the last decade of peril in Afghanistan, it is evident the Taliban would neither succumb nor agree to America's five demands, announced by Bush, that led to a declaration of war in which they were demanded to:

> (i) Deliver to United States authorities all of the leaders of al-Qaeda who hide in your land; (ii) Release all foreign nationals, including American citizens, you have unjustly imprisoned; (iii) Protect foreign journalists, diplomats, and aid workers in your country; (iv) Close immediately and permanently every terrorist training camp in Afghanistan, and hand over every terrorist and every person and their support structure, to the appropriate authorities; [and] (v) Give the United States full access to terrorist training camps, so we can make sure they are no longer operating.[5]

Notwithstanding the president offering what appeared to be an objective presentation of the likely problem, as commander in chief of the United States of America, Bush's actions, between 2001 and 2008, would both contradict and distort any favorable efforts to restore trust with Muslims by agencies such as the State Department or the US Agency for International Development. While an absence of a grand strategy (rooted in a two-way dialogue-based public diplomacy) and a reliance on Cold War communication approaches were paramount during this period, Bush's erratic public behavior and off-hand religious rhetoric toward Muslims abetted in distorting the communication process. Despite providing a disclaimer that "The enemy of America is not our many Muslim friends. It is not our many Arab friends. Our enemy is a radical network of terrorists and every government that supports them," Muslims throughout the world would view America's leadership and military activity in South Asia with suspicion.[6]

Despite outlining a strategic plan for the War on Terror to contain radical Islamic ideals and counter future terrorist attacks, it is apparent that both the White House and State Department failed in producing a practicable strategy to effectively engage the *Islamic Street*. When looking closely, it appears that the absence of a grand strategy (that exercised dialogue-based public diplomacy via trained professionals to engage the religio-cultural dimensions of Islamic society) permitted a pivotal opportunity for a set of ad-hoc engagement approaches to materialize that achieved the goal of pacifying global Islamic communities in order that Washington reach its post-9/11 covert interest. Such actions to controvert global Islamic aspirations and perspectives included distorting the communicative context on four specific levels: first, by exercising one-way transmission models of communication to pacify global Islamic communities by selling American values; second, by omitting religious nonstate actors from the engagement process; third, by inciting cultural wars in the United States that pitted America Judeo-Christian aspirations against the religion of Islam in the public sphere; and most importantly, fourth, which led to promoting a staunch neoconservative agenda that functioned in concert with set of neoconservative values.

The Promise of an American Century

The neoconservative movement cast itself into the American political sphere during the Cold War as a staunch supporter of an aggressive US foreign policy and national security agenda. Its leading convictions were to: (i) give credence to the *American Century*—a period in history where US primacy has no competition and US purposes are fully realizable; (ii) hold that America's values are "universal" and should be installed with democracy around the world; and (iii) regard America as an exceptional nation.[7] Its most prominent organization after the Cold War, The Project for a New America Century (PNAC) captured this conviction in its statement of purpose by promoting four specific aims that set out to: increase US defense spending significantly if America would carry out its global responsibilities today and modernize its armed forces for the future; strengthen America's ties to democratic allies and to challenge regimes hostile to its interests and values; promote the cause of political and economic freedom abroad; and accept responsibility for America's unique role in preserving and extending an international order friendly to its security, prosperity, and principles.[8]

Charles Krauthammer captures this vision in the post–Cold War essay, "The Unipolar Moment," outlining the post-Reaganite era neoconservative agenda. Beyond laying out a new direction in US foreign policymaking immediately after America's support for Kuwait in the Gulf War, he reflected that the latter part of the twentieth century was an opportune period for the United States to seize global dominance considering that it had entered an era where its power was unchallenged since the fall and dismantling of the Soviet Union. Expanding America's preeminence across the globe meant exercising unilateralism—accompanied by a coalition of willing states unified behind America's national security agenda. Making his case on the value of promoting US primacy, Krauthammer says,

> International stability is never a given. It is never the norm. When achieved, it is the product of self-conscious action by the great powers, and most particularly of the greatest power, which now and for the foreseeable future is the United States. If America wants stability, it will have to create it…[Hence], we are in for abnormal times. Our best hope for safety in such times, as in difficult times past, is an American strength and *will*–the strength and *will* to lead a unipolar world, unashamedly laying down the rules of world order and being prepared to enforce them.[9]

Emerging as the dominant nation-state after the Cold War for neoconservatives meant leading from a position of absolute strength and implementing a unilateral foreign policy agenda to ensure US security, while extending its predominance to keep in check purported "Weapons States."[10] Prominent neoconservative figures like William Kristol and Robert Kagan introduced their own reinterpretation of Krauthammer's vision, outlining that in order to bring this post–Cold War promise into being required the use of force both *unilaterally* and *preemptively* in the essay, "Toward a Neo-Reaganite Foreign Policy" (1996). Responding to the Clinton administration's foreign policies that neocons were convinced had compromised American security, Kristol and Kagan argued,

> Having defeated the "evil empire," the United States enjoys strategic and ideological predominance. The first objective of US foreign policy should be to preserve and enhance that predominance by strengthening America's security, supporting its friends, advancing its interests, and standing up for its principles around the world. The aspiration to benevolent hegemony might strike some as either hubristic or morally suspect. But a hegemon is nothing more or less than a leader with preponderant influence and authority over all others in its domain.[11]

The political liberalism of Clinton's first term, according to Krauthamer, Kristol, and Kagan reflected the trepidation that purported "Weapons States" might threaten America's unipolarity and interest in South Asia and the Middle East. Moving beyond this suggested fear meant that

American leadership after the Cold War needed to apply the necessary physical force and unilateral measures to ensure US national security. The writings of several neoconservatives during this period provided the backdrop of what later became an aggressive agenda of George W. Bush's administration after 9/11, a decade later contending that "the Weapons State is an unusual international creature marked by three characteristics as being failed a state as Iraq, generally oil states with a repressive state apparatus that dominates civil society, and in 1990 that Iraq would soon become a weapon's state in ten years, or a nation with deep grievances against the West."[12] As argued later on in this chapter, the neoconservative language that persisted in the writings of key neocons during the 1980s and 1990s would soon become instrumental in shaping the Bush Doctrine after 9/11.

Clearly, the political and security agenda of neoconservatives to install an American hegemony across the globe is exclusive in both framework and interpretation. This conservative interest-based interpretation presented, for example, by Kristol and Kagan at the outset, restricted both America's foreign policy and prospective communication relations with the post–Cold War world's new nonstate actors to advance multilateralism. To a large degree, the neocons' vision functions in an imperial context that sets out to sever ties with nations and actors who appear to be at odds with its national security and foreign policy agenda, thereby shrinking the opportunity for Washington to enter into a mutually beneficial context, leading to the establishment of a common ground. This neoconservative agenda meant looking beyond valuable opportunities after 9/11 to appraise the aspirations of moderate Islamic voices and their objections. Furthermore, this posture shaped itself into a threefold foreign policy, public diplomacy, and a staunch military agenda to advance the US's preeminence in South Asia.

Meeting America's national security interest in South Asia after 9/11, on the surface required converging the principles of this new conservative advocacy movement with publicly expressed faith-based values represented by *fear* and *dominance* of an American president to shape the new international context. While projecting American Judeo-Christian ideals into American politics is not a leading neoconservative position—after 9/11—little, if any, objections were raised by neocons about George W. Bush exercising political moralism in context with a neocon-led foreign policy to win the War on Terror. For example, Mel Gurtov reminds us that "Two foreign policy implications flow from Bush's moralism. One is a faith-based certainty in the rightness of his actions and a strong tendency to ignore facts that get in the way of decisions already made. Another is his belief in the oneness of God's and [America's purpose]."[13] Bush's determination after 9/11 meant carrying out his duties as president, while adhering to his own faith-based convictions. Gurtov claims, "Moral certainty and religiously informed devotion to the national interest are a dangerous combination. They create a sense of destiny that mirrors the vision of fundamentalist regimes and movements. In the hands of a leader with awesome military and economic power at his disposal, they have the potential to convert U.S. exceptionalism into U.S. adventurism."[14] Because of Bush's position as commander in chief, his reliance on his religious convictions would inevitably clash with his liberal-secular obligation to pursue unbiased decision making. By relying instead on these instincts, after 9/11, the president along with his administration contributed to distorting the larger communicative engagement process.

Projecting Compassionate Conservatism and God-Talk

Stephen Mansfield, in *The Faith of George W. Bush,* says that the president's major policies were influenced by his newfound commitment to Christianity.[15] Unlike previous American presidents, who were often reluctant to project their religious commitment publicly, Bush's presidency after 9/11 was defined by a barrage of religious rhetoric and a reliance on religious convictions, while acknowledging that evangelical Christians in particular had a religious partner in the Oval Office.[16] In his campaign biography *A Charge to Keep: My Journey to the White House*, Bush reaffirms his commitment to Christianity and his devotion to lead the United States compassionately, identifying this specific task as "God's calling and a sacred opportunity to improve history."[17] Bush recognized this not just as his calling, but as the obligation of all Christians, as citizens, to improve America.[18] The same "doomsday" rhetoric upheld decades earlier resurfaced, with Bush stressing that America was on the brink of "moral decay" and Christian ideals are likely to steer the young nation in the right direction. Bush writes in *A Charge to Keep*:

> During more than half a century of my life, we have seen an unprecedented decay in our American culture, a decay that has eroded the foundation of our collective values and moral standards of conduct. Our sense of personal responsibility has declined dramatically, just as the role and responsibility of the federal government have increased...We can now say, without question, that

the belief that government could solve people's problems instead of people solving people's problems was wrong and misguided.[19]

Bush's political moralism reasserted the late twentieth-century Moral Majority's central argument that only a moral solution could solve America's moral decay. This moral solution became apparent in his governing philosophy, *compassionate conservatism*—a commitment to limit the role of the government in addressing social issues.[20] This position argues that government should be focused, effective, and close to the people, but not the sole actor in reconciling domestic matters related to health, poverty, and social welfare. Introducing his governing philosophy, Bush emphasized, "I call my philosophy and approach, compassionate conservatism. It is compassionate to actively help our fellow citizens in need. It is conservative to insist on responsibility and results. And with this hopeful approach, we will make a real difference in people's lives."[21]

According to Michael Gerson (Bush's chief speechwriter between 2001 and 2006), "Compassionate conservatism is the theory that the government should encourage the effective provision of social services without providing the service itself."[22] This conservative conviction permeated the Bush administration's domestic and foreign policy agenda. For example, this would be the case with the administration's position on American public school education with its presentation of the No Child Left Behind policy, combating poverty in the United States by relying on faith-based charities as partners, and providing massive aid packages to underdeveloped countries around the globe.

In a real sense, this governing philosophy provides the starting point to comprehend why this administration set out, months prior to and after 9/11 to engage with Muslim audiences at arm's length. First, compassionate conservatism shapes the context of how US policy would approach both domestic and foreign affairs between 2000 and 2008; while second, after 9/11, efforts to restore trust with the Muslim world resulted in Washington either outsourcing engagement opportunities to nongovernment organizations, or engaging with the *Islamic Street* at arm's length by exercising outdated one-way transmission models of communication.

Bruce Lincoln remarks that Bush "understands compassion to be quality of spirit that characterizes (religious) individuals and groups, but is categorically different from the soulless, bureaucratic nature of the state."[23] President Bush did not shy away from applying his religious conviction to ensuring a moral solution to promote a conservative vision for America. Strangely, he identified his role as president as a *calling* to bring America out of its dependency on liberal ideals. As the Moral Majority's most staunch advocate, Bush insisted that America was a "soulless bureaucracy," deserving of compassionate leadership capable of restoring the "soul of the nation" by exercising a conservative policy agenda. Hence, the translation of Bush's religious convictions into public rhetoric went on to be the foundation of what scholars like Lincoln regard as "Bush's God-Talk". Lincoln establishes that Bush's God-Talk included "an evangelical theology of 'born again' conversion; a theology of American exceptionalism as grounded in the virtue of compassion; a Calvinist theology of vocation; and a Manichean dualism of good and evil."[24]

Bush's God-Talk gained traction after 9/11 with several offhand remarks regarding the War on Terror and negative references regarding Islamic society. Bush's exclusivist worldview clashed with political Islamist's anti-Western worldviews that criticized America's hegemonic position as an imperialist state. For example, just five days after 9/11, Bush's reference to the War on Terror as America's crusade against radical Islamic forces heightened objections in the Muslim world toward America's role in Afghanistan, while forcing Charlotte Beers and other public diplomacy practitioners to apply damage control. Commenting on America's efforts to combat terror in an interview, the president stated, "This crusade, this war on terrorism is gonna take awhile. And the American people must be patient. I'm gonna be patient...We haven't seen this kind of barbarism in a long period of time...This is a new kind of evil."[25] Bush's use of the term "crusade" incited controversy in the Muslim world and especially among key Islamic leaders in Europe embroiled in an ongoing Muslim-West debate. James Carroll makes the case in *The Bush Crusade*:

> For George W. Bush, [the term] crusade was an offhand reference. But all the more powerfully for that, it was an accidental probing of unintended but nevertheless real meaning. That the president used the word inadvertently suggests how it expressed his exact truth, an unmasking of his most deeply felt purpose...He defined crusade as war. Even offhandedly, he had said exactly what he meant...A coherent set of political, economic, social and even mythological traditions of the Eurasian continent, from the British Isles to the far side of Arabia, grew out of the transformations wrought by the Crusades. And it is far from incidental still, both that those campaigns were conducted by Christians against

Muslims, and that they, too, were attached to the irrationalities of millennial fever.[26]

Bush's use of a biased term like "crusade" incited fear and suspicion among Muslims about Washington's policies to "rid the world of evil."[27] Drawing from the academic playbooks of confrontationalists like Lewis and Huntington—both of which provided substantial advisement to the president after 9/11—Bush fell in line with manufacturing fear and a sense of phobia to galvanize America's conservative base. In fact, cultivating this fear was in fact a necessity to point to the tension between East and West as a cosmic battle that only a moral Western solution could resolve.[28] Such solutions include the promotion of American values, which neocons agree are universal, spreading Western democracy, and combating radical Islam with a right-wing Christian political moralism.

Bush's God-Talk resurfaced again in Egypt at the Israeli-Palestinian Sharm el-Sheikh summit in 2005, with the president affirming his religious convictions, exclaiming:

> I am driven with a mission from God, God would tell me, "George go and fight these terrorist in Afghanistan." And I did. And then God would tell me "George, go and end the tyranny in Iraq." And I did... And now, again, I feel God's word coming to me, "Go get the Palestinians their state and get the Israelis their security, and get peace in the Middle East." And, by God, I'm gonna do it.[29]

Crystallizing his commitment to lead this new "crusade" to contain the spread of radical Islamic ideology and combat terror, Bush announced to the world on September 24 that all nations must make a choice, insisting, "There could be no neutrality in the coming struggle. Every nation, in every region, now has a decision to make," adding that, "Either you are with us, or you are with the terrorist."[30] Such an ultimatum would not attract non-Western nations without the coercion of foreign aid and political arm-twisting. Nevertheless, this religious rhetoric and Bush's neocon-led agenda would shift America's position in the international system from the potential post–Cold War multilateral leader to predominant unipolar hegemon.

In contradicting the US Establishment Clause—*"to not favor one religion over another within the US political realm"*—as president, Bush failed in upholding this commitment. However, Bush's open devotion and religious convictions interfered with sound decision making and the clear-mindedness needed to embrace religious pluralism and tolerance when dealing with emerging postsecular issues. Despite Bush's repeated attempts to present olive branches to Muslim majority nations, asserting that "America is not at war with Islam," such promises fell on deaf ears. With a commitment to rid the world of terrorism by spreading America's influence and power in key parts of the Arab and Muslim world, his agenda succeeded in alienating Muslims by projecting an exceptional American worldview that showed little if any regard to either the cultural or ethical dimensions of Islamic society. By taking this approach, the Bush administration thereby promoted three all-important components to aid in advancing American security and predominance in South Asia after 9/11. They included Bush's misguided religious rhetoric that infuriated global Islamic communities while cultivating "cultural wars" at home, a narrow neoconservative strategy that presented a fierce political realist agenda on extending American predominance in South Asia, and the Bush Doctrine that saturated US foreign policymaking at all levels in the US government—including the US Department of State's mission to engage the Muslim world months prior to and after 9/11—leading to adverse exchanges between Washington, US state actors, and key nonstate actors in the Muslim world.

The Bush Doctrine

Prior to President Bush assuming office on January 20, 2001, American neoconservatives and conservative special interests groups were consumed with seizing the right post–Cold War moment to project their worldview into reshaping America's national security agenda. Prominent Washington-based conservative advocacy groups dedicated to preserving and even projecting this worldview included the US Committee on NATO, the Committee on the Present Danger, Clifford May's Foundation for Defense of Democracies (2001), and the Committee for the Liberation of Iraq (2002). Among these influential organizations with the ability to garner national attention within the Washington Beltway was PNAC, chaired by neo-Reaganite William Kristol and led by prominent neoconservatives like Donald Rumsfeld, Dick Cheney, Paul Wolfowitz, Robert Kagan, Frank Gaffney, Fred Iklé, Zalmay Khalilzad, Richard Perle, Elliot Abrams, Francis Fukuyama, and Peter W. Rodman. Given the opportune moment, one might agree that PNAC's political and military influence might soon become a driving force in twenty-first century American foreign policy. Considering the events of 9/11, its influence was relentless in ensuring America's dominance in the international system against challengers such as smaller "Weapons States." Meeting the neoconservative movement's objectives meant shaping and providing a firm national security agenda.

Furthermore, PNAC's inflexible agenda conveyed a seriousness toward installing US global leadership after the Cold War by applying a narrow American foreign policy built on the successes of the Reagan administration dedicated to promoting a US military strong and ready to meet both present and future challenges; a foreign policy that boldly and purposefully promotes American principles abroad; and national leadership that accepts the United States' global responsibilities.[31] Demonstrated in its statement and principles, PNAC sets out that American foreign policy had fallen adrift after the Cold War, due in part to the Clinton administration's commitment to liberal internationalism and its resistance to "isolationist impulses from within its ranks."[32] According to PNAC's leadership, "[cuts] in foreign affairs and defense spending, inattention to the tools of statecraft, and inconstant leadership" contributed to a set of opportunities that makes it "increasingly difficult to sustain American influence around the world."[33] Hence, defending America's new post–Cold War responsibility meant taking seriously the need to increase US defense spending, strengthening ties with democratic allies, promoting economic and political freedom, spreading American values, and expanding US military primacy.

Both the election of US President Bush and the terrorist attacks of 9/11 created the opportune moment for PNAC to inject its neo-Reaganite national security agenda. Acknowledging this position, Mel Gurtov reminds us that the terrorist attacks had three transforming effects on American foreign policy.

> First, it elevated neocon thinking—a vigorous US nationalism— to the intellectual center... Second, 9/11 downgraded the particularities of traditional realism and globalism in favor of a new crusade akin to the Cold War crusade that fused anticommunism with an open-door world economy... [and] Third, 9/11 crystallized two simple but very expansive strategic objectives: winning the war on terror and undermining rogue states that possess, or might possess, weapons of mass destruction.[34]

US National Security Strategy (2002 and 2006)

For example, several key recommendations introduced by leading neocons like Charles Krauthammer, William Kristol, and Robert Kagan were adapted into core pillars of the Bush Doctrine and US National Security Strategy, 2002 and 2006.[35] The three core components of the Bush Doctrine are: (i) the endorsement of preemptive strikes against potential targets linked to terrorist activity, (ii) advancing military primacy, (iii) supporting a new multilateralism by establishing a coalition of the willing, and (iv) the spread of democracy to combat terrorist ideology within the Middle East.[36]

The premise of the Bush Doctrine is unraveled in the following NSS 2002 statement highlighting the Washington post-9/11 agenda to combat terror:

> The security environment confronting the United States today is radically different from what we have faced before. Yet the first duty of the United States Government remains what it always has been: to protect the American people and American interests. It is an enduring American principle that this duty obligates the government to anticipate and counter threats, using all elements of national power, before the threats can do grave damage. The greater the threat, the greater is the risk of inaction—and the more compelling the case for taking anticipatory action to defend ourselves, even if uncertainty remains as to the time and place of the enemy's attack. There are few greater threats than a terrorist attack with WMD.
>
> To forestall or prevent such hostile acts by our adversaries, the United States will, if necessary, act pre-emptively in exercising our inherent right of self-defence. The United States will not resort to force in all cases to pre-empt emerging threats. Our preference is that nonmilitary actions succeed. And no country should ever use pre-emption as a pretext for aggression.[37]

Reflecting on the 2002 NSS at the Waldrof Astoria, US Secretary of State Condoleezza Rice said that, "President Bush's new National Security Strategy offers a bold vision for protecting our nation that captures today's new realities and new opportunities. It calls on America to use our position of unparalleled strength and influence to create a balance of power that favors freedom."[38] In pursuing a strategy of unparalleled measures to tackle asymmetrical warfare inflicted by nonstate combatants after 9/11, the neocon agenda was upheld to address the purported rise in "Weapons States," and several strategies such as the National Strategy to Combat Weapons of Mass Destruction (NSCWMD) were implemented to promote counter weapons proliferation, particularly in South Asia. In carrying out this agenda, NSCWMD identified three central components to the proliferation of WMDs from falling into the hands of terrorists. They include: counterproliferation to combat WMD use; strengthening nonproliferation to combat WMD proliferation; and establishing a consequence management unit to respond to WMD use.

When considering the NSCWMD impact on a more nuanced level, its first component highlights the imperative counterproliferation to offset the flow of WMDs from reaching the hands of Islamic extremists involved directly or indirectly with the Taliban or al-Qaeda. Countering the development of nuclear arms by interdiction was the chief interest of the president's national security plan and was also seen as a means of assuring counterproliferation after 9/11. Efforts to counter WMDs were reinforced by US military and intelligence agencies at the Department of Defense, the CIA, the National Security Agency and National Intelligence Council, in efforts to deter cross-border transactions of arms proliferation and the financing of terrorist cells. Tactics involve preemptive measures, and analyzing of these agencies's "capabilities of detecting and destroying an adversary's WMD assets before these weapons [were] used."[39]

The second component centered on "diplomatic approaches in bilateral and multilateral settings in pursuit of [Washington's] nonproliferation goals."[40] Suppressing terrorist organizations and countries that purportedly posed an imminent threat to US national security interests by the development and selling of nuclear arms, chemical and biological weapons, and ballistic missiles, were to be carried out under this component, therefore setting, to a degree, the foreign policy and diplomatic agenda. In doing so, the Bush administration proposed measures that openly supported the Nuclear Nonproliferation Treaty and the International Atomic Energy Agency's objectives on a number of levels, including UN sanctions against foes.[41] The selling of chemical and biological weapons was halted through a US government alliance with the Organization for the Prohibition of Chemical Weapons. Conversely, in its pursuit to halt missile production by rival states and international terrorist organizations, the United States would lapse in reinforcing its position in the Missile Technology Control Regime by offering strategic "support for universal adherence to the International Code of Conduct Against Ballistic Missile Proliferation."[42]

The final component of this strategy provided a central outline of how the United States might protect and defend the "American homeland" in the event of future terrorist attacks by establishing a Department of

Homeland Security. The objectives of the *National Strategy of Homeland Security* falling under this third component addressed the role of the White House Office of Homeland Security, first in "[coordinating] all federal efforts to prepare for and mitigate the consequences of terrorist attacks within the United States, including those involving WMDs", and, second, in committing the Office of Homeland Security to "[working] closely with state and local governments to ensure their planning, training and equipment requirements [were] addressed" in the event of another terrorist attack. [43]

In establishing these three components to combat WMDs, an upgraded US *National Security Strategy* was introduced in March 2006 after Bush's reelection, shifting the focus of the global War on Terror from being combat and weaponry intensive to containing the flow of radical Islamic ideology by promoting nation building, the spread of democracy and support for democratic regime change in order that Muslim majority nations such as Afghanistan and Iraq might combat Islamic extremism. The NSS 2006 set out with the objective to ensure that the Middle East no longer served as a breeding ground for recurring terrorist activities. In taking proactive measures, the Bush administration implemented alternative steps. The NSS 2006 states:

> The long-term solution for winning the War on Terror is the advancement of freedom and human dignity through effective democracy. Elections are the most viable sign of a free society and can play a critical role in advancing effective democracy. But elections alone are not enough . . . They are responsive to their citizens, submitting to the will of the people. Effective democracies exercise effective sovereignty and maintain order within their own borders; address causes of conflict peacefully, protect independent and impartial systems of justice, punish crime, embrace the rule of law and resist corruption. Effective democracies limit the reach of government, protecting the institutions of civil society. In effective democracies, freedom is indivisible.[44]

Among other important objectives like containing the spread of radical Islamic ideals throughout the Arab world, regime change became an essential component of the new paradigm. The 2006 NSS accomplished, on the surface, two specific goals: (i) identifying in clear terms America's new enemy as extreme Islamic ideology, terrorists, and rogue states that the US government planned to defend against at all costs militarily; and (ii) it included the course of action for rebuilding key nations such as Iraq and Afghanistan in an effort to promote effective democracies within countries identified as failed states.

While the Bush Doctrine set out to ensure American security, its rigid approach came with a price that meant alienating the political opinions of some Western allies in the international system, while projecting unfavorable unilateral policies that cut off prospective opportunities to recognize the interests of state and nonstate actors throughout the Middle East and Arab world. Between *Bush's God-Talk* and *a hard-line neoconservative agenda*, the prospects of endorsing a dual communication and security strategy capable of working within a postsecular context was far removed from the Bush administration's grasp. Washington did not make the world any safer prior to 9/11 by exercising a rigid neocon national security agenda to extend America's predominance. This posture, however, planted a seed of insecurity that flourished into widespread apprehension by US state actors toward the religion of Islam and political Islamists. In clear terms, America's insecurity over the last decade has inevitably cost Washington its reputation throughout the Muslim world and the possibility of improving international ventures to restore trust with global Islamic communities.[45]

The Limitations of the Bush Doctrine

On the whole, the political framework of the Bush Doctrine is limiting in two regards: First, it promotes a hyperrealist strategy to contain the spread of radical terrorist ideology to combat against future terrorist attacks and, second, it is shortsighted in acknowledging the unpredictable nature of religion in post-9/11 US foreign policymaking. Drawing on the traditions of political realism, the Bush administration's approach centered on projecting power politics that excluded building valuable relations with key nonstate actors in South Asia and the Arab world prior to and after 9/11. While it is true that the US Department of State held extensive ties with nongovernment organizations in both regions, US policymakers in Washington were reluctant to realize that establishing relations with key tribal and religious nonstate actors is a valuable tenet in the War on Terror. Hence, while both the National Security Strategies of 2002 and 2006 firmly outline Washington's foreign policy agenda to combat global terrorism and the spread of Islamic extremism, they fail to present a comparable strategy on engaging the base of global Islamic communities to build strong relations through dialogue-based engagement. After 9/11, the consensus in US policymaking circles hinged on applying ad hoc approaches to engage the base, which as chapter one mentioned, had previously existed to sell American values and ideals to European public behind the Iron Curtain.

In a real sense, the Bush Doctrine fails at recognizing that America (as the rest of the world) has entered a period of postsecularism, which suggests that Washington's post-9/11 policies must be updated to function competently in this new era. This highlights the imperative of setting policies that move from identifying the religion of Islam as a potential threat to US policymakers to comprehending its role as an entry point and instrument of peacemaking to deter Islamic-based terrorism. Hence, the aim of the Bush Doctrine served a larger agenda to extend US primacy vis-à-vis the promotion of democratization. In turn, it really succeeded in "expanding its material military capability and the presence of a U.S. domestic ideology cultivated by fear."[46] Jonathan Monten arrives at this point in the essay "Roots of the Bush Doctrine," stating:

> In an approach variously characterized as "democratic realism," "national security liberalism," democratic globalism" and "messianic universalism" the Bush administration's national security policy [centered] on the direct application of U.S. military and political power to promote democracy in strategic areas...More broadly, the Bush administration [proposed] a liberal international order grounded in US military and political power, as its 2002 National Security Strategy NSS contends, the unparalleled US position of primacy creates a moment of opportunity to extend the benefits of freedom across the globe...[to] actively work to bring the hope of democracy, development, free markets, and free trade to every corner of the world.[47]

As acknowledged above, the Bush Doctrine contributed a lot to: (i) distorting US-Muslim world communication, (ii) ensuring the spread of American values to global Islamic communities, and (iii) replacing the spread of radical Islamic ideals with a Western worldview. Joshua Marshal acknowledges that Bush's unilateralist policies on the whole "produced quick victories in Afghanistan and Iraq but have yet fractured the nation's alliances causing the world system to be more chaotic and unfriendly and the United States to be less secure."[48]

Looking back in detail at the Center for Strategic and International Studies' report, *Mixed Blessings*, that drew our attention earlier to the three obstacles related to US engagement with religion and culture during the Bush era, we gathered that misreading the Establishment Clause, Washington's narrow bureaucratic framework, and its ability to discount religion as nonsubstantive would work in concert with the Bush Doctrine and the president's religious rhetoric to distort US-Muslim relations. When looking more closely at these obstacles, Danan and Hunt reveal, first, that misunderstanding the Establishment Clause provided the political context that led US state actors to be more apprehensive about challenging the Bush administration, or entertaining any form of critical analysis of international religious issues or state-religious nonstate actor engagement into its larger policymaking discussion. According to *Mixed Blessings*, when US government department and agency officials were interviewed:

> Some officials said they believe the Establishment Clause categorically limits government activities related to religion, while others said they were not sure of the specific ways the clause should shape their actions and decisions. This lack of clarity on the rules regarding religion can hinder proactive engagement. Some government officials said they are sensitive about approaching religion because they fear being personally attacked—via litigation or public opprobrium—for possibly violating the Establishment Clause. Although usually unclear on the legal parameters of this engagement, government officials are often certain of the political risks involved.[49]

This level of apprehension has penetrated the US government system, leading policymakers to be apprehensive about religious nonstate actors, especially in the Muslim world. In this case, the Bush administration—despite the president's contradictory projection of religious rhetoric—"comprehended religion as a dangerous or divisive issue best left out of analysis."[50] It appears, however, that further discussion between USG agencies on its parameters and its gathering a definitive understanding of the Establishment Clause deserves greater attention. This discussion is one that would initially broaden the conversation on how the administration could possibly engage religion to employ strategic nonviolent peacemaking as a first option.

Second, this report maintains that the US government's contemporary framework for "approaching" religious issues is too restricted and narrow. It implies that the framework generally lacks a progressive focus when confronted by emerging religious and cultural elements in global politics. After 9/11, this restricted framework would intersect with a narrow vision toward the religion of Islam, fostering an insular US government culture skeptical of analyzing the religion of Islam to promote peacemaking.

> Despite the fact that religion is seen as powerful enough to fuel conflict, policymakers less often [engage] with its peacemaking potential. The current focus on extremism...skewed official US policy toward viewing Islam through a threat lens, rather than as a community of actors who may also be able to play a positive role in international relations.[51]

The final, but most important, obstacle identified recounts how the Bush Doctrine influenced the overall framework of US departments and agencies, whereby actors reduced the concept of religion to a nonsubstantive topic in American foreign policymaking discussions. It is clear here how a neocon-led national security agenda might permeate through the US government system. For example, the Defense Intelligence Agency, the Central Intelligence Agency, and the Department of Defense would each take narrow approaches toward engaging global Islamic communities keeping within the parameters as set forth by the Bush Doctrine. Reflecting on the reluctance by US departments and agencies toward training or recruiting actors adept in international religious affairs, Danan and Hunt say:

> Although mainstreaming religious awareness across the government will be critical to improving engagement abroad, many government officials mentioned the lack of religious experts as a particular problem. Hiring of religious experts has recently been emphasised by some government officials, but their use has been ad hoc and resource-constrained and there is often a lack of incentive for these experts to join the government.[52]

J. Bryan Heir interjects in *Religion, Realism and Just Intervention,* "The separation of religion from political discourse and the broader assumption that religion may be treated as a 'private phenomenon,' significant in the lives of individuals but not a force of public consequence, has been treated as a given in the discipline of international relations and in the discourse of [American foreign policymaking after 9/11]."[53] Barry Rubin however, adds, "U.S. foreign policy, in recent decades, has often misread the importance of religion as a factor in the national politics and international behaviour of some countries and regions. This has sometimes led to incorrect analysis and erroneous policy responses which have proven quite costly."[54]

Ensuring that the Bush administration met its post-9/11 "unilateral" objectives to win the War on Terror and curb the spread of global WMDs required creating a distorted political atmosphere—driven by Islamophobia. This chapter makes the case that events after 9/11 served as a pivotal moment for "neocons" to converge the personal religious beliefs of US President George Bush with the neo-Reaganite principles of the neoconservative movement. With such a narrow view as a starting point, we gather exactly why the Bush administration adopted such a shallow approach to engage the Muslim world (an approach limited in offering equal attention to the vast majority of Muslims). Thereby, two essential points are evident. First, given the Bush administration's hesitation to engage the vast majority of the Muslim world, the US government, at present, has no alternative but to move beyond its division of the sacred and secular in American politics. This in turn means welcoming a more integrated approach that promotes communicative interchange to ensure that the perspectives and aspirations of key nonstate actors and grassroots' networks are included in the overall foreign policy discourse. Second, in order to put this point into practice, Washington must take seriously the task of redefining a strategy that deals with concrete postsecular issues that transcends the voices of both state and nonstate actors in the political realm. In order to accomplish this goal, US government agencies must:(a) better comprehend vital aspects within Islamic society by broadening their narrow bureaucratic framework, (b) build more direct relations with Muslim audiences that pay due heed to the traditional voice of Islamic society—religious leadership, and (c) set out to restore relations with global Islamic communities from the bottom-up that build on mutual understanding and mutual interest.

CHAPTER FIVE

Marketing the American Brand

This chapter shifts from appraising the role of communication distortion as exercised by US policymakers after 9/11 to an evaluation of how the absence of a dialogue-based public diplomacy approach greatly impeded US-Muslim outreach between 2001 and 2008. In making the case, this draws attention to what occurs within the US foreign policy environment when postsecularism is not taken seriously by US State Department officials, and what became of US public diplomacy after 9/11 when a long-term dialogue-based approach was neither considered nor exercised to directly engage global Islamic communities. These and other major considerations are raised in this discussion in light of the new trend established during the Bush era to nominate former corporate marketing executives to the seat of US Undersecretary for Public Diplomacy and Public Affairs to market the American brand by overlapping the practices of public diplomacy and nation branding. The epic failure of Charlotte Beers and Karen P. Hughes to trumpet America's brand to a value-defined socially constructed Muslim world is carefully assessed. This chapter uncovers that post-9/11 public diplomacy efforts by the US Department of State hinged on applying these and other ad hoc one-way transmission models of communication that provided short-term solutions rather than a long-term dialogue-based focus with key religious nonstate actors. Such lackluster attempts set out to engage with global Islamic communities at arm's length, consequently widening the contemporary US-Muslim world trust deficit.

Institutional Limitations

In comprehending the role of post-9/11 US-Muslim world engagement, it is appropriate that we raise the question as to which is more important, the *means* or the *ends* by which the US Department of State engages global Islamic communities. Months prior to and after 9/11, US Muslim outreach efforts focused primarily on the *means*, which included the application of one-way transmission models of communication that inevitably discounted both the religious and cultural dimensions of Arab society. Such efforts were short-term in their approach in juxtaposition to the long-term two-way communicative relationships required when engaging value-defined societies like global Islamic communities. While practitioners may argue that the *means* are important, the argument here is that the public diplomacy focus must begin with the *ends* in mind. Thus, when the *ends* are discounted, state actors are likely to apply ad hoc measures that are reluctant to make a viable connection with nonstate actors.

Throughout the post–Cold War era, misinformation and reluctance by US policymakers to take seriously the religious dimension in global politics has often led to poor decision making, misguided policies, and setbacks when engaging global Islamic communities. Part I of this study addressed two major shortcomings contributing to misguiding post-9/11 US public diplomacy: the application of adverse foreign policies to promote a War on Terror to target key audiences in the Arab world (against the backdrop of a chaotic history of US-Middle East foreign relations), and the US government openly discounting the role of both religion and culture when analyzing the sociopolitical terrain of target audiences in the Arab and Muslim world. From these two shortcomings additional blunders such as Bush's God-Talk and a staunch neoconservative agenda constructed the foundation and provided the context leading to a reluctance by key US state actors to take seriously the aspirations and perspectives of nonelites throughout the Muslim world.

To comprehend this case better, it is important that we delve deeper to appraise the ad hoc function of the post-9/11 State Department communication apparatus of public diplomacy and its exercise of short-term one-way transmission models of communication that overlapped both the practices of public diplomacy and nation branding. In understanding this perspective, it is imperative to openly acknowledge the influence that a narrow bureaucratic framework and the present institutional limitations have on ensuring that Washington has adept professionals committed to researching and addressing international religious concerns and vital intercultural issues. The absence of a forward-thinking body or office at the State Department devoted to these concerns contributes to key US policymakers and diplomats focusing more on the short-term *means* rather than on the long-term *ends* of post-9/11 public diplomacy engagement. A lack of comprehension about the role of international religious affairs and how state actors might effectively engage social worlds successfully is the central reason behind the State Department's public diplomacy missteps that relied on overlapping public diplomacy and nation-branding practices to win the hearts and minds of Muslims. This point is first made clear while looking at the narrow framework and limitations at the State Department as associated with the Office of Religious Freedom, located in the Bureau of Democracy, Human Rights and Labor.

Relying on International Religious Freedom

The International Religious Freedom Act, passed in 1998 "established the promotion of religious freedom as a US foreign policy objective, (mandating) the creation of an Office of International Religious Freedom (IRF)."[1] Further responsibilities of the office include mandating all US embassies to produce a comprehensive final report on the status of religious freedom, which, along with the United States Commission on International Religious Freedom, provides foreign policy insight to the White House and State Department, and key US government agencies on Countries of Particular Concern. The religious freedom agenda was promoted in the mid-1990s by activists who focused on the importance of preventing Christian persecution abroad, and a broader coalition of faith-based and human rights groups rallied around the larger religious freedom issue. But how does this institutional limitation and narrow framework reflect throughout the US government system?

Since the mid-1990s, the White House and State Department have promoted programs whose titles connote interest in religion or faith, but whose agendas are far from critical thinking about the resurging international religious issues or exercising a forward-thinking project supportive of interreligious relations, religio-political analysis, conflict resolution or staffing and training key personnel within the US government system to address international religious communities through dialogue-based engagement. This is highlighted, for example, with President Obama's White House Office of Faith-based and Neighborhood Partnerships (and previously, President Bush's White House Faith-based and Community Initiatives) serving primarily as a hub for American faith-based organizations to receive public sector funding to provide social welfare across the United States. Of the 15

US cabinet-level departments in the executive branch with interagency specific foreign policy agendas, none have a mission on international religious concerns in global politics in this postsecular era. Considering the new levels of global religious intensity, to date the United States has neither taken up the challenge to establish an agency or central office concerned specifically with these issues like previous approaches taken by the Departments of Labor, Treasure, Energy or Defense that recruits, trains, and deploys interagency attachments to US embassies to carry out their mission-specific tasks.

Despite having an office of IRF that serves as the only serious outlet at the State Department to address international religious concerns, in recent years it has garnered criticism from within and from former administrators about the way that it prioritizes concerns. US diplomats, on occasion, have suggested that "the issue of [religious freedom] has often been limited conceptually and structurally."[2] Indicated in the IRF mandate, the primary goal of the office is promoting religious freedom as a core objective of US foreign policy. With international attention in recent years placed on human rights and the Abu Ghraib and Guantanamo Bay prisons torture issues, additional focus has been placed on religious persecution and support for freeing religious prisoners. Critics of the IRF suggest that this redirection currently limits and narrows the attention available for meeting the initial IRF goal of promoting religious freedom and places it on more formidable issues for the present international community.

A US Department of Peace

Recognizing the needs of a broad forward-thinking agency committed to research and analysis on religion, culture, and peace calls for a new way forward and new tradition, which takes seriously the promotion of peace through nonviolence. Liberal special interests groups and key US policymakers suggest that Congress consider passing the H.R. 808 *Department of Peace and Nonviolence Act,* which calls for the establishment of a Department of Peace and Non-violence. Setting up a US Department of Peace (S. 1756) was first proposed in the US Senate by Senator Mark Dayton (D-MN) on September 22, 2005 (but returned to the House on February 7, 2007. Congressional Representative Dennis Kucinich reintroduced it on February 18, 2011 (H.R. 808), and it is currently gathering legislative support). H. R. 808, as a groundbreaking congressional proposal, concentrates on the cornerstones of promoting peace and nonviolence in establishing a comprehensive Peace

Department. As idealistic as this modern proposal may appear—this recommendation is not far-fetched—because such a department was first proposed more than two centuries ago (in 1792) by Benjamin Rush and Benjamin Banneker. Rush's proposal, published in Banneker's *Almanac*, envisaged an additional executive branch department to serve as a counterpart to the US War Department (Department of Defense).

The concept of H. R. 808 introduces a grand vision of a Department of Peace led by a Secretary of Peace, who will set its tactical agenda that includes: (i) working proactively and interactively with each branch of the USG on all policy matters relating to conditions of peace; (ii) serving as a delegate to the National Security Council; (iii) drawing from the intellectual and spiritual wealth of the US private, public and nongovernmental sectors for the development of coherent policy; and (iv) monitoring and analyzing the causative principles of conflict while making policy recommendations for developing and maintaining peaceful international conduct.[3] It is within the confines of such bureaucratic infrastructure that opportunities to promote analysis on international religious concerns may seriously be developed by well-trained US state actors.

Hence, the absence of a forward-thinking body or ministry to handle international religious concerns stifles US government's outreach capabilities within the Muslim world, especially on comprehending how to effectively engage socially constructed value-defined societies. This could contribute to potential communicative failure, considering the fact that most predominantly Muslim countries (and those with significant religious populations) have a Ministry of Religious Affairs with trained diplomats that deal with broad international religious issues. This is the case today, for example, with countries such as Turkey, Pakistan, Oman, Burma, Myanmar, China, Indonesia, the Philippines, Bangladesh, Greece, Iraq, Brunei, and Saudi Arabia—which have Ministries of Religion led by a Minister of Religious Affairs to address key international religious concerns confronting their nation's foreign agenda.

If most predominantly Muslim countries have Foreign Ministries with specific departments to address emerging religious concerns with trained offices adept in interreligious relations, conflict resolution, or religio-political analysis, what is the equivalent for this within the State Department's Office of International Religious Freedom—whose officials are generally cultural affairs officers limited in resources, and are based solely in Washington DC? After 9/11, Washington's reading of the Muslim world was limited in part to focusing on the short-term means, due to the absence of a serious forward-thinking body with an approach broader than international religious freedom or trumpeting America's brand, which might aid the Office of Public Diplomacy and Public Affairs. As we acknowledge this unique institutional limitation and a narrowness in comprehension about religion—due in part to America's marginal bureaucratic framework—its evident how one-way transmission models of communication surfaced as the State Department's primary ad hoc resource, which ran counter to the engagement norms of Arabs and the larger Muslim world that rely upon two-way communication when building new relations or restoring trust.

Insufficient Analysis

Arguably, absence of a forward-thinking body that takes serious international religious concerns beyond religious freedom and the US government misreading the sociopolitical terrain of the Muslim world after 9/11, contributed to the application of Cold War public diplomacy models of communication to reach global Islamic communities. The unavailability of a forward-thinking body contributed to an inadequate diplomatic environment subject to reapplying Cold War one-way communication models that received relative success by disseminating persuasive propaganda messages to European publics behind the Iron Curtain. The use of propaganda by the United States Information Agency (and other outlets like Voice of America), provided a means of support during the Cold War period in combating Communist-led propaganda campaigns disseminated by the Kremlin.

While the term and field of *public diplomacy* are presently evolving, its core component—of setting out to ensure long-term two-way communication opportunities—was (and still to date is) omitted from Washington's engagement with Muslims. It is for this reason that practitioners in the field recognize post-9/11 public diplomacy efforts as a mere extension of the one-way transmission models applied by the United States Information Agency during the middle and late twentieth century. However, in recent years practitioners are challenging the concept and practice of public diplomacy through the lens of the *new public diplomacy*, a substantive alternative to the ambiguous and poorly defined concepts of twentieth-century public diplomacy. Let us turn our attention here to survey how this poorly defined conception, nonetheless, led to erratic communication approaches in the Arab and Muslim world after 9/11 under the leadership of both Charlotte Beers and Karen P. Hughes.

Engaging Global Islamic Communities (2001–2005)

In January 2001, Washington's newly appointed Secretary of State, Colin Powell, introduced a robust agenda to reorganize the State Department's post–Cold War infrastructure and improve America's ailing image. Both agendas were confronted by new challenges and demands linked to budgetary cuts and transitioning America's public diplomacy focus from Eastern Europe to the Arab and Muslim world. As a first priority to bring the State Department into a new global era and revive its outdated infrastructure, Powell introduced a two-pronged strategy: to change the leadership culture so that managers at all levels focus on training, empowering and taking care of their people and remedying critical management deficiencies. The latter included: (a) restoring diplomatic readiness by rebuilding the State Department's diplomatic corps, (b) providing State with modern information technology, (c) focusing on the security of the nation (including the interests of Americans abroad), (d) assuring safe, healthy, and secure US embassy and consulate facilities overseas, and (e) relating the budget to agreed strategies, policies, and priorities.[4]

Powell's mission to restore the US's diplomatic infrastructure included training and ensuring that US diplomats were adept in meeting the new demands the new era offered with respect to the closing of key US embassies throughout Europe. Powell's visibility as a Four Star General and Washington insider made it possible to rally key support for his proposed *Diplomatic Readiness Initiative*, which aided his first agenda to restore the State Department's infrastructure. Lauded as a success during Powell's tenure, the November 2004 Foreign Affairs Council's Independent Assessment acknowledges that the initiative was influential between 2001 and 2003 in hiring 1,158 new diplomats (which included 561 consular and 608 diplomatic security hires); revising the State Department's recruitment system; in increasing US Foreign Service applicants from 8000 during FY 2000 to nearly 20,000 in FY 2004 (marked by the hiring of new recruits with advanced foreign language skills); in implementing biannual Employee Satisfaction and Commitment Surveys; and in increasing courses offered at the Foreign Service Institute.[5]

As attention turned to America's ailing image in the Arab world, the view from the top-down by State Department officials on the question of improving relations ensued, but with a lack of coherence on why Arab audiences displayed unfavorable perceptions toward the United States. Like other US agencies, the State Department perceived the problem as an isolated regional matter instigated by Arab media outlets and influential nonstate networks (i.e., radical Islamic groups) that might potentially be countered by a sharp well-funded information campaign that resembled one-way transmission models from the Cold War era. Further, Powell and other insiders missed the mark by succumbing to the perspective that "America's increasing trust deficit with Arab audiences was associated with the spread of inaccurate information as opposed to Washington's chaotic foreign policies in the Arab world."[6] By promoting vague, short-term communication symbols that later served as a major alternative to long-term two-way relationship based strategies included, but were not limited to, increasing foreign aid to Arab countries, promoting cultural and academic exchanges and lecture tours, and disseminating media programming to boost a favorable image of the United States. Arguably, these one-way efforts, at best, succeeded at keeping global Islamic communities at arm's length, dismantling any possibility of building a genuine connection with Muslim audiences at the grassroots level. Essentials such as comprehending the sociocultural terrain and the role the religious dimension contributes to the construction of communication in Islamic society were neither considered nor applied from the outset by Washington after 9/11, leading to dysfunctional communicative relations.

Selling the American Brand

Convinced that America held a distinct national brand and sellable story that Arab audiences might readily consume, Secretary Powell turned to the private commercial sector, hiring former marketing CEO of Ogilvy & Mather, Charlotte Beers. As America's new "Brand Ambassador," Beers's chief responsibilities were to improve America's ailing image in the Arab and Muslim world and to establish public diplomacy outreach initiatives targeting key audiences to transmit "accurate" information. In 2002, Beers launched her maiden nation-branding effort, the *Shared Values Initiative* (SVI) to connect the United States with Arab audiences, stimulate dialogue between the United States and Muslim world, and establish a forum to disseminate one-way messaging to counter terrorist's propaganda. SVI's central objectives included "highlighting the common values and beliefs shared by Muslims and Americans, demonstrating that America is not at war with Islam and stimulating dialogue between the United States and the Muslim world."[7]

Costing around $15 million, SVI spotlighted the life of Muslims living in America through a well-funded market-driven television campaign, developed by the New York based McCann-Erickson global advertising firm. Disseminated in six languages throughout the Arab world, the five-series media campaign included a booklet entitled, *Muslim Life in America* (distributed by local embassies), instructional websites, cultural and academic exchanges, lecture tours, and additional information-based programs targeting primarily women and children. Despite the State Department's attempts to reach a broad Muslim audience by promoting common values between American society and the Muslim world, the SVI media campaign and "television advertisement turned into embarrassments when countries such as Egypt, Lebanon and Jordan refused to air them."[8] Hence, SVI's centerpiece television campaign, which it hoped would be broadcast on multiple occasions, had lackluster appeal and was only aired briefly through the winter months of 2002 and 2003.

> This multimedia campaign also included a booklet on Muslim life in America, speaker tours, an interactive Web site to promote dialogue between Muslims in the United States and abroad and other informational programs. The initial phase of the Shared Values Initiative was aired in six languages in Pakistan, Indonesia, Malaysia and Kuwait, as well as on pan-Arab media. The State estimates that 288 million people were exposed to these messages, but television stations in several countries, including Egypt and Lebanon, refused to air them for political and other reasons.[9]

Ironically, three signature public diplomacy campaigns (SVI, *Hi* Magazine and the Partnership for Leadership) implemented under Beers were eventually terminated and replaced with similar programming initiatives by Undersecretary Karen P. Hughes in 2003. The task of setting up public diplomacy programs that fell under the auspices of marketing America's brand and selling values to State Department diplomats was not an easy sell for Beers. Hence, the Beers's legacy is marred by criticism that its application of commercial marketing approaches to sell rather than genuinely share America's values with global Islamic communities vis-à-vis well-funded media and exchange outlets ran counter to the religious and cultural dimensions of Islamic society. After the SVI media campaign failure, additional initiatives were introduced. With a budget of $4.5 million, Beers launched *Hi* magazine throughout the Middle East and North Africa.

Hi publications were produced by a private sector firm, with the State Department estimating its "circulation to be about 50,000 in the Arab world. For example, one official in Egypt, however, said that of 2,500 copies the embassy distributed monthly to newsstands in Cairo, often as many as 2,000 copies were returned unsold."[10] In effect, the *Hi* publication, according to Middle East critics, lacked substance and meaningful content. While the magazine "focused on articles with subjects like internet dating, snowboarding and yoga [its content was] criticised at home and abroad."[11] Thus, key religious nonstate actors throughout the Muslim world regarded the magazine as an insult. The magazine went on to dampen the fact that critical social issues between the United States and the Muslim world were occurring as it overlooked consideration of both the religious and cultural dimensions of the Muslim world by presenting a Western portrait to Middle East youth. Beers's last initiative during her tenure, the $150 million Partner for Leadership Program, was eventually suspended after three years, while avenues were investigated as to how the State Department might reach more young adults, with lowering the cost of operations.

Inspite of the State Department's ability to employ high cost corporate marketing approaches when engaging target Muslim audiences, such efforts proved unreliable. Of the US Government Accountability Office's (GAO) numerous reports during this period, the office recommended that while the State Department incorporated communication elements used by the private sector, these elements should include "having core messages, segmented target audiences, detailed strategies and tactics, in-depth research and analysis to monitor and evaluate results and a communication plan which brings it all together."[12] During the Bush era, American public diplomacy focused primarily on reaching unclear *ends* to US-Muslim engagement by applying short-term distorted *means* to engage the core of Islamic society. Beginning first, under the leadership of Charlotte Beers, and to a great extent later, under the tenure of Karen P. Hughes, the Bush administration established a new trend by nominating former corporate marketing executives to serve as the US Undersecretary for Public Diplomacy and Public Affairs to sell America's brand by overlapping the practices of public diplomacy and nation branding to market American values.

Overlapping Public Diplomacy and Nation Branding

In recent years, several public diplomacy practitioners and internal government agencies such as GAO have asked: "How could a well-funded post-9/11 public diplomacy campaign miss the mark to directly connect the United States with its target audience in the Arab world?" While the conventional argument suggests shortage of funding and a lack of resources as nominal reasons, others agree that the State Department's misconception that selling its message without making a genuine connection with a value-defined traditional society is why America's post-9/11 public diplomacy campaign failed. Hence, under the direction of Charlotte Beers and Karen P. Hughes, contemporary nation-branding approaches were applied in conjunction with one-way transmission models of communication in a concerted effort to market American values. Relatively new to the discipline of marketing, nation branding is *success-over-understanding* oriented and insistent in its attempt. The application of this approach raises questions as to whether nation branding is in fact an effective communication approach to connect with value-defined societies as the Muslim world to build or restore trust.

Focusing primarily on promoting a country's image as a tool to conjure international attention, British place branding expert Simon Anholt illustrates this position in the study *Brand America* with a hexagon having six points of interest: Tourism, Exports, Governance (foreign and domestic policy), Immigration, Culture, and People. Recognizing in *Brand America* that key vectors upon the hexagon that underlie the Anholt-GfK Roper Nation Brand Index (an international survey that measures the quality and power of a country's brand image) determines a country's marketability.

In the case of the United States, Anholt suggests that America has an identifiable brand and sellable story linked to an American history of liberation and freedom that foreign audiences are likely to find appealing.

> America has taken so naturally to being a nation brand partly because it has always been a country that stands for things, both for itself and for people. It has always been fond of big ideas. It's a country that has always liked to feel that its actions reflect deeply held beliefs about itself and about the way the world works, or should work.[13]

While the Anholt study attempts to put forward a strong case, it sidesteps acknowledging the overwhelming failure of liberal secular states in their endeavor to brand Western values to value-defined and often religion-based non-Western societies. Anholt's argument, particularly about America, surmises that the world is a marketplace where ideas and traditions may be readily consumed, if a nation's hexagon is balanced. The major misconception perceived in the Anholt study is that the world will readily welcome America's perceptible brand and story. Both Powell and Beers held this presumptuous perspective after 9/11, maintaining that the rich values present in traditional societies throughout the Muslim world might be redefined within a short period if met by a persuasive message. As the field of marketing and advertisement makes room for nation branding to contribute to enriching a country's overall image, arguably its convergence with public diplomacy is particularly detrimental to post-9/11 US-Muslim relations.

By taking a *success-over-understanding* posture, brand ambassadors as Beers tend to bypass critical analysis and the emerging realities linked to culture and tension created by previous historical relations as in the case of US-Middle East foreign policy. Their focus is often shifted toward reaching quick results by exercising short-term symbols that attempt to pacify target audiences. Comparing the roles of *nation branding* and *public diplomacy*, Jan Melissen argues, "Branding's level of ambition easily outflanks that of the limited aims and modesty of most public diplomacy campaigns."[14] By nature, public diplomacy, in contrast, is *understanding-over-success* oriented and "based on the common sense assumption that state actors are not the decisive factors in determining foreign perceptions."[15] Furthering this perspective, Gyrogy Szondi introduces the comparative nature of both perspectives into this debate:

> Branding is very much image-driven, with the aim of creating positive country images. It is largely one-way communication where the communicator has control over the message, which tends to be simple and concise and leaves little space for dialogue and interactions... Nation branding has more visibility as it relies heavily on visual sand symbols and therefore target audiences are able to detect that they are exposed to another country's branding campaign, unlike public diplomacy, which is a more subtle operation, which relies more on behavior than symbols.[16]

Public diplomacy's reliance on behavior is linked to its function as a communicative instrument dedicated to relationship building. Whereas nation branding is indirect in its approach toward foreign audiences in the sense that it is less concerned with the intricacies of interpersonal relations that are central in traditional societies that comprise large parts of the Muslim world.

Beers announced her dependency on image-driven programming as the sole option to connect with Arab audiences during the Committee on Foreign Relations Hearing on American Public Diplomacy and Islam in February 2003. Presenting her case on Washington's new way forward, just two years after launching the SVI, proposing increased branding and image-driven programming efforts, Beers announced "We need to take the best of America to other countries, to offer who we are honestly and sincerely, to share with them our exceptional gifts in English teaching, literature, science, and technology."[17]

SVI's *Hi* magazine campaign, academic exchanges, and Reward for Justice information pamphlets (geared toward women) were developed as one-way transmission models to disseminate Washington's message (which as well included utilizing SVI's radio and television initiatives and the establishment of Al-Hurra Satellite Network). Additional outlets included: booklets and brochures such as *Iraq: From Fear to Freedom, Iraq: A Population Silenced, and Iraqi voices for Freedom*; and cultural exchanges that included invitations to Arab women to witness the American political process; women from Afghan government ministries to receive training in leadership management; and northern Iraqi/Kurdish television producers who visited the United States to learn about American journalism. Pressing her case in front of the Council on Foreign Relations, Beers pointed to additional lackluster recommendations insisting, "[America] can do a better job of sharing what's already known and written through television and the Internet... There are brave and bold plans in front of you now. Prominent among them are a Sesame Street for teens, an Arabic-language television channel, an Arabic-language magazine, the Middle East Partnership Initiative and its important exchange component, and a global Partnership for Learning initiative aimed initially at the Muslim world."[18] Ensuring a steady flow of congressional funding support for existing and future projects meant identifying in clear terms that image-driven projects are a valuable resource in reaching Washington's *end* goal to improve its ailing image.[19]

This study contends that public diplomacy and nation branding are constructive tools to approach foreign audiences, but when overlapped to advance US-Muslim outreach, their convergence proves to be deleterious. Additionally, the State Department's post-9/11 public diplomacy agenda to influence Arab audiences was led by the White House's impatience to restore America's ailing image. Further, haste led to an

unsuccessful public diplomacy campaign that owes its primary failure
to misreading the social and religious terrain of the Arab and Muslim
world. Washington's distorted view of the Muslim world and a lack of
attention given to key elements as *culture* and *religion* and their influence in constructing communicative actions in Islamic society led to
America's post-9/11 public diplomacy failure. By misreading the social
terrain of traditional societies that comprise many predominantly
Muslim nations, key state officials believed that traditional communication approaches used to connect with Western audiences were sufficient to engage global Islamic communities. It is evident that post-9/11
public diplomacy experienced a cross-cultural communication clash
in its endeavor to pursue one-way transmission models, while engaging Arab audiences that by nature respond confidently to two-way
communication. Taking this analysis a step further, let us survey how,
after Beers's tenure that relied to a great extent on overlapping nation
branding and public diplomacy, Karen P. Hughes's legacy would both
triumph over the Beers project and establish a new communicative
tradition at the State Department committed to relying on commercial
marketing approaches to win the hearts and minds of Muslims.

Branding America (2005–2007)

When taking over as Undersecretary of State for Public Diplomacy
and Public Affairs in September 2005, former Texas communication
director for George W. Bush, Karen P. Hughes, continued in the State
Department's new tradition to sell America to global Islamic communities. Reaching this goal meant updating preexisting State Department
academic and professional exchange programs into massive marketing
campaigns. In carrying out this short-lived mission over a two-year
tenure, Hughes public diplomacy contribution focused on three specific areas: expanding academic and professional exchange programs,
modernizing state and intergovernmental agency communication
efforts, and expanding US foreign assistance by placing an emphasis on
promoting a diplomacy of deeds.

Ensuring the facilitation of these goals, the Policy Coordination
Committee (PCC) was established and led by Hughes in April 2006.
The high-level PCC held the responsibility for convening senior-level
USG officials from all agencies to promote a strategic plan for new
program opportunities in predominantly Muslim countries. Additional
subcommittees were also introduced: the Rapid Response Unit,

which monitors the coverage of US policies and anti-American propaganda on foreign media outlets; the establishment of three international media hubs located in London, Brussels, and Dubai, providing US government officials access to foreign audiences via television and radio; and the Counterterrorism Communication Center, established in 2007 with aims to counter terrorist messaging that runs counter to US national interests.

Academic and Professional Exchange programs

A core component of marketing American values to foreign audiences has centered on building strong relations through cultural exchange. Giles Scott-Smith of the Roosevelt Study Centre argues:

> The ability of individuals to cross national boundaries has been a matter of major consequence since the arrival of the nation-state, and exchanges are naturally no exception. Even the most politically neutral of exchanges, such as those between high schools, have either political intent behind their creation or are promoted from the purpose of developing cross-border relations that can subsequently lead to political outcomes, such as a reduction in conflict.[20]

The first academic and professional exchange developed by Hughes expanded preexisting exchanges or *people-to-people* programming under the Bureau of Education and Cultural Affairs (ECA). Historically, many of the State Departments professional exchanges have serviced the State Department by promoting US foreign policy while targeting specific audiences. One specific program initiative that Hughes offered to key Arab and Muslim audiences was sponsored through ECA and the Bureau of International Information programs was the International Visitor Leadership Program. To ensure Powell's objective, Hughes spent much of her time as undersecretary winning the hearts and minds of Arab and Muslim teenagers.

Some of the major academic and professional exchanges launched under her tenure included The *Youth Exchange and Study Program* (YES Program), introduced in 2003 after Beers's resignation. It was set up to provide high school students from significant Muslim populations an opportunity to spend an academic year or semester in select countries. *The English ACCESS Micro Scholarship*, launched in 2004 centers on teaching English to nonelite Muslim teenagers in over 85 countries and has a current base of over 70,000 participants. *The National Security Language Initiative* (NSLI-Y) launched in 2006 is an exchange program between American and foreign teachers to teach and/or study critical foreign (e.g., Arabic, Chinese, Mandarin, Hindi, Korean, Persian, or Russian). *The Community College Initiative* launched in 2006 by Dina Habib Powell launched in 2007, aimed to attract 1,000 Egyptian students to study in US community colleges for up to one year. It has expanded its reach to include academics from Brazil, Cameroon, Costa Rica, Ghana, and Turkey to study in eligible fields as agriculture, business management and administration, allied health care or information technology. *The Global Cultural Initiative*, launched in 2006, continued to promote cultural diplomacy by advancing cultural partnership between American and foreign artists. The Iraqi Young Leadership Exchange Program, which is a six-week leadership program that provides training and instruction in leadership development, diversity, American culture, history and society, was launched in 2007.

Promoting Mass Communication to Arab Youth

Second, Hughes focused on meeting strategic State Department imperatives to raise favorability and connect with Muslims by expanding mass communication efforts that included applying corporate logic to nation branding. In an effort to reach a broader, but much younger audience (in multiple languages), Hughes used one-way communication projects that relied upon social networking and television, radio, and multimedia resources. To better prepare US state actors for the mass media, US ambassadors and diplomats were provided with media training through the Foreign Service Institute to promote pro-American sentiments in the Muslim world. According to the 2008 State Department *Major Accomplishments 2005–2007*:

In May 2007, [State officials in Europe] did 45 media interviews and top officials such as Secretary of Homeland Security Michael Chertoff, Assistant Secretary of State Daniel Fried, Assistant Secretary David Welch, Undersecretary Hughes, as well as Secretary Rice, appeared in multiple overseas media interviews. In June 2007, USG officials made 89 appearances on Middle East media, including Al Hurra, Radio Sawa, BBC Arabic, Al Jazeera English, Al Jazeera Arabic, VOA Persian and Al Arabiya.[21]

Relying upon media outlets to curb radical Islamic ideals, promoting key State Department officials in front of the international eye became a principal public diplomacy approach by Hughes in her attempt at combating anti-Americanism toward US policy.[22]

However, a big part of Hughes's branding campaign was given to engaging with younger audiences and women within the Muslim world. Efforts grew tremendously between 2006 and 2007 with the creation of a flagship website, *America.gov*. This and other sites targeting Muslim youth provided an in-depth look at the American story, international news from a US perspective, foreign policy and the benefits of practicing democracy, continuing the attempt to win the hearts and minds of youth. This approach was employed with the aim of developing a younger generation of Muslims who would be more accepting of US foreign policy and America's value system. This is highlighted, for example, with the State Department's leading radio program, *Greetings from America* (GFA). Launched in 2005, GFA's core objective includes encouraging foreign citizens studying in the United States to relate their experiences with US culture, customs, values, education, lifestyle, and more on radio stations in their home country. Reaching over 25 million listeners from 15–25, GFA is today functional in Nigeria and holds broadcasting ties in both Indonesia and Pakistan.

Reform through Foreign Aid

The third approach taken to market America's values focused on promoting what Hughes regard as a "diplomacy of deeds" program. In remarks made on June 2007 at the Washington Foreign Press Center, she recalled that a "diplomacy of deeds" was one of "the concrete ways in which [the United States would partner] with people around the world to help them improve their lives, particularly in the areas of education and health and economic opportunity."[23] Promoting a "diplomacy of deeds" is indicated by the Office of Public Diplomacy and Public Affairs as a premiere area of US public diplomacy. Considering its impact of reforming Muslim countries through foreign aid, it is the most important. Most efforts during Bush's presidency were made possible by the United States Agency for International Development (USAID) and private sector outlets. Each year, USAID manages around $10 billion in US foreign aid, which supports joint USAID and State Department projects.

A range of projects with attempts to reshape America's image and bolster US favorability through foreign assistance were the President's Emergency Plan for AIDS Relief, the US Middle East Breast Cancer Awareness and Research Partnership, the US Malaria Initiative and the use of Navy Hospital Ships (for disaster relief after the tsunami). As a US government agency, USAID does not allocate funding according to a country's religion, but according to acting USAID Deputy Administrator James Kunder, "Over 50 percent of total U.S. foreign assistance managed by USAID [in recent years] goes to countries with Muslim majority populations."[24] Take, for instance, the Middle East Partnership Initiative (MEPI), established in December 2005 as a platform to oversee the vast majority of US foreign aid distributed to Middle East NGOs. Its founding objectives are to ensure fair disbursement of funds across the Middle East region, while promoting within each country political, economic, educational, and women's empowerment reform. "From the 1950s through 2001, U.S. bilateral economic assistance to the Middle East and North Africa focused on promoting regional stability by providing funding for large bilateral military and economic programmes, chiefly in Egypt, Israel and Jordan and by fostering development."[25] Under this third goal to raise US favorability ratings, billions of US dollars in funding have gone toward restoring confidence in the United States in Muslim audiences by working with NGO and private sector outlets that attempted to strengthen the ties between Muslim audiences and the US government through political and social reform.

Maintaining Bush's governing philosophy of *compassionate conservatism,* which meant outsourcing social welfare initiatives, in the fiscal year 2002–2003 MEPI reported distributing 33 percent of $129 million to Middle Eastern NGO and private sector organizations to disburse grants to local companies. "According to MEPI, their grants are intended to support innovative ideas which can be implemented quickly to produce concrete results, such as increasing women's political participation."[26] Since 2002, sources indicate that over $430 million were distributed to over 350 projects in 17 countries. However, the clear finding thus far suggests that such projects by the State Department and USAID during this period failed to raise US favorability (or touch the core of Muslim publics by engaging critical religious infrastructures to influence serious change).

Approaching the Religious Dimension

In trying to comprehend the State Department's efforts to engage global Islamic communities and the religion of Islam after 9/11, let us turn to two concepts regarded as *direct* and *indirect* communicative relations that aid this discussion. Direct communicative relations are identified here as dialogue-based engagement that is underpinned by a strategic project to acknowledge and incorporate the ideals, perspectives and aspirations of both state and nonstate actors. The concept of a direct approach is not state-centric, but materializes from a realization that in a postsecular era, state actors must embrace nontraditional means in order to engage the new religious dimensions of global politics. On the contrary, indirect communicative relations often set out, first to discount and later, to engage with the religious dimension at arm's length, which often leads to symbolic relationships to shore up quick public support. For example, indirect communicative relations often give limited attention to key socioreligious issues. Hence, Karen P. Hughes's public diplomacy doctrine used indirect relations, as indicated in September 2005 with Hughes's Middle East tour to listen to the voices of Islamic communities to win hearts and minds. During her 2005 Middle East public diplomacy tour, she visited Egypt, Saudi Arabia, Turkey, and Indonesia, in what Hughes believed might be an opportune period to trumpet the American story, preferably among women and children. Rather than this tour serving as a genuine "listening tour," it marks an epic failure in American public diplomacy that deepened divisions in an already existing US-Muslim world trust deficit.

On September 27, in Jeddah, Saudi Arabia, Hughes verbally trumpeted America's brand via an indirect communicative relations approach by relying on one-way assaults and less-informed rhetoric speaking to more than 500 Saudi women making the erratic prediction that Saudi women, "would soon be able to drive as American women and be fully incorporated into Saudi society."[27] Countering Hughes, the university auditoriums erupted in dismay with women objecting to her crude assumption about the disenchantment of all Saudi women with their status, as perceived by the West. One Saudi woman openly disputed Hughes's position, stating, "The general image of the Arab woman is that she isn't happy... well, we're all pretty happy."[28] Trumpeting American ideals through a one-way communication assault that ran counter to the religio-cultural norms of Arab and Islamic society created more resistance than acceptance between Saudi women and Hughes. Rather than listening and cultivating direct communicative relations based on mutual respect and understanding, Hughes attempted to exercise an elitist position with clear intention to win the hearts and minds at the expense of cutting off the ear—the vital tool required to understand America's target audience.

The same outcry among Muslim women followed the next day in Ankara, Turkey, with a group of 20 Turkish feminist leaders after Hughes had identified herself as "a working mother." Rather than listening, Hughes lectured to this group on the benefits of the Iraq War—despite widespread Turkish opposition to it. Acknowledging the Turkish audience, she noted, "I can appreciate your concern about war. No one likes war [but] . . . It is impossible to say that the rights of women were better under Saddam Hussein than they are today."[29] Regarding Turkey's opposition to the Iraq War, Hidyet Tuskal emphasized that Turkish feminists regarded America's mass killing of women and children as a threat to human rights and a severe concern for all feminists in the region. Hughes's clash with this small group of feminists is a microcosm indicative of the current trust deficit and the fact that there has never been a period in history where safe space has existed between the United States and the Muslim world. Notwithstanding her setbacks in Ankara, Hughes captured the attention of Muslims during her Middle East public diplomacy tour, exercising a makeshift interfaith dialogue event (after touring Istanbul's Topaki Palace) with Muslim, Eastern Orthodox, Jewish, and Roman Catholic religious officials. While participating in a prime opportunity to promote interreligious engagement to resolve deep-seated conflicts in the region, Hughes discounted this opportunity by lowering the engagement process to a rallying of talking points and symbolic gestures rather than elevating the engagement process as a genuine opportunity to engage critical religio-cultural affairs. Thus, the 2005 Middle East public diplomacy tour is dubbed as a gross attempt to "directly" engage global Islamic communities at the expense of overlooking key opportunities to punctuate critical dialogue to promote regional conflict resolution. This event did not produce a critical dialogue session that focused on peace-making or the application of conflict resolution issues, but rather served as a symbolic gesture to trumpet and market America's brand and its popular position on religious tolerance and religious freedom.

Several opportunities, however, materialized under Hughes's tenure within the international community, but considering the US government's limited infrastructure, the United States neither has participated or pursued critically engaging international religious concerns at the diplomatic level. Since 2007, the State Department's efforts to "encourage" or "facilitate" interfaith activity is often promoted through the Bureau of Education and Cultural Affairs, the International Information Programs, and the International Visitor Leadership Program. Often these initiatives support academic and professional exchange efforts to the Muslim world, thereby employing the proverbial phrase "interfaith dialogue" in order to convene religious leadership for symbolic "meet and greets" to bolster US morale. Unfortunately, none of these initiatives directly engage religious elements within a sociopolitical forum to build sacred-secular relations beyond symbolic presentations or the promotion of conflict resolution through peace-making initiatives. Many of these staged events are associated with ECA and IIP bureau-sponsored programs such as the new Fulbright Interfaith Community Action Program, which in the past convened Muslim clerics in the United States with the central aim of providing a remote forum where religious scholars and academics might converse with US religious leaders. For example, the principal objective of the Fulbright Interfaith Dialogue and Community Action Program is "to engage in inter-religious dialogue with both lay and clerical counterparts from the broader American community of believers and to observe the compatibility of religious belief and practice in democratically oriented social and political structures."[30]

Between 2005 and 2007, Undersecretary Hughes was successful in encouraging interfaith relations, but failed significantly at introducing a strategic plan that utilized contemporary interfaith relations between state and religious nonstate actors on issues related to counterterrorism and improving US–Muslim world relations beyond one-way transmission models of communication. Addressing the UN High Level Dialogue on Interreligious and Intercultural Understanding and Cooperation for Peace, Hughes indicated that having a deep respect for and knowledge of other cultures advances mutual understanding.[31] Despite the impact of Hughes's address and the need for the United States to attend the high-level panel at the United Nations, she evaded the prospect of direct engagement, indicating to panel members that US officials would participate with representatives from the Alliance of Civilizations (AOC), keeping religious leaders at arm's length. At first glance, one is led to believe the United States might fully cooperate with the AOC agenda to employ nonviolent tactics for finding peace through sacred-secular interfaith practices. However, Hughes does not suggest that the United States will adopt, for example, a new dialogue-based public diplomacy with global Islamic communities, but ensures the US government is conducting its own engagement efforts that do not require stipulations or requirements which are binding by transnational organizations such as the United Nations:

We all have a role. America wants to partner in this dialogue. Through websites and communication alerts, we are working to highlight the many voices speaking out against terrorist violence and of greater inter-faith understanding. We are encouraging inter-faith dialogue and conversations between cultures. Through a new programme called "Citizen Dialogue," we've sent Muslim American citizens across the world to engage with grassroots citizens in Muslim communities. We've brought clerics here and sent American clerics abroad. We've sponsored programmes for young people, teaching respect for diversity.[32]

Key efforts by Hughes to directly engage the religious dimension came at the expense of Washington not entirely capitalizing on annual interfaith events. This point is made in the context of President Bush and Hughes encouraging US ambassadors to conduct personal outreach in local Muslim communities by hosting Iftaar dinners at US embassies, which to date serve symbolic opportunities to promote dialogue-based public diplomacy with religious actors. While Iftaar dinners are valuable, the concept of working within such religious-cultural settings offers an opportunity to promote two-way communicative engagement between state and nonstate actors. The hosting of annual Iftaar dinners within the White House and State Department community under the Bush Administration was not uncommon. Between 2001 and 2008, President Bush hosted an annual Iftaar dinner with a twofold mission: to demonstrate that the United States is not at war with Islam, and to celebrate the Islamic faith while acknowledging the Muslim holy month of Ramadan.

Assessing Secular Marketing Approaches after 9/11

Arguably, the State Department's new tradition beginning under the Bush administration to nominate former secular-based marketing executives to the seat of Under Secretary of Public Diplomacy and Public Affairs needs reassessing. The secular consumer marketing culture that appeals to a broad Western audience stands in contrast with value-defined socially constructed global Islamic communities. This leads to my closing position here on the setbacks of post-9/11 public diplomacy as related to the State Department's leadership, and its inability to comprehend how an effective direct communicative way forward to engage the religious dimension of global politics is imperative to US national security and building genuine relations with value-defined religious societies.

The State Department's organizational structure, and its inability to retain a devout Under Secretary of State for Public Diplomacy and Public Affairs between 2001 and 2008, contributed to the absence of a long-term communication strategy reflective of the Arab and Muslim communicative tradition (see table 5.1). Since 1998, the Office of International Religious Freedom has held the responsibility to publicly address specific religious issues—as opposed to broad international religious affairs. Unlike Ministries of Religious Affairs throughout the Muslim world with government officials who are trained at carrying out religio-political analysis, peace-making and conflict resolution, the State Department (after 9/11) was forced to redirect efforts to conduct Muslim world outreach through the office of Public Diplomacy and Public relations.

For the first time in the State Department's history, it bore the responsibility for rebuilding America's image among the foreign public since terminating the United States Information Agency in 1998 and President Clinton's creation of a new position of Under Secretary for Public Diplomacy and Public Affairs. By Bush's term, the trend included nominating former Madison Avenue marketing executives to the post, convinced that brand management approaches would resolve a long-standing image problem that affected American foreign policy.

Throughout Bush's term in office this post would be held by four different undersecretaries, three of whom would resign at the height of the US's Muslim world outreach campaign: Charlotte Beers unexpectedly resigned after a year, serving today as Director of Martha Stewart's Living Omnimedia Inc.; Margaret D. Tutwiler resigned after six months of service to take a post with the New York Stock Exchange Euronext; and Karen P. Hughes resigned after two years of service, serving as vice chairman with the Burson-Marsteller PR

Table 5.1   US Undersecretaries of State for Public Diplomacy and Public Affairs 2001–2012

Undersecretary	Term in Office	Administration
Evelyn Lieberman	October 1, 1999—January 19, 2001	Bill Clinton
Charlotte Beers	October 2, 2001—March 28, 2003	George W. Bush
Margaret D. Tutwiler	December 16, 2003—June 30, 2004	George W. Bush
Karen P. Hughes	September 9, 2005—December 14, 2007	George W. Bush
Position Open (1yr)	December 14, 2007—June 10, 2008	George W. Bush
James K. Glassman	June 10, 2008—January 15, 2009	George W. Bush
Judith McHale	May 26, 2009—June 2011	Barack Obama
Kathleen Stephens	February 6, 2012—April 4, 2012	Barack Obama
Tara D. Sonenshine	April 6, 2012—present	Barack Obama

firm. Between 2007 and 2008, the undersecretary position remained vacant until James K. Glassman (former business journalist) served a short term of seven months before resigning. Thus, for this office to bear the responsibility of crafting America's communicative message to the Muslim world, the Bush administration's inability to nominate a set of skilful professionals capable of comprehending the social terrain of the Arab and Muslim world demonstrates a lack of attention to, and an inconsistency with, leading the Office for Public Diplomacy and Public Affairs in a postsecular era.

Maintaining the Bush tradition under the Obama administration, former MTV and Discovery Network executive, Judith A. McHale assumed the position in May 2009 as undersecretary, only to resign in June 2011. Perhaps taking into consideration several recommendations put forth by the USC Center on Public Diplomacy at the Annenberg School, the Obama administration has recently turned the page on this long-standing tradition of hiring former marketing executives and public affairs professionals to hire for the first time in history a career US Foreign Service office to the seat of Under Secretary of State for Public Diplomacy and Public Affairs. At this time of writing, Kathleen Stephens, former US Ambassador to the Republic of Korea (September 2008 to October 2011) assumed the role of Undersecretary in February 2012 only to be replaced two months later in April by, Tara D. Sonenshine, the former Executive Vice President of the United States Institute of Peace. It is uncertain as to whether Undersecretary Sonenshine will grasp the complexity of moving from the long-standing tradition to overlap nation-branding and public diplomacy in a deleterious fashion to market the American story to Muslim audiences.

Washington's post-9/11 national security objectives came at the expense of exercising a failure to develop a strategic communication approach that magnified dialogue-based public diplomacy. Essentially, integrating corporate logic and secular communication were paramount between 2001 and 2008 in marketing the American brand to pacify global Islamic communities. In making this case, this chapter examined how institutional limitations within the US government system led to injurious decision making as it related to engaging value-defined socially constructed societies as the Muslim world. Clearly, a stronger form of analysis is required in this postsecular era when approaching the religious dimension in global politics. In moving forward after 2008 with the presidency of Barack Obama, the world anticipated that America's new president might follow through on campaign promises made to improve US-Muslim world relations. Confronted with a prime opportunity, evidence indicates that the Obama administration's military and diplomatic posture aiming to succeed in South Asia and reach stability in the Middle East reflects a similar set of actions taken during the Bush era. While overt religious rhetoric and a reliance on trumpeting the American brand are not prominent features of the current administration, an inconsistency in keeping political promises with Muslim majority audiences broadens the ongoing trust deficit that inevitably requires reshaping the communicative context.

CHAPTER SIX

Shifting the Tide

Upon taking office in 2009, the world anticipated that US President Barack Obama might follow through on campaign promises to improve America's tenuous relationship with the Muslim world. While reluctant to blatantly trumpet the American brand, it has instead relied upon Bush era top-down engagement approaches and the persuasive single-actor model to bolster target audience confidence in the Muslim world. Presently, Washington is confronted with the enormous task of defining a new way forward that takes into consideration both the perspective of nonelites at the grassroots level, while sustaining ties with state actors in Muslim majority nations. Based on the many missteps encountered, it is evident the US Department of State has no alternative but to take seriously the prospects of exercising bottom-up engagement measures that operate within a fair and balanced communicative context. Despite shifting the tide by promoting a more conciliatory tone in the 2010 US National Security Strategy, red flags appear as to whether the Obama White House and State Department are equipped with sufficient tools to restore relations with global Islamic communities beyond applying short-term symbolic gestures. Given the strategies exercised since 2009, this chapter argues that a commitment to restore relations with 1.5 billion Muslims necessitates exercising a new form of public diplomacy capable of convening state and nonstate actors in dialogue-based engagement.

The Transition

On November 4, 2008, America embarked upon a historic political transition, presenting a fresh signal to the world by electing its first

African American president, Barack Hussein Obama.[1] His ascendancy to the Oval Office was ushered in part by his grassroots background as a community organizer and his ability to galvanize the American public with a set of political promises to restore confidence and hope to the US general electorate. Richard Wolffe reasons that Obama's political charisma coupled by his persuasive rhetoric looked more hopeful than the policies pursued under President George W. Bush's presidency. Additionally, Obama's candid, direct communicative approach that ran counter to Bush's neoconservative agenda supported the argument that effective change came not from the top down, but from the bottom up. Ensuring this new way forward meant embracing a change in course capable of restoring American values at home, promoting transparent domestic and foreign policies, and improving both America's international standing in the world and its ailing economy.[2]

Adopting a set of new approaches to pursue peace that values both allies and adversaries by pursuing comprehensive engagement is a key cornerstone to the Obama administration's commitment to engaging global Islamic communities. This is particularly the case in its effort to curb escalating international terrorist activity and sectarian conflict in parts of the Middle East and South Asia. During the 2007 Democratic primaries and the 2008 general election, it appeared risky for either a Republican or Democratic presidential candidate to staunchly oppose the ultra-patriotic policies that dominated Washington's post-9/11 agenda. Notwithstanding Obama's political platform on introducing new paths on engaging, for example, Iran and Syria, Candidate Obama outlined in *The Blueprint for Change: Obama's Plan for America*, three major platforms of engagement. If given the opportunity as commander in chief, he stressed that his administration would: (a) rely on the nonmilitary peacemaking options in confronting potential threats; (b) oppose any effort to extend the present Iraq war into Iran; and (c) employ direct presidential diplomacy with Iran without preconditions.[3]

From January 2009, several political and diplomatic developments have transpired since Obama assumed the presidency, which challenge his commitment to achieve these and other campaign promises linked to the Muslim world. The most pertinent of which includes restoring America's ailing economy, bringing both the Afghan and Iraq wars to an end, and maintaining regional stability in the Middle East and South Asia. Upon taking office, academics and fellow state actors queried whether Obama might be capable of translating what Deborah P. Atwater refers to as a *political rhetoric of hope* into specific occasions of meaningful engagement between state and nonstate actors in the

Muslim world.[4] While Obama's *political rhetoric of hope* is persuasive in some respects to galvanize and invoke global attention, a gap exists between this rhetoric—which transcends borders—and the application of authentic diplomatic solutions that critically address the aspirations and perspectives of global Islamic communities.

Guidance on Engagement

A substantial number of Muslim majority nations are presently skeptical of Washington's political promises because of the inconsistencies and the State Department's failed outreach attempts throughout the Muslim world. In an effort to correct Washington's missteps in 2008, the US–Muslim Engagement Project presented an appeal to both the Bush and new presidential administration to take seriously the prospect of employing an updated strategy to advance four specific goals in the issue areas of improving diplomacy, increasing civic participation, job creation, and advancing mutual understanding. Of the 34-member committee, Madeline Albright, Joseph S. Nye, and Richard Armitage were outspoken on the argument that improving America's deteriorating relations with global Islamic communities requires that attention is given to both the dynamics of communication, the prospects of engaging the grassroots, and building relations with nonstate actors. The report of the leadership group stated:

> During the past several years, it has become clear that military force may be necessary, but is not sufficient, to defeat violent extremism in Iraq, Afghanistan, and Pakistan, or to prevent attacks elsewhere. Moreover, military action has significant costs to US standing in the world, and to our ability to gain the cooperation of other countries in counterterrorism, and counterinsurgency operations. Senior US defence and military leaders have recognised the primary importance of diplomatic, political, economic, and cultural initiatives in combating extremism.[5]

The project maintains that a staunch military agenda should not be exercised to support a unilateral US-led agenda, but only be a last resort to sustain peace. Additionally, it recommended that it might be advantageous for Washington to pool its secular resources with religious, political, and cultural assets (at home and abroad) to reconcile deep-seated tensions ignited by hostile factions. Acknowledging this guidance, the Obama administration agreed with several think tanks and study groups that US diplomacy should serve as a first option in hostile settings opposed to military force in most cases.

However, guidance in the issue area of public diplomacy and Muslim outreach is not a new concern. The Government Accountability Office maintains this specific position in a set of clear recommendations in its 2005 report, U.S. Public Diplomacy: Interagency Coordination Efforts Hampered by the Lack of National Communication Strategy, and again in 2005, in State Department Efforts to Engage Muslim Audiences Lack Certain Communication Elements and Face Significant Challenges.[6] Its 2006 report identified a set of clear observations for the State Department to consider: implementing guidance modeled on private sector best practices for its public diplomacy strategy, establishing a sample country-level communication plan that could be adapted for local use by US embassies, and setting up a systematic mechanism for sharing best practice data to address long-standing program challenges. Its analysis states:

> In May 2006, GAO reported (U.S. Public Diplomacy: State Department Efforts to Engage Muslim Audiences Lack Certain Communication Elements and Face Significant Challenges) that State Department efforts to communicate with the Muslim audiences faced challenges related to staffing and security at posts in the Muslim world and that State lacked a systematic mechanism for sharing best practices, which could help address these challenges. GAO recommended that State strengthen existing systems of sharing best practices in order to more systematically transfer knowledge among embassies around the world.[7]

Near the end of Bush's term, findings conclude that the State Department recognized GAO's recommendations through a follow-up communiqué acknowledging its intentions to correct these practices—but no concrete efforts were implemented. In addition to this appeal, the US-Muslim Engagement Project has since called for a new strategy that proposes four immediate goals: (i) the elevation of diplomacy as the primary tool for resolving key conflicts involving Muslim countries by engaging both allies and adversaries in dialogue; (ii) supporting efforts to improve governance and promote civic participation in Muslim countries; (iii) helping to catalyze job-creating growth in Muslim countries to benefit both them and the US; and, (iv) improving mutual respect and understanding between Americans and Muslims around the world.[8] Arguably the *symptoms* of insufficient and indirect

US communication with global Islamic communities are materializing into a labyrinth of miscommunication. These symptoms are caused in part by the many grievances held by political Islamists and some moderate Muslims over US foreign policies and the impact of secular political approaches that influence state actors to discount religious and cultural elements as unimportant in decision making.

Treating Communication Differently

In an initial effort to treat communication and engagement differently with the Arab world, both Senator George Mitchell and Richard Holbrooke were sent as special envoys to the Middle East and South Asia. Their tasks included rebooting the Middle East peace process and reinforcing the president's tough stance against a nuclear Iran, while reviving US foreign relations with Russia, thereby introducing the New START Treaty. As commander in chief, Obama pledged publicly that his administration would pursue direct engagement with the Muslim world, adopting a set of similar proposals comparable to the US-Muslim Engagement Project. Emphasizing the role of the United States in ushering a new way forward, the president stated in his January 20, 2009 inaugural address:

> To the Muslim world, we seek a new way forward, based on mutual interest and mutual respect. To those leaders around the globe who seek to sow conflict or blame their society's ills on the West, know that your people will judge you on what you can build, not what you destroy... To those who cling to power through corruption and deceit and the silencing of dissent, know that you are on the wrong side of history, but that we will extend a hand if you are willing to unclench your fist.[9]

In setting a precedent just seven days into the presidency, Obama affirmed his new stance in his first prime-time interview to target Muslim audiences. Rather than addressing the global Islamic communities via a US news agency (*CNN*, *NBC* or *CBS*), surprising both the Muslim world and the American public, the Dubai-based and part Saudi owned Arabic and Farsi language news agency, Al-Arabiya syndicated the interview.

Unlike previous cabinets, the Obama administration moved immediately to address the ongoing Middle East peace process. Initial steps in 2009 included taking a broad, yet holistic approach to the region, affirming the Israeli–Palestinian crisis is not a solitary event, but more accurately an interrelated episode fueling intractable conflicts in Pakistan, Syria, Lebanon, Afghanistan and Iraq, Iran. He reminds us,

> [Even] as we engage in this direct diplomacy, we are very clear about certain deep concerns that we have as a country, that Iran understands that we find the funding of terrorist organizations unacceptable, that we're clear about the fact that a nuclear Iran could set off a nuclear arms race in the region that would be profoundly destabilizing. So there are going to be a set of objectives that we have in these conversations, but I think that there's the possibility, at least, of a relationship of mutual respect and progress. And I think that if you look at how we've approached the Middle East, my designation of George Mitchell as a special envoy to help deal with the Arab-Israeli situation, some of the interviews that I've given, it indicates the degree to which we want to do things differently in the region.[10]

Though wavering on several occasions, the Obama administration early on acknowledged its foreign policy position regarding the Middle East Peace Process, calling for a two-state solution. However, Obama has dithered on several occasions to stand firm against Israeli settlement construction in East Jerusalem and supporting Palestine's bid at the U.N. for permanent statehood in October 2011. Thus, the current administration finds that restoring trust requires taking seriously the regional aspirations and perspectives present throughout the Arab world, especially on the question of Palestine. According to John Esposito, ending such events demands that a presidential administration be diplomatically prepared from the outset to acknowledge the turmoil of the Israeli-Palestinian debacle and the necessity of a change in course.[11]

Smart Power

Extending the administration's position to listen to both state and nonstate actors, as nominee Secretary of State, Hillary Clinton disclosed in her senate confirmation hearing that the State Department was prepared to move in a new direction, ready to lead this shift by exercising the strategy of *smart power* to deter attacks from America's adversaries, while encouraging peaceful relations through the channels of diplomacy.[12] Coined by distinguished Harvard University professor Joseph S. Nye Jr., *smart power* is a relevant term that highlights how a new direction in both posture and policy could improve America's dealings in the world.[13] Instead of relying solely on *hard power* "to ensure America's place as a strategic player on the world stage, both *hard* and *soft power* must be incorporated to assure that a complex interdependence is established."[14] The *2006 CSIS Commission on Smart Power* led by Richard Armitage and Nye established:

> Smart power is neither hard nor soft—it is the skilful combination of both. Smart power means developing an integrated strategy, resource base, and tool-kit to achieve American objectives, drawing on both hard and soft power. It is an approach that underscores the necessity of a strong military, but also invests heavily in alliances, partnerships, and institutions at all levels to expand American influences and establish the legitimacy of American action.[15]

Since 2009, the Obama-administration's strategy to exercise smart power has resulted principally in an imbalance, where US military strength presently outflanks the soft power option. Despite emphasizing America's commitment to pursue comprehensive engagement with allies and adversaries, and a new way forward comprised of direct communicative approaches, the administration struggles with moving beyond strong military and intelligence activities to pursue diplomacy as a favorable option.

In this case, two additional efforts are required that warrant further consideration from the administration, apart from the five critical areas both the State Department and the Pentagon should focus their attention on, as proposed by the *CSIS Commissions on Smart Power* which includes: (i) rebuilding the foundation to respond to global challenges; (ii) developing a more unified approach through global development; (iii) improving access to international knowledge and learning; (iv) increasing benefits of trade for all people; and (v) addressing climate change and energy insecurity.[16] Additional efforts by both the State Department and the Pentagon must pay close attention to relate especially to Washington recalibrating its perceptions of the Muslim world, which means not solely recognizing it as a set of countries where the practice of Islam is central to the culture, but as being comprised of multiple value-defined socially constructed societies and traditional frameworks that must be engaged as a whole for the promotion of healthy *smart power performance*. Thus, it's vital both departments reach the conclusion that this recalibration in perspective must be accompanied by a strategy of smart postsecular communication, which aids in facilitating state and religious nonstate actor relations to promote a dialogue-based public diplomacy.

Foundations of the Obama Doctrine on Muslim Outreach

President Obama has taken into consideration several proposals and recommendations since 2009, on pursuing robust engagement between state and nonstate actors that runs counter to the Bush Doctrine, which wrestled openly with linking the religion of Islam to terrorism. Further, the Obama administration is adamant about projecting a respectful tone in communication by omitting loaded religious rhetoric like what was taken up during the Bush era. Bush's God-Talk and the influence of post-9/11 era confrontationalist ideology led by Bernard Lewis and Samuel P. Huntington contributed to key terminology and questionable phrases implemented in the 2006 US National Security Strategy. On the surface, the 2006 National Security Strategy (as highlighted in chapter four) accomplished two specific goals that identified in clear terms America's new enemy—Islamic radicalism, terrorist, and rogue states—against whom the United States planned to defend itself at all costs using the military, thus setting out a course of action for rebuilding key nations in an effort to promote effective democracies within countries identified as failed states.

In pursuing a new way forward, administrative officials such as Senior Director for Global Engagement at the National Security Staff, Pradeep Ramamurthy and deputy Jenny Urizar, led a study group to remove negative language leading to shortcomings in US-Muslim engagement. Several considerations included *Words that Work and Words that Don't* by the Counter Terror Communication Center and *Terminology to Define the Terrorist: Recommendations from American Muslims* by the Department of Homeland Security. The Department of Homeland Security advised that the terminology used by senior government officials must accurately identify the nature of the challenges that face our generation... At the same time, the terminology should also be strategic—it should avoid helping the terrorists by inflating the religious bases and glamorous appeal of their ideology.[17]

The Obama administration's shift in tone is symbolic as it ventures in a new direction to agree that a civil voice in communication is vital to advance US-Muslim world relations. This position is backed by the 2010 National Security Strategy's central pillar that maintains, "Currently, the United States is focused on implementing a responsible transition as we end the war in Iraq, succeeding in Afghanistan, and defeating al-Qaeda and its terrorist affiliates, while moving our economy from catastrophic recession to lasting recovery."[18] In pursuing this objective, the current administration is taking an alternative path from its predecessor. Strengthening ties with allies have included deepening America's relationship between Washington and wavering allies like Russia and Pakistan, constant partners such as the United Kingdom and Turkey, and strategic players like China and Saudi Arabia. However, pursuing comprehensive engagement as a national security strategy extends to relationship building with adversaries by offering a clear choice that they:

> [A]bide by international norms, and achieve the political and economic benefits that come with greater integration with the international community; or refuse to accept this pathway, and bear the consequences of that decision, including greater isolation. Through engagement, we can create opportunities to resolve differences, strengthen the international community's support for our actions, learn about the intentions and nature of closed regimes, and plainly demonstrate to the publics within those nations that their governments are to blame for their isolation. Successful engagement will depend upon the effective use and integration of different elements of American power.[19]

Extending efforts to restore relations with the Muslim world, the administration has paid heed to an additional set of recommendations from the Chicago Council on Global Affairs, highlighting the frequent imperative of broadening the United's State's bureaucratic framework in the 2010 report, *Engaging Religious Communities Abroad: An Imperative for US Foreign Policy*. Among the key objectives introduced, the most essential puts forward that Washington upgrade its communicative strategy while promoting religious tolerance and cooperation, reminding it is imperative to:

> Establish religious engagement within the government bureaucracy; Provide mandatory training for officials on the role of religion in world affairs; Utilize the expertise of military veterans to enhance peaceful engagement; Clarify the parameters of the

US Establishment Clause; Engage religious communities at a societal (grassroots) level; Launch special initiatives; Tackle religious extremism by addressing political issues; Avoid pejorative terminology when describing religious players; Reaffirm the U.S.'s commitment to religious freedom; Embrace a comprehensive approach to democracy promotion; and Work with international multilateral organizations.[20]

Since 2009, the Obama administration has incorporated several of these recommendations to form a concise position on US-Muslim world outreach. When viewed comprehensively, it forms an Obama Doctrine on US-Muslim world engagement that is comprised of eight components. The general proposition of this doctrine between 2009 and 2012 includes: (i) promoting efforts to disrupt, dismantle, and defeat al-Qaeda and its violent affiliates in Afghanistan, Pakistan, and around the world, (ii) Reconciling with moderate members of the Taliban through special Afghan reintegration programs, (iii) Responsibly ending the war in Iraq and withdrawing troops by 2010, (iv) Pursuing a regional peace agreement between Israel and Palestine, (v) Reversing the spread of nuclear and biological weapons and secular nuclear material (which has lately included levying sanctions against Iran), (vi) De-linking pejorative terminology from US national security documents, (vii) Promoting special people-to-people initiatives that seek to cultivate mutual interest and mutual understanding between the United States and Muslim world, (viii) And, maintaining a commitment to restore trust at a societal/and governmental level which since 2009 included the appointments of both Farah A. Pandith (US Special Representative to Muslim Communities) and Rashad Hussain (US Special Envoy to the Organization for Islamic States).

Persuasive Single-actor Model

The Obama administration's commitment to comprehensive engagement with allies and adversaries indicates that the White House is serious about restoring trust, though many efforts over the last few years were piecemeal. While the administration is laying a foundation that takes seriously publicly recognizing and engaging allies and adversaries, its current public diplomacy approach revolves around upgrading preexisting programs and relying upon a persuasive single-actor to win over Muslim audiences. With respect to the latter, such actions since 2009 have included attempts at managing global perceptions by placing reliance on the expertise of Farah Anwar Pandith and what is regarded as the *Obama effect*.

Accentuating this task at the State Department on June 23, 2009, Secretary of State Hillary Clinton appointed Pandith as the United State's first Special Representative to Muslim Communities. A prominent American Muslim (born in India administered Kashmir), Pandith was sworn in on September 15, 2009, to draw attention to President Obama's inaugural call to put forth a new strategy to engage global Islamic communities. As Special Representative, Pandith's office is responsible for executing Clinton's vision on Muslim outreach, which to some extent parallels Karen P. Hughes's agenda, placing an emphasis on promoting people-to-people engagement specifically with younger Muslim audiences at the organizational level.

Hired by the State Department in 2007 to serve as former President George W. Bush's senior advisor to the Assistant Secretary of State for European and Eurasian affairs on Muslim Outreach, several insiders pondered on whether Pandith's venerated role might be any different from Beers's or Hughes's commitment to market American values throughout the Arab and Muslim world. Remarking on Secretary Clinton's vision and her new commitment to serve as America's liaison to Muslim communities she announced:

> [Clinton] has asked me to find ways to build strong partnerships and create new connections and joining together with grassroots organisations to effect positive change. Under the leadership of Secretary Clinton, the Department of State is recalibrating the way in which we work with Muslim communities around the world. Guided by her passion, leadership and dedication to an issue that is not new to her—she has been active on these issues for decades—this office will advise her and the Department on issues related to Muslim engagement. Through this office we will engage Muslim communities to solve collaboratively the most pressing problems facing these communities around the world.[21]

Here, Pandith affirms the US's proposed top-down approach and how it fits into her role as a *persuasive single-actor*. Upon assuming this position, both study groups and global public diplomacy practitioners warned the State Department of any new measures that lead to rebranding America by overlapping nation branding and public diplomacy activities that especially target youth and women audiences. Nearly four years into this strategy, two major concerns are present that question whether the

United States is really willing to implement a broad postsecular approach (beyond pacification) that engages global Islamic communities directly and that channels nonelite aspiration back into the foreign policy sphere and the reality that the Pandith-Clinton posture is not in lock-step with leading recommendations by public diplomacy practitioners like Jan Melissen, Phillip Seib, or R. S. Zahrana in pursuing a *new dialogue-based public diplomacy* that takes effect from the bottom up. Pandith's current approach is plausible in the sense that it galvanizes target audiences from the top-down, but it is communicatively unsound for reaching the core of Islamic society, beyond occasional lecture tours and community talks that capture the short-term attention of Muslims.

Calling attention to this top-down measure at the "Forum for the Future," held in Marrakesh, Morocco, on November 3, 2009, Clinton opened by indicating three uniquely secular-based, but broad areas that the administration, in 2010, would gear its attention toward: an emphasis on job creation in the Muslim world, advancing science and technology, and promoting widespread educational opportunities. However, none, as of today, take seriously the dynamics of communication and the role that a special set of US state actors (Foreign Service Officers) will need to contribute to the overall grand strategy to restore trust with global Islamic communities. It may very well be the case that multiple dialogue-based efforts by such a cadre or corps deserve immediate deliberation.

Yet, considering both the value and setback presented by the Pandith-Clinton approach, we gather: First, their top-down measures are not in lock-step with key recommendations on employing a new public diplomacy beyond relying on a persuasive single-actor to shore up quick attention to win Muslim hearts and minds. Second, the US's move to appoint Pandith has failed to strengthen US engagement with global Islamic communities at the grassroots-level or in restoring fractured relations in key regions as the Middle East or South Asia. A reliance on Pandith (or any US state actor) brings up the point that relying upon a single actor is seemingly unrealistic, thereby reinforcing consideration of the need for a broader approach. And third, the State Department's present deficiency in having a readily accessible cadre of specialists indicates that it is time Washington consider shifting its focus from short-term public diplomacy programming to communication-building at the grassroots level.

Former US Chairman of the Joint Chief of Staff, Admiral Michael Mullen, is correct in his 2009 assessment, *Strategic Communication: Getting Back to Basics*, that America is not facing a horrific problem of capturing "men in caves," but it is faced with defeating a long-standing credibility problem that is linked to Washington's unwillingness to deliver on its promises with the Muslim world. Elaborating on the role effective communication training will have on US engagement with Muslim audiences, Mullen writes:

> The irony here is that we know better. For all the instant polling, market analysis, and focus groups we employ today, we could learn a lot by looking to our own past. No other people on Earth have proven more capable at establishing trust and credibility in more places than we have. And we've done it primarily through the power of our example...And make no mistake—there has been a certain arrogance to our "strat comm" efforts. We've come to believe that messages are something we can launch down range like a rocket, something we can fire for effect. They are not. Good communication runs both ways. It's not about telling our story. We must also be better listeners. We cannot capture hearts and minds. We must engage them; we must listen to them one heart and one mind at a time—over time.[22]

Mullen is correct in making the case that credibility is not earned by relying on marketing American values. In fact, it is earned when trained US state actors are deployed to restore relations by first listening and later taking a dialogue-based approach. After addressing The Washington Institute for Near East Policy in August 2009, Pandith raised eyebrows in the Arab world about her ability as a *persuasive single-actor* in approaching the core of US-Muslim world relations when addressing the pro-Israel think tank in August 2009 remarking, "I come to you just days after Secretary Clinton talked about the need for a new mindset about how America will use its power to safeguard our nation, expand shared prosperity, and help more people in more places live up to their God-given potential."[23] Providing a sharp analysis on Pandith's comments, Senior Fellow at Harvard University's Belfer Center, Rami Khouri states in a nutshell:

> Everything that Pandith said is exactly what Admiral Mullen seemed to criticise in his article. She listed an impressive list of activities to engage Muslim communities worldwide on the basis of "mutual interest and mutual respect"—break down stereotypes, work with youth at the grassroots level, and build new partnerships via education, technology, business, sports and culture.

None of Pandith's rhetoric has a chance in *hell* of going anywhere, while the majority of Muslims, Arabs and others in our region broadly perceive American foreign policy as being tilted toward Israeli priorities or the incumbency of Arab autocrats, as has been the case for about four decades now. Tough American patriots like Gen. Petraeus and Adm. Mullen seem to grasp this, probably because they have escaped the diversionary lunacy of American "public diplomacy" and the choke-hold of single-interest lobby groups in Washington.[24]

Improving the US Department of State's engagement strategy is essential to restoring relations with global Islamic communities and requires setting an agenda that is broad enough to integrate the perspectives of key nonstate actors, but substantive enough to reach the core of Islamic society to curb and halt the spread of radical Islamic ideals. However, supporting this administration's efforts to galvanize Muslim audiences are the narrow attempts taken by the White House, which to a certain extent relies upon the *Obama effect* to lure Muslim audiences at the expense of broadening an already existing trust deficit between Muslims and the United States.

America's Persuader-in-Chief

In recent years, relying on President Obama's mosaic biography and hybrid heritage has been essential in both the White House and State Department's efforts to galvanize Muslim audiences.[25] Obama's willingness to disclose his background or speak candidly on the topic of his heritage enriches Washington's efforts at connecting with nonelite Muslim audiences. It is Obama's ties through his father to the religion of Islam, his coming of age in Indonesia, and Arabic middle name—Hussein—which distinguishes him as a unique symbol of America's engagement process. America would be reminded of Obama's symbolism as he extinguished the flame of racial tension ignited by his former Chicago-based pastor, Jeremiah Wright in 2008 defending publicly:

I am the son of a black man from Kenya and a white woman from Kansas. I was raised with the help of a white grandfather who survived a Depression to serve in Patton's Army during World War II and a white grandmother who worked on a bomber assembly line at Fort Leavenworth while he was overseas. I've gone to some of the best schools in America and lived in one of the world's poorest nations. I am married to a black American who carries within her the blood of slaves and slaveowners—an inheritance we pass on to our two precious daughters. I have brothers, sisters, nieces, nephews, uncles and cousins, of every race and every hue, scattered across three continents, and for as long as I live, I will never forget that in no other country on Earth is my story even possible.[26]

Obama's mosaic biography on occasion ensures his administration a unique entry-point to connect with global Islamic communities, but at the cost that "feel-good rhetoric" bears a short life span. Though the *Obama effect* presents an everlasting impression, it is in fact a short-term symbolic gesture that wrestles with Washington's present foreign policy reality and the fact that the State Department is lacking a long-term communication approach to engage Muslim audiences beyond generic programs and consumer marketing campaigns.

Appraising the *Obama effect*, public diplomacy practitioner Nancy Snow argues, "His rhetoric has helped reshape America's image in the world from being perceived as a unilateral, arrogant power to being seen as a humble nation that listens to and partners with others to achieve shared objectives." She contends, "Public diplomacy is best practiced as a symphony, not a one-man band. National reputation does not reside in one person, much less in one electoral outcome. It is deeply buried in the perceptions of countless people around the world, often rooted in their own national cultures, and can be rebuilt slowly and painstakingly only by altering the root causes of a country's good or bad name."[27] In 2009, Washington relied upon what Snow regards as the impact of America's *Persuader-in-Chief* to connect publicly with Arab audiences during the president's first Middle East tour.[28] At best, Obama's actions in the Arab world (especially at Cairo) bolstered immediate support for the president's political promises between 2009 and 2011 which today are called into question by Muslim audiences, since the onset of the 2010 Arab Spring.

Obama at Cairo

Stops on President Obama's first Middle East tour included a short visit to France, Dresden, Germany, and Buchenwald concentration camp to commemorate the 65th anniversary of the allied D-Day invasion. The president's immediate objective on this first tour was to fulfill his campaign promise to reach out to citizens of Muslim majority nations to chart a new course since the attacks of September 11. In pursuing this new course, first in Saudi Arabia on June 3rd, Obama exchanged views with Saudi Arabian King Abdullah on key regional matters such as relaunching the 2002 Arab-backed Middle East peace process, and mutual concerns related to US energy interests and counterterrorism. Then he traveled to Cairo, Egypt, to meet with then President Hosni Mubarak before delivering his "New Beginning" address at Cairo University.

Taking note of America's new set of challenges, Senior White House advisor, David Axelrod, noted ahead of Obama's address to reporters that, "There has been a breech, an undeniable breech between America and the Islamic world, and that breech has been years in the making...It is not going to be reversed in perhaps one administration. But the president is a strong believer in an open, honest dialogue."[29] According to President Obama, mending this breech required capturing the attention of Muslims by laying out a clear agenda on a new way forward, with Washington to consistently engage Muslim audiences—especially Muslims living in the Arab world. The short list of Muslim majority nations to host the "New Beginning" address were Indonesia, Morocco, Turkey, and Jordan. While US-South Asian issues held center stage in 2009, the instability mounting in the Arab world served as one of the determining factors on where Obama would give his long awaited address. Stephen R. Grand maintains,

> After weighing many options, the White House probably settled on Cairo as the location for the speech because Egypt has long been the leading intellectual and cultural force as well as the most populous country, in the Arab world. But the choice of Egypt as a venue comes with a distinct negative its poor record on democracy and human rights. Hosni Mubarak is in his fifth six year term as Egypt's president, and his regime has beaten, locked up, and/or exiled most of his political opponents. On the surface, President Obama would appear to confront the agonizing choice of neither insulting his host by raising these issues or be seen to be abandoning America's longstanding commitment to the promotion of democracy and human rights by not doing so, thereby disappointing the millions who will be listening careful for any sign of change in U.S. policy in the region.[30]

Grand's assertion on the Egyptian location is correct in that a contradiction might later aid Obama's case on improving relations with 1.5 billion Muslims. Instead of addressing many of the factors that later gave rise to the Arab Spring, Obama's address centered on secular-based issues as science/technology, education, and equality over outlining how violent extremists have exploited the opportunity of building equitable relations between the United States and Muslim world around the intended role of Washington in creating a new way forward. In presenting his case at Cairo, Obama's "New Beginning" address to convene global Islamic communities was executed in four parts: recognizing the problem, acknowledging actions to solve the problem, political promises, and a resolution.

In first *recognizing* the disturbing nature of US-Muslim relations, Obama stresses:

> I've come here to Cairo to seek a new beginning between the United States and Muslim and Muslim around the world, one based on mutual interests and mutual respect, and one based upon the truth that American and Islam are not exclusive and need not be in competition. Instead, they overlap, and share common principles—principles of justice and progress; tolerance and the dignity of all human beings. I do so recognizing that change cannot happen overnight...no single speech can eradicate years of mistrust, nor can I answer in the time that I have this afternoon all the complex questions that brought us to this point.[31]

Here, Obama takes a radical shift to publicly recognize that a distinct problem exists between the United States and Muslims throughout the world. Notwithstanding this point, he implies clearly that the tension experienced between the United States and global Islamic communities is linked to a broad historical relationship between Islam and the West that involves centuries of conflict and religious wars as the Crusades.

Second, before inviting Muslims into his proposed dialogue, the president takes this recognition further, to *acknowledge* (as in the Philadelphia message) by utilizing his mosaic biography and its link to human civilization, reminding the Muslim world:

> I'm Christian, but my father came from a Kenyan family that includes generation of Muslims. As a boy, I spent several years in Indonesia and heard the call of the azan at the break of dawn and at the fall of dusk. As a young man, I worked in Chicago communities where many found dignity and peace in their Muslim faith. As a student of history, I also know civilization dept to Islam. It was Islam—at places like Al-Azhar—that carried the light of

learning through so many centuries, paving the way for Europe's Renaissance and Enlightenment. It was innovation in Muslim communities—(applause)—it was innovation in Muslim communities that developed the order of algebra; our magnetic compass and tools of navigation; our mastery of pens and printing; our understanding of how disease spread and how it can be healed.[32]

Such public acknowledgment crystallizes Obama's relevance and legitimacy to stand before the Muslim world and convey empathy and respect for Islamic civilization as the United States is engaged in subsequent conflicts in several regions throughout the Muslim world. While Muslims indicate their appreciation toward an American president who is capable of remarking on the problem, consensus indicates that Muslims would like to see an Obama administration taking-to-task the very policies that are instrumental in inciting precarious relations between the United States and Muslims.

The third component of the "New Beginning" address accents seven political promises to *promote* a mutually beneficial way forward between the United States and Muslim world committing Washington to:[33]

a) ***Combating against violent extremism in all forms***—"So America will defend itself, respectful of the sovereignty of nations and the rule of law. And we will do so in partnership with Muslim communities which are also threatened. The sooner the extremists are isolated and unwelcome in Muslim communities, the sooner we will all be safer."

b) ***Addressing the tense situation between Israelis, Palestinians, and the Arab world***—"America's strong bonds with Israel are well known. This bond is unbreakable. It is based upon cultural and historical ties, and the recognition that the aspiration for a Jewish homeland is rooted in a tragic history that cannot be denied... On the other hand, it is also undeniable that the Palestinian people—Muslims and Christians—have suffered in pursuing of a homeland. For more than 60 years they've endured the pain of dislocation."

c) ***Expressing shared interests in the rights and responsibility of nations on nuclear weapons***—"I understand those who protest that some countries have weapons that others do not. No single nation should pick and choose which nation holds nuclear weapons. And that's why I strongly reaffirmed America's commitment to seek a world in which no nation holds nuclear weapons... And any nation—including Iran—should have the right to access peaceful nuclear power if it complies with its responsibilities under the nuclear Non-Proliferation Treaty."

d) **Promoting democracy**—"Suppressing ideas never succeeds in making them go away. America respects the right of all peaceful and law-abiding voices to be heard around the world, even if we disagree with them. And we will welcome all elected, peaceful governments—provided they govern with respect for all their people."

e) **Addressing international religious freedom**—"Freedom of religion is central to the ability of peoples to live together. We must always examine the ways in which we protect it. For instance, in the United States, rules on charitable giving have made it harder for Muslims to fulfill their religious obligation. That's why I'm committed to working with American Muslims to ensure that they can fulfill zakat. Likewise, it is important for Western countries to avoid impeding Muslim citizens from practicing religion as they see fit—for instance, by dictating what clothes a Muslim world should wear. We can't disguise hostility towards any religion behind the pretence of liberalism."

f) **Encouraging international women's rights**—"I do not believe that women must make the same choices as men in order to be equal, and I respect those women who choose to live their lives in traditional roles. But it should be their choice. And that is why the United States will partner with any Muslim-majority country to support expanded literacy for girls, and to help young women pursue employment through micro-financing that helps people live their dreams."

g) **Advancing economic development and educational opportunities**— "Many Gulf States have enjoyed great wealth as a consequence of oil, and some are beginning to focus it on broader development. But all of us must recognize that education and innovation will be the currency of the 21st century—(applause)—and in too many Muslim communities, there remains underinvestment in these areas...On education we will expand exchange programs, and increase scholarships, like the one that brought my father to America...On economic development, we will create a new corps of business volunteers to partner with counterparts in Muslim-majority countries...On science and technology, we will launch a new fund to support technological development in Muslim-majority countries, and to help transfer ideas to the marketplace so they can create more jobs."

Lastly, the final section of Obama's "New Beginning" address is defined here as presenting a *resolution* to the Muslim world that established that any action pursued must work in concert with global Islamic communities. Making this point clear, Obama announced, "Americans are ready to join with citizens and governments; community organizations, religious leaders, and businesses in Muslim communities around the world to help our people pursue a better life."[34] Scoring immediate points with global Islamic communities, Obama's address has since come under fire from nonstate actors at all levels, especially throughout the Arab world.

Deliverables the administration has since met include: (i) drawing down American troops from Iraq and presenting a projected 2014 timetable to withdraw troops from Afghanistan, (ii) the launch of the Global Technology and Innovation Fund providing between $25 million to $150 million to catalyze private sector investment (additional projects include initiating The Global Entrepreneurial Project, Partners for New Beginning, EMentor Corps, the Silicon Valley Partnership: Global Technology and Innovation Partners), (iii) hosting the Presidential Summit on Entrepreneurship to spur economic development and business innovation in Muslim majority countries (held April 23–27, 2010), (iv) upgrading US Department of State exchange programs to encourage engagement with Muslims, (v) and an expansion of foreign aid to Pakistan—which fell under criticism in 2010 after US government officials learned al-Qaeda's principal leader, Osama bin Laden was living in Abbottabad, Pakistan, probably with the knowledge of Pakistani authorities. There are more concrete promises mentioned at Cairo that have yet to be addressed, like the failure of the administration to close Guantanamo Bay prison by early 2010, dithering on the Middle East peace process as it relates to the continued building of Israeli settlements, and trepidation toward building a new way forward with Iran.[35]

Since addressing the Muslim world at Cairo, subsequent short-term communication attempts and piecemeal public diplomacy initiatives have materialized, most of which are an extension of previous programming efforts introduced under the Bush administration. It might be assumed that the Obama administration is lapsing into the same problem as the Bush administration by overly relying on short-term public diplomacy initiatives (as the persuasive single-actor model and one-way transmissions of communication and programming) to boost target audience confidence especially throughout the Arab world. Initiatives such as government-private sector led summits like the

US Islamic World Forum, educational exchanges like the Fulbright Program, and advertising campaigns like the Shared Values Initiative at best spark interests, but fail in their attempts to reach the core of Islamic society where the authentic conversation with vital nonstate actors like nonelite religious and tribal leadership exist. Currently, America's foreign policy in the Near East and South Asia coupled by its short-term public diplomacy initiatives contributes to a shrinking of its standing abroad and the widening of an already increasing trust deficit.

Expanding Outreach

As addressed above, the general position of the Obama doctrine on US-Muslim outreach encompasses seven central objectives: defeating al-Qaeda and its terrorist affiliates, reconciling with moderate members of the Taliban to bring an end to US-led combat in Afghanistan by 2014 (and troop withdrawal by 2024), responsibly ending the war in Iraq, pursuing a regional peace agreement between Israel and Palestine based on promoting a two-state solution, reversing the spread of nuclear and biological weapons and nuclear material, de-linking pejorative terminology from US national security documents, employing special people-to-people initiatives that seek to cultivate mutual interest and mutual understanding, and maintaining a commitment to restore trust at a societal and governmental level that in recent years relies on applying a *persuasive single-actor* to galvanize Muslim audiences. Since 2010, the Obama administration has added an additional aim extending beyond traditional boundaries to promote strategic engagement with key nonstate actors in South Asia like the Taliban's Quetta Shura. While two-thirds of the world's growing Muslim population live in ten countries, the Obama administration's outreach set a historic precedent in that it creates new paths that broaden America's Muslim outreach framework beyond a narrow Middle East and North African focus. Further, this shift proves tactically astute, despite sharp criticism by US state actors and private sector analysts on the irrelevance of engaging *nonstate combatants* and the perspectives they will bring to high-stakes political negotiations.

Materializing as a military force in South Asia in 1994, the Taliban's roots derive from a "mixture of Mujahadeen who fought against the Soviet invasion in the 1980s, and a group of Pashtun tribesman who spent time in Pakistani religious school, or madrassas, and received assistance from Pakistan's Intern Services Intelligence agency."[36] The

Taliban's draconian social and political agenda gained prominence between 1996 and 2001, capturing the world's attention with its strict fundamentalist decrees inspired by Sharia law, clashing significantly with the Northern alliance leadership led by anti-Taliban leaders Ahmad Shah Massoud and Abdul Rashid Dostum (of the Massoud and Dostum territories).[37] A deep contradiction was present in Afghanistan during this period with reference to women's rights. During the Taliban's 1996–2001 rule, Massoud's opposition movement integrated women into Northern Afghanistan's social system by relaxing strict Taliban decrees that enforced burqas, human rights violations toward young women, and discounting human equality and dignity between women and men—a goal widely recognized by the international community. Executed just two days before the September 11 attacks, Massoud's legacy of establishing an Afghan society free from the Taliban's draconian rule emerged just months afterward with the US-NATO led Operation Enduring Freedom, launched in retaliation for the al-Qaeda 9/11 attacks. Though well-funded by Osama bin Laden in the late 1980s, al-Qaeda's narrow fundamentalist reading of Islam which "seeks to rid Muslim countries of what it sees as the profane influence of the West and replace their government with fundamentalist Islamic regimes" is marked as the new ideological catalyst that is presently intertwined with the Taliban's political philosophy of self-determination (whether in Afghanistan or in North-West Pakistan).[38]

Pursuing Peace talks

After weighing the political and economic cost of US military action in Afghanistan and Iraq (totaling nearly $1.283 trillion by March 2011) and the reality that US public opinion about the Afghan War is largely negative, President Obama announced drawing down troops by 2014 while maintaining a US military presence until 2024. In addition to anticipated troop withdrawal, the administration is expanding efforts to pursue a negotiated settlement with top Afghan Taliban leaders willing to break ties with al-Qaeda and accept the Afghan constitution. Initial Afghan-led efforts have included launching an Afghan High Peace Council led by former Afghan President Burhanuddin Rabbani (before his assassination in 2011). Additional US-backed efforts were launched in January 2010 at the International Conference on Afghanistan in London, England. Among the vital interests discussed, such as transitioning security to Afghan forces the conference was recognized as a credible success in bringing together Afghan President Hamid Karzai, UN Secretary General Ban Ki Moon, UK Prime Minister Gordon Brown, UK Foreign Secretary David Milband, UN Envoy Kai Eide and US Secretary of State Hillary Clinton to discuss the feasibility of reconciliation and reintegration of moderate and low-level members of the Afghan Taliban back into Afghan society. The London Conference backed Afghan-led reconciliation by establishing a $500 million Peace and Reintegration Trust Fund to support international peacemaking efforts with the Afghan Taliban. However, more concrete efforts supporting the pursuit of comprehensive engagement have included Hamid Karzai's 2010 Loya Jirga tribal peace summit, Kai Eide's UN-led talks with high-level members of the Taliban, and secret US-led talks (between 2010 and 2012) with key members of the Taliban on four separate occasions (twice in Germany and Qatar).[39]

According to Richard Barrett, coordinator of the al-Qaeda Taliban Analytical Support Monitoring Team at the United Nations, making a concrete effort to talk to the Taliban is the first step to solving the decade long conflict and restoring regional stability. With the assistance of the Gulf State of Qatar, the State Department and key intelligence officers have carried out several rounds of clandestine talks with high-level proxies to Afghan Taliban leader, Mullah Mohammad Omar. In March 2012, several rounds of talks would center on the prospects of the United States taking into consideration two of the Taliban's conditions: removing the Taliban as a terrorist organization from the UN Security Council's watch-list, and releasing key members of the Taliban from Guantanamo Bay prison. On the contrary, US conditions call for members of the Taliban to sever ties with al-Qaeda and agree to a ceasefire zone leading to a cessation of hostilities between the United States and Taliban forces in Afghanistan. Among the invaluable gems of this process is the influence of the Gulf State of Qatar and key actors such as negotiator Mullah Abdul Aziz (a former secretary for the Taliban's embassy in the United Arab Emirates) who are responsible for facilitating aspects of the peace-talks. While Qatar is expected to host the site of the Taliban's new political office, its role as a high-stakes actor was confirmed in March 2012 with the transfer of five senior Taliban fighters held at Guantanamo Bay to prison facilities in Qatar in return for Western prisoners.[40]

Alongside efforts to omit polarized rhetoric linking the religion of Islam to terrorism, the Obama administration is taking strides to broaden Washington's diplomatic framework to engage vital nonstate actors. This radical shift in direction by the Obama administration was first recorded in the 2010 National Security Strategy outlining its commitment to engage adversaries alongside Western allies to pursue deeper cooperation on the basis of mutual interests and mutual respect.

> To adversarial governments, we offer a clear choice: abide by international norms, and achieve the political and economic benefits that come with greater integration with the international community or refuse to accept this pathway, and bear the consequences of that decision, including greater isolation. Through engagement we can create opportunities to resolve differences, strengthen the international community's support of our actions, learn about the intention and nature of closed regimes, and plainly demonstrate to the publics within those nations that their governments are to blame for their isolation. Successful engagement will depend on the effective use and integration of different elements of American power.[41]

Actions ranging from the overthrow of the Taliban in 2001 to covert military operations led by unmanned drones along the northwestern Af-Pak border demonstrate Washington's commitment to counterinsurgency in the region. This commitment is highlighted in the March 2009 *White Paper of the Interagency Policy Group's Report on U.S. Policy toward Afghanistan and Pakistan*, which asserts "the core goal of the U.S. must be to disrupt, dismantle, and destroy al-Qaeda and its safe haven in Pakistan, and to prevent their return to Pakistan or Afghanistan."[42] In the administration's efforts to converge hard and soft power to achieve maximum results, it acknowledges that achieving Washington's core objectives is contingent upon disrupting terrorist networks in Afghanistan and especially Pakistan; promoting a more capable, accountable, and effective government in Afghanistan; developing increasing self-reliant Afghan security forces; assisting efforts to enhance civilian control and a stable constitutional government in Pakistan, and involving the international community to actively assist with these objectives. The Interagency Policy Group has also been an instrumental force in fostering the position that Washington and its allies publicly support the Karzai government, which in turn will bolster its legitimacy and thereby encourage Afghan-led efforts to integrate former insurgents into Afghan society.

Rethinking Peace-talks with the Quetta Shura?

Ahead of US talks with the Afghan Taliban, staunch critics opposing the current efforts include Carnegie Endowment Senior Expert on South Asia, Ashley Tellis, who presents the case that talks with the Afghan Taliban will only weaken regional security and make the United States politically vulnerable in the eyes of its adversary. According to Tellis, engaging with the Taliban relinquishes any chance for the United States to meet its military objective to dismantle and destroy the Taliban and its rogue accomplice (al-Qaeda, operating in nearby Pakistan). In addition, such engagement might have severe consequences for India's future security interests. The Tellis argument implies that "Any effort at reconciling today will, therefore, undermine the credibility of American power and the success of the Afghan mission. Most important, reconciling with the Taliban is both premature and unnecessary for the success of Western aims."[43] This argument claims that success in Afghanistan would be strengthened by Washington's commitment to a negotiated settlement led first by US military action.

Tellis establishes that the Taliban is an unwarranted diplomatic priority to ensure regional stability. Hence, his position is grounded in the traditional state-centric view that enters state affairs by subjectively discounting the viability of working with key nonstate actors. But there is a concrete reason behind such position, based on the level of atrocities inflicted by such actors, which have neither acted rationally nor prudently toward international consensus. Tellis contends:

> Reconciling with the Taliban is a deceptively beguiling strategy for pacifying Afghanistan—and one that is doomed to fail presently. Not only is the Taliban leadership uninterested in such conciliation even initiating it could lead to a perverse set of consequences. It could exacerbate the ethnic fissures within Afghanistan; it could signal to both opponents and bystanders within the country that a Western defeat was imminent and, hence, did not warrant any premature compromise—ironically making the success of reconciliation itself more improbable; and worse, it could open the door to a renewed civil war that inveigles all the major regional actors and creates fresh opportunities for al-Qaeda to nourish itself amid the resulting lawlessness and attack the West with renewed vigor.[44]

Gilles Dorronsoro adds that restoring Washington's failed strategy requires International Coalition Forces to sharpen their core interests, which include "preventing the Taliban from retaking Afghan cities, avoiding the risk that al-Qaeda would try to reestablish sanctuaries there, pursue a more aggressive counterinsurgency strategy in the North, and reallocate its civilian aid resources to places where the insurgency is still weak."[45] Since the publication of both reports and the 2009 US troop surge that included the deployment of an additional 30,000 US troops in Afghanistan, the NATO-led International Security Assistance Force presence (comprised of military soldiers from 46 countries) has neither been successful at pushing the Afghan Taliban into Pakistan nor disrupting Taliban–al-Qaeda sanctuaries in the Federal Administered Tribal Areas (FATA) of North-West Pakistan. Since 2001, a NATO-led presence in the region has inspired extensive recruitment of Taliban militants from Pakistan into Afghanistan.

While it is arguable the International Security Assistance Force is losing the ground offensive, CIA-led drone strikes in FATA since 2004 are relatively successful at targeting and eliminating high-ranking al-Qaeda and Taliban militants with an increase from 50 to over 300 missions launched under Obama's presidency. Maintaining that both the United States and India have equally suffered from terrorist threats that emanate from Afghanistan, Tellis' argument in 2011 raises the point that beyond winning in Afghanistan, Washington's real commitment must be to ensure that Afghanistan does not decelerate into a pre-Karzai state led by or permitted to share power with the Taliban. This position emerges from a deep concern about the Taliban's Af-Pak presence and the implications it might soon have on shared US-Indian security.

In a November 2011 written testimony presented to the House Foreign Affairs Committee Tellis argues, "The United States should stop employing talks with the Quetta Shura and Haqqani network as the solution to Afghanistan's problem. The insurgency has virtually no incentive to negotiate when its adversaries are headed for the exit."[46] According to Tellis, moving ahead requires postponing Washington's proposed 2014 withdrawal of US forces, thereby delaying a troop withdrawal. Instead, emphasis must be placed on consolidating security gains in the south and east, expanding US networks of air and ground lines in Afghanistan, and securing long-term basing rights with Kabul to conduct continued counter terrorism operations while supporting Afghan national security forces.[47] Considering this and similar recommendations, President Obama traveled secretly to Afghanistan in May 2012 to meet with President Hamid Karzai to sign the Strategic Partnership Agreement. This new measure outlined several updated provisions that included transitioning power to Afghan forces in 2013, and a gradual troop withdrawal from 2014–2024.

The Tellis argument cuts against this study's position on engaging the Taliban to assist in reaching an Afghan-led negotiated settlement, and it suggests that Washington's pursuit of regional security must take into account India's national security interest while highlighting the uncertainty that a Taliban power-sharing government or a return to a vast Taliban presence in Kabul may bring. Notwithstanding the economic and political burden of the Afghan quagmire, the Obama administration is taking the correct measures that might possibly lead toward a new path to ensure troop withdrawal and a workable settlement on some level with the Afghan Taliban despite its radical extension of an American troop presence until 2024.

The many setbacks to engaging the Muslim world since 2001 proves that working to restore trust with 1.5 billion Muslims is a labor intensive process requiring a long-term commitment. This educative moment suggests that key US diplomats consider broadening both their intellectual and bureaucratic framework to respond to a new set of global affairs, necessitating state-nonstate actor engagement. As this chapter illustrates, the real battle lies at the grassroots level, forcing a reassessment of the Obama administration's reliance on the persuasive single-actor model. Four points of consideration, however, are all-important as Washington moves forward in South Asia. First, maintaining regional security must include acknowledging the common security shared between the United States and India. "India's growing national capabilities give it ever greater tools to pursue its national interest to the benefit of the United States."[48] With the world's third-largest army, fourth-largest air force, and fifth-largest navy, India is a proven strategic ally with common security interests to curb the spread of global terrorism and weapons of mass destruction throughout South Asia. Second, incorporating both hard power and robust peace-talks with key Taliban leaders such as Mullah Mohammad Omar (or high-ranking proxy willing to ensure a ceasefire)—assuming that the Taliban is willing to renounce al-Qaeda—can provide a foundation that supports a realistic timetable to withdraw troops from Afghanistan. Third, ensuring an Afghan-led peace process guarantees that any attempts toward peace and security remain organic, but are largely supported by the United States and its allies. Utilizing Washington's diverse channels of diplomacy can prove beneficial in facilitating and training Afghan leadership after America's departure. And fourth, the US-led drone attacks throughout northwest Pakistan, which have increased considerably under President Obama's leadership must work to lessen civilian casualties often caused by failed US intelligence.

Considering the proliferation of nonstate actors in global politics, it is essential for Washington to comprehend that casting aside the perspectives of key religious and tribal leadership may contribute to damaging the engagement process in the near future. The next chapter builds upon this claim by exploring a new context that takes seriously the communication training and presence of a special cadre of US Foreign Service Officers adept in carrying out new public diplomacy measures at the grassroots level that move beyond resting on the laurels garnered at Cairo.

PART 3

Reshaping the Communicative Context

CHAPTER SEVEN

Considering a Corps of Specialists

Moving beyond the laurels garnered at Cairo in 2009 as well as the many missteps experienced over the last decade requires that the 2013 White House and State Department reexamine its reliance on short-term measures and symbolic gestures. This includes administering a bold set of practicable alternatives to enhance direct engagement with global Islamic communities. Neither the "Obama effect" or Pandith's short-term presence have proven capable of shoring up long-term support. Recent uprisings throughout the Middle East and North Africa reaffirm this study's argument that collective grassroots level engagement with global Islamic leadership must soon become a national security priority. These and other developments in the near future will drive US government officials to move beyond employing antiquated one-way transmission models of communication that stop short of reaching the core of Islamic society. This chapter proposes that the US Department of State consider the many worthwhile suggestions that call for the establishment of a new corps of religio-cultural specialists to pursue collective engagement. A dialogue-based "new public diplomacy" requires that we grasp several noteworthy recommendations, which serve as a starting point to initiate a new beginning, which takes seriously state/nonstate actor engagement at the grassroots level. In making this case, this chapter considers Douglas Johnston's Religion Attaché model to determine the value and limitations of this new specialist as a valuable component in the State Department's public diplomacy strategy to engage Muslim audiences.

Religion and the New Public Diplomacy

The University of Southern California Center on Public Diplomacy (CPD) at the Annenberg School of Communication has taken bold measures in its call for practitioners to exercise a "new public diplomacy" that employs dialogue-based engagement with key nonstate actors. Leading this commitment, CPD held its first conference on Faith Diplomacy in March 2011 tackling "key issues of faith in an increasingly connected world to provide a better understanding of the role religion plays in foreign policy."[1] The Faith Diplomacy conference led to an instrumental follow-up briefing the following month in Washington, DC, that launched a platform to advise key US government officials on the best approaches for engaging global religious communities. Among numerous recommendations presented, several called for the US Department of State to consider updating its antiquated public diplomacy structure by collaborating with both nongovernmental organizations and private sector public diplomacy practitioners to educate and train diplomats to publicly engage with religious affairs. As a remedy to address emerging postsecular issues, Faith Diplomacy seeks to bring awareness to "incorporating religion into public diplomacy, with particular emphasis on engaging the global Islamic community and examining religious organizations as public diplomats."[2]

Douglas Johnston, one among the many contributors to the *USC Faith Diplomacy Initiative*, is the president and founder of the Washington-based International Center for Religion and Diplomacy. Johnston's persistent call since 2002 that the State Department broaden its diplomatic and policymaking framework between state and religious nonstate actors adds strength to this study's case on how Washington might guarantee a new way forward with global Islamic communities, given the recent developments of the Arab Spring.

An Unexpected Revolt

Despite Washington's extended relationship with autocratic regimes in the Arab world over the last three decades, the embarrassment of knowing that US government officials were blindsided by the developments that swept through the Middle East and North Africa (between 2010 and 2012) remains an unsettling blow. Soon after the start of the Arab Spring, the Obama administration dithered a great while on properly addressing its developments—due to its antiquated public diplomacy structure that over the last decade failed to *build substantive relations with the Islamic/Arab Street* and *implement a two-way communication structure on the ground to feedback vital aspirations held by key opinion-formers.* After decades of ignoring Muslims at the grassroots level, the Obama administration is entangled today in an outmoded web that warrants a contemporary solution. The defining moment was its initial days in Washington, where momentum was lost due to an antiquated public diplomacy system, which since the Cold War, has relied on projecting one-way transmission models of communication as a reactionary measure to engage foreign audiences. Civil unrest spreading throughout the Arab world, ignited by a frustrated Libyan produce vendor, Mohammed Bouazizi, and transmitted via Facebook, reinforces my position that an approach that connects with the streets from the bottom up may ensure that US actors make the substantive connection required to engage key opinion formers.[3]

The two central narratives of the Arab Spring—the proliferation of social media as a tool to promote social justice and the impact of the "collective voice" in the public arena—elevate this study's discussion on the role a dialogue-based "new public diplomacy" should have with Muslim audiences. For some time Washington's interest in the Arab world has centered specifically on strengthening relations at the state actor level with autocratic leaders and curbing the spread of radical Islam, while employing ad hoc public diplomacy measures to pacify nonelite Arab audiences. The reality is that never has there existed a period of consistent interchange between the United States and Arab world leading to Washington getting feedback about the aspirations of key opinion formers at the grassroots level. While discounting these opinion formers has proven unproductive at keeping a lid on Arab frustration, it is today apparent the real disappointment held among US policymakers is that they must hasten to implement new measures that incorporate the aspirations of disenchanted youth throughout the Arab and Muslim world. Though the State Department's one-way transmission model of communication failed to rapidly inform government officials of major developments unfolding in the region, new social media tools such as Facebook, Twitter, and YouTube are proving instrumental in promoting social justice, thus shedding light on a common experience held by millions throughout the Middle East and North Africa.

New Social Media

The essential contribution of social media in the Arab Spring is linked to its ability to message in real-time to the international community the mass atrocities incited by the regime, and its power to undermine the same regime's legitimacy through social media and through media channels like two-way text, email, photo-sharing, and live video chat. Based on the limits of nation-state cyber diplomacy and Internet state-craft we are able to determine both are complex measures that practitioners must be reluctant to rely upon in the coming years. Clay Shirky writes in the essay, "The Political Power of Social Media,"

> The more promising way to think about social media is as long-term tools that can strengthen civil society and the public sphere...According this conception, positive changes in the life of a country, including pro-democratic regime change, follow, rather than precede, the development of a strong public sphere. This is not to say that popular movements will not successfully use these tools to discipline or even oust their government, but rather that U.S. attempts to direct such uses are likely to do more harm than good.[4]

Crystallizing Shirky's argument, Egyptian blogger, Wael Abbas argues, " Social media is a tool. But revolution is the decision of many people. Once we [in Egypt] decided to have a revolution, once people decided to stay in the square, social media was a helpful tool to call for support."[5] Considering the limits of Washington's public diplomacy program to deliver insight, social media served as Washington's eyes and ears on the *Arab Street*. As the medium of social media raised Americans' awareness of the Arab Spring, its ability to disseminate facts in real-time exposed the inadequacies of Washington's supposedly well-oiled intelligence and diplomatic services. Thus, defending the National Security Council, spokesman Tommy Vietor reminds us that, During the early days of the revolution, social media served as Washington's eyes and ears along the Arab streets. The real distress toward the power of social media websites was in fact the public fact that US intelligence agencies were unable to adequately inform key US policymakers of the unfolding events as rapidly as they were occurring. National Security Council spokesman Tommy Vietor stated in an interview, "Did anyone in the world know in advance that a fruit vendor in Tunisia was going to light himself on fire and start a revolution? No. But for decades, the intelligence community and diplomats have been reporting on unrest in the region that was a result of economic, demographic and political conditions."[6] Despite Principal Deputy Director of National Intelligence Stephanie O'Sullivan's statement that forewarned of instability, Washington's inadequacy highlights the overarching reality that effective two-way communication structures were in fact nonexistent at the grassroots level.

If pondering on this case closely, it's reasonable to ask if whether a two-way communication structure were present prior to the uprisings, might key government officials have anticipated its development sooner? Yes, but when assessing the absence of a substantive two-way communication structure that connects Washington to the *Arab Street*, we gather much attention over the last decade has centered on galvanizing attention around combating global terrorism and curbing the spread of Islamism in the Middle East and South Asia. Less attention is given to the growing disenchantment held among Arab youth toward rising unemployment and other conditions leading to the Arab Spring. Next, the absence of this two-way communications structure reinforces the well-established argument by former State Department officials that Washington, sooner than later revaluates the vital role dialogue-based engagement might inevitably have on building genuine relations in an era where officials are today reliant upon cyber diplomacy and social media tools to disseminate rapid messaging. Facebook, Twitter, YouTube, and Skype are capable of informing mass audiences instantaneously of the many atrocities occurring in the Arab world in real-time; however, none of them have proven successful at replacing direct human-to-human engagement.[7]

While the Internet and social media websites are instrumental in highlighting the conditions and voices of millions of Arab youth, new social media tools helped to give voice to a voiceless movement. Despite the accolades we might bestow upon social media websites, without the physical presence and collective voice of millions taking to the Arab streets, the uprisings would never have happened. For this reason, it is imperative that US diplomats do not complacently rely on social media tools as a substitute for direct dialogue-based engagement. As Philip Seib reminds us in *Real-time Diplomacy*, while surveying the impact of real-time media transmission and the role of diplomacy, "Effective diplomacy cannot be done on the fly; it requires back-and-forth among parties, an ability to listen and respond carefully. During much of the twentieth century, speed steadily encroached on the diplomatic process as the public came to increasingly rely upon radio, and then television, and then Internet as principal sources of information."[8] One essential challenge in the days ahead will include redefining its role at the grassroots level, where the collective voice of the masses resides. Decades of ignoring the Arab masses is transpiring into a new wave ushering regime change and the political presence of Islamist parties as an alternative to Western-backed tyranny in the region.

Embracing the Collective Voice

In December 2010, the world witnessed the determination of Arab youth in Tunisia to assert their collective voice in protest toward President Zine El Abidine Ben Ali. Conflated political promises over 23 years had reached a boiling point earlier in the month when Tunisian hip-hop artist Hamada "El-General" Ben Amor released the contentious single, "Rais Lelbled," which openly criticizing Ben Ali's kleptocratic rule. Forced to record in a dilapidated "underground" recording studio—in fear of breaching Tunisia's censorship laws—Hamada's lyrics echoed throughout the country, establishing a pretext that provided the flame for the Jasmine Revolution, which later ousted Tunisia's dictator. Permeating south to the city of Sidi Bouzid, El General's anthem intersected with the social frustrations of produce vendor, Mohamed Bouazizi. Hard-pressed and facing the universal condition of many college educated youth in the Arab world unable to find work, Bouazizi resorted to selling produce without a vending license from a borrowed cart to earn a day's wage. After a routine stop resulting in officers confiscating his property, a quarrel ensued with a female officer slapping him, thereby involving public humiliation.

After repeated attempts to regain his property, Bouazizi's final act of self-immolation in front of a city municipality building served as the spark igniting the Arab Spring. "Bouazizi's death triggered the revolt in Tunisia, serving as a 'last straw' for thousands of Tunisians who saw in his frustration as a mirror image of their own lives."[9] As the events were captured on cell phone and instantaneously uploaded onto Facebook (and later Twitter), Bouazizi's resistance inspired Arab youth to replace authoritarian regimes with democratically elected officials to liberate the masses from mounting unemployment and corruption. Contrasting the average Tunisian reality against the opulence of Ben Ali's lifestyle, Michele P. Angrist writes of the Tunisians' reality reminding us, "dissidents were tortured and everyday Tunisians struggled to build livelihoods, while the families of the president and those connected to him enriched themselves and flaunted their wealth. The Ben Ali regime was contemptuous of its citizens, treating them as too unsophisticated to entrust with freedoms—and betting that they would be too meek to call the regime to account for its excesses."[10] Following nearly a month of protest, both President Ben Ali and Prime Minster Mohamed Ghannouchi resigned from office, leading to the dissolution of the political police, release of political prisoners, dispersing the ruling Constitutional Democratic Rally party, which later ushered in a new political era and constitutional assembly in October 2011.

Inspired by concurrent regional protest in Algeria, Jordan, Morocco, Sudan, Oman, and Saudi Arabia, young antigovernment demonstrators in Egypt rallied around similar frustrations such as mounting corruption and increased food prices under President Hosni Mubarak's 30-year rule. Despite spurring foreign investments and pursuing economic reforms for nearly a decade, Egyptians' living conditions coupled by the nation's skyrocketting unemployment rate held little hope for college educated students in a country marred by kleptocracy and military rule. Since 1953, the military arrangement worked in the favor of Egypt's despots, whether in the case of Nasser's secret police force, Sadat's public relations with the United States, or Mubarak's enforcing a three-decade-long state of emergency. Underneath the initial layer of frustration, leading Arab masses to exercise civil disobedience to bring awareness to their deplorable economic conditions and for the right to broader freedoms, lies the underbelly of the Arab condition, linked in part to Western exploitative interests.

The United States (as France in Algeria, Italy in Libya, or Russia in Syria) has profited from its highly exploitative relationship with Egypt as a financial surrogate to the military as a strategic ploy to cushion Israel. As Steven A. Cook reminds us,

> The original sin was Sadat's separate peace with Israel, which Mubarak inherited and scrupulously upheld. From the perspective of many Egyptians, this arrangement hopelessly constrained Cairo's power while it freed Israel and the United States to pursue their regional interests unencumbered. For the United States, Mubarak was pivotal in creating a regional order that made it easier and less expensive for Washington to pursue its interests, from the free flow of oil to the protection of Israel and the prevention of any one country in the region from becoming too dominant. The benefits to Mubarak were clear: approximately $70 billion in economic and military aid over thirty years and the ostensible prestige of being a partner of the world's superpower.[11]

However, a grim reminder that tyrannical rule is not linked to nonviolent civil disobedience is underscored by the nearly 50,000 protestors killed between 2010 and 2012. Following the onset of Egypt's revolution were subsequent uprisings in *Yemen,* calling for President Ali Abdullah Saleh's resignation; *Iraq,* where the provisional governors and local council resigned at the behest of antigovernment demonstrators; *Bahrain,* where sectarian strife between its Shiite Majority and Sunni minority has led to scores of deadly violence; *Kuwait,* which was followed by the resignation of Prime Minster Nasser Mohammed Al-Ahmed Al-Sabah and dismantling parliament; *Morocco,* where King Mohammed VI promised constitutional reform; and even with episodes throughout the Palestinian territories with the Palestinian Liberation Organization undermining both Israel and the United States by making it bid for statehood at the United Nations.

The act of inflicting gross atrocities and Arab dictators giving orders to carry out torture are not new occurrence. Among the two most deadly uprisings at the time of this writing are the 2011 and 2012 atrocities in Libya and Syria. Estimates indicate that nearly 35,000 demonstrators and innocent civilians were killed in Libya's uprising-turned-civil-war between NATO-backed insurgents and pro-government loyalists. However, violence ceased in October 2011 with the murder of Muammar Gadhafi in the northern town of Sirt. Taking similar measures to crackdown on antigovernment protestors, Syrian President Bashar Shar al-Assad, as of March 2011, ordered the Syrian armed forces to violently suppress protestors throughout the country in their call for regime change and elimination of Syria's Ba'th Party. While supporting its geopolitical interests in early 2012, China and Russia together contributed to impeding the Arab League peace plan, led by Kofi Annan, by wielding their veto power in the United Nations Security Council, which subsequently added to an estimate 13,000 deaths.

Arguably, without our many new social media tools, the Arab Spring would neither have gained traction nor wide-scale international support. While they are capable of placing the Arab and Islamic streets in contact with the West, they expose the deficit of not having a readily available two-way communication structure or effective public diplomacy apparatus to first engage and later feedback perspectives from the grassroots into the foreign policy discourse. In recent years, an overemphasis on Cyber Diplomacy as a serious avenue to connect with Muslim youth stops short at building the relations required in this era from the bottom up. "Diplomats who claim to be up-to-date because they have their own Twitter feeds or Facebook pages miss the point. Many of them are enamored of gadgetry without recognizing what media tools can really do on a macro level. The foreign policy establishment in many countries is exceedingly slow to recognize change, in this case the impact of networks that communication-based connectivity enables."[12] Appreciating the perspective of secular youth in the Muslim world, grassroots organizations, and Islamist groups such as the Muslim Brotherhood requires that the State Department reach beyond reactionary digital tools and step onto the streets. Being proactive in the days ahead requires US government officials to consider direct two-way communication structures that ensure broad relationship building with the core of global Islamic societies.

Reaffirming Broad Engagement

Among the many false starts and missteps that gripped US public diplomacy over the last decade, it is sensible that the State Department enhance all opportunities to appreciate the perspective of secular Arab youth, and Islamist leadership (such as the Muslim Brotherhood), which necessitates moving beyond one-way communication models to connect with the *Arab* and *Islamic Street*.[13] As new social media tools like Facebook and Twitter share a unique place in the public sphere, it is imperative that government officials are mindful these instruments function in a reactionary capacity, merely allowing Washington to gather "inside stories" from one direction in real-time. Improving relations dictates we take into account new dialogue-based public diplomacy opportunities that employ broad engagement efforts at the grassroots level. For this matter, this study forecasts the next wave of the Arab Spring will be incited by anti-Western undertones led by emerging Islamist opinion formers. This prospect reinforces the argument as to why it is vital that US policymakers and diplomats begin thinking about moving beyond antiquated measures to link communication opportunities to the potency of nonviolent Arab youth and their call for civil disobedience to replace autocratic regimes with democratically elected officials, and the determination of Arab youth to work at the grassroots level with local networks and nonstate actors to improve sociopolitical conditions.

In moving forward, it is recommended here that Washington consider employing innovative measures to broaden its diplomatic framework by adopting previously recommended proposals like those put forth by former US policymakers like Douglas Johnston and that the State Department launch a Religion Attaché corps to provide expert advisement and mediation at US embassies where religious issue are salient. This measure may contribute significantly to the "New Beginning" vision as proposed by the Obama administration to restore trust with global Islamic communities. Considering the current developments unfolding throughout the Arab world and South Asia, the Johnston model demonstrates a resolve by providing extensive ground support to facilitate in promoting a *dialogue-based new public diplomacy* and *state/nonstate actor relationship building*, two chief component's of restoring trust.

Revisiting the Johnston Model

In considering a new way forward, the US Department of State will find it suitable to take into account Edward Luttwak's 1994 proposal that state and its intelligence services consider recruiting a corps of specialists to provide adequate assistance in analyzing international religious affairs, honing capabilities to perform multiple task to improve direct communicative engagement, and employ existing foundational skills to make clear emerging religious matters pertinent to US national security.[14] Considering the role of this new actor requires a trained human presence stationed at the grassroots level to conduct direct two-way dialogue-based engagement with key players, whether religious nonstate actors, youth leadership, nongovernmental organizations or Islamist political party figures. This presence will additionally ensure that a robust communication structure exists at the grassroots level.

Envisioning this major approach in the 2002 *Foreign Service Journal* article, "The Case for a Religion Attaché," Johnston reintroduced Luttwak's proposal—nearly a decade later—a practical model. Making this case in the study *Faith-based Diplomacy*, he writes, "Consideration of religious factors within US foreign policy would be considerably enhanced by the creation of a new Religion Attaché Officer position within the Foreign Service. These attachés would be assigned to those [diplomatic] missions in countries where religion has particular salience in order to deal more effectively with complex religious issues."[15]

In a more recent study entitled, *Religion, Terror, and Error: U.S. Foreign Policy and the Challenge of Spiritual Engagement*, Johnston points to the responsibilities of a new specialist, who will build new partnerships across sacred-secular lines, restoring trust with religious communities, and most importantly, creating effective peace-building frameworks by conducting on-the-ground assessments.[16] This new actor will help in working with reestablishing local embassy contacts to support drafting the annual report on international religious freedom. Additional responsibilities as employed by public diplomacy and cultural affairs officers, bearing program responsibilities and carrying out training in "nonrational complexity" to accommodate with "(i) understanding religious motives and priorities, (ii) the specific language of local resolution expression, and, above all, (iii) how faith inspires action."[17]

Recruitment and Finance

Generally, when recruiting US Foreign Service Officers an open application process is held whereby candidates are pooled and later selected based on written merit and oral distinction. While this process is beneficial as standard criteria, an additional vocation-specific element is essential to fulfill the role of this new specialist. With any labor, financial, cultural, or agricultural attaché assigned to a foreign embassy, it is imperative this candidate is trained with an interdisciplinary skill-set in religious studies and culture to perform proficiently. With an increase in American students since 9/11 peering into the fields of religion and conflict resolution studies both American seminaries and international studies programs may serve as a valuable recruiting ground due to their interdisciplinary training and potential background in religio-cultural affairs and foreign language. The State Department will benefit greatly by taking into account this recruitment pool considering the high probability of getting culturally astute candidates. In the case of restoring trust with Muslim audiences, Johnston asserts, "Because it will take some time for the bureaucracy to address this need once the decision has been made to do so, consideration could be given to bridging the gap in Muslim countries by recruiting qualified American Muslims or other suitable experts to perform the function, while serving as a special assistant to the ambassador."[18]

Consideration regarding the cost of funding this new specialist was taken in 2002. Agreeably, funding a corps of specialist/attaché, will be substantially less than fiscal expenditures spent to fund the War on Terror. Since 2001, the United States Congress has approved over $1.23 trillion for defense-related activities such as Operation Enduring Freedom, Operation Noble Eagle, and Operation Iraqi Freedom, which includes base security, reconstruction, foreign aid, and embassy costs.[19] Johnston interjects that funding a corps would be unlikely to reach even half of US defense spending by some top departments/agencies.[20]

According to the Johnston study, "A conservative estimate of global requirements suggests the need for a corps of 30 at an initial total of $10 million. The figure is based on a State Department budget office estimate of $250,000 to $300,000 per year to field a person in a new position (including salary, benefits, transportation to and from the post, shipping of household effects, outfitting of a new office and any allowances for hardship, danger pay, cost of living adjustment and housing)."[21] However, this study finds that since 2002, a slight rise in funding 30 or more attaché is possible. It is believed that $300,000–$350,000 per attaché would suffice to ensure their deployment, whether or not they are serving at a hardship embassy post in a conflict-prone setting. Despite this minimum cost adjustment, the cost for assuring peace through proactive public diplomacy measures is not comparable to the surmounting cost of $1.23 trillion to maintain America's military presence in both Afghanistan and Iraq, which has yet to curb increasing religious and sectarian strife where US national security interests are pivotal.

Considering the Two Limitations

As vital as expanding the State Department's bureaucratic framework to recruit religion specialist will be to ensuring Washington remains in front of the curve, two perceptible shortcomings are present with respect to the Johnston model. First, if the State Department were to consider launching a corps of specialist, it will be beneficial if key officials (such as the Secretary of State) give serious consideration to its descriptive limitations. Acknowledging its limitations in this area, Johnston adds,

> Whether the religion specialists are designed as Religion Attaches or some other title is far less important than the fact that embassy staffing would include the requisite expertise to take the religious imperative fully into account in the conduct of our relations with the particular country. This position would also go a long way toward ensuring that foreign policy mistakes resulting from ignorance or the conscious exclusion of religious factors are minimized, if not eliminated altogether.[22]

While the actors' description should neither matter nor impede its development, considering Washington's polarized environment is led by political pundits and opinion formers, we must consider that this actor's *title/description* will in fact define its role and suspected political limitations. A more inclusive description as *Human Communication Specialist* (HCS) provides a concise characterization of the new specialist. Here are the reasons why the description Religion Specialist or Religion Attaché is limiting on three grounds:

1. A cosmic war lasting more than a decade between Islamist and the West will generate a negative backlash in the public sphere. Further, it is highly probable that either title will become misinterpreted or easily co-opted by US special interests groups, considering their legacy to intertwine religious interests with US national security.
2. The description and role of this actor should not denote that it will limit its interaction solely between Specialist/Attaché and religious actors. Its description must reflect its willingness to engage broadly with civil society, key nonstate actors, and foes alike at the grassroots level to build and restore relations.
3. Extensive speculation exists as to whether the title Religion Attaché or Religion Specialist titles might gain the proper traction before members of Congress, thereby proving to be a tough sell. Holding to the "religious" description will surely incite chaos between lawmakers thus dissuading support of a brilliant recommendation.

While ensuring its description is more inclusive, it is imperative this new actor incorporates a substantive, but missing element into its equation—*postsecular communication*. If the specialist's chief task will include engaging across sacred-secular lines, it is appropriate the State Department provide an adequate measure of communication training that works complementary to both actors. This form of grassroots engagement that works from the bottom up will be beneficial in decreasing the current trust deficit, especially with Muslim majority audiences. Further, the description *HCS* is broad in scope, but provides the latitude to implement core components that may include comprehending "nonrational complexities," religio-cultural analysis, conflict resolution, and communication intensive roles, each of which will aid in furthering peace-building opportunities.[23]

Secondly, if the State Department were to adopt the Johnston model, serious consideration to upgrading aspects of US public diplomacy that utilizes this new actor within a dialogue-based setting will deserve immediate consideration. This necessitates taking seriously the communication functions of this new actor, especially as it relates to communicating across sacred-secular lines. US government agencies have yet to seriously place major emphasis on the role and responsibility of communication in the engagement setting. While Johnston provides a clear description of this actor's role outside of the embassy, his and Luttwak's proposals overlook the core element to ensure a favorable outcome—two-way communication training. If this actor were to carryout its duties in a predominantly Muslim majority country it will be advantageous if she/he: (i) comprehends vital aspects within Islamic society by depending more on its socioreligious infrastructure; (ii) builds direct relations with Muslim audiences that pay due heed to the traditional voice of Islam; (iii) restores relations at a grassroots level that build on mutual understanding and mutual interests, thus extending the voice of key religious players within Islamic society; and (iv) grasps that fulfilling such task will require employing a productive two-way postsecular communication approach.

In reimagining the role of US-Muslim world engagement as it functions in the public diplomacy arena, let us remember that such innovative proposals may likely be confronted by bureaucratic limitations that to a great extent may impede recruitment. Notwithstanding the fact that an office of International Religious Freedom exists with a primary role to promote religious freedom as a core objective of US foreign policy, hence, the State Department's bureaucratic framework is limited both conceptually and structurally.[24] *This deficiency in the US government structure underscores its lack of having diverse resources as a specialty department, agency, or an office to specifically deal with broad international religious affairs. Arguably, such limitations contribute to countless episodes linked to communicative failures and limited analysis on the social terrain of Muslim majority nations—especially those with Ministries of Religious Affairs and trained diplomats who handle clearly defined international religious issues.*

In the case of connecting with key actors throughout the Muslim world, the State Department must set out boldly to launch a corps of specialists and shift its focus toward providing two-way communication training that these new actors might draw upon when in the dialogical setting. This requires comprehending best practices that will enrich interaction between sacred-secular players, in and outside of the embassy. In taking on this bold new approach, the new actor will be able to effectively engage the core of the Islamic society by practicing human-to-human engagement. This more engaged approach on the whole is capable of sharing space with or being incorporated into the practice of a new dialogue-based public diplomacy. If this model is considered as a serious option to engage key nonstate actors throughout the Muslim world and in areas where religion is salient for that matter, then it is only appropriate the HCS practice postsecular communication to ensure equitable dialogical opportunities for both sacred and secular actors. Considering the magnitude of this recommendation, the next chapter will explore this dynamic of surveying the Theory of Communicative Action and Coordinated Management of Meaning, two communication theories that when intersected, provide a foundation to commence two-way postsecular communication between diplomats and key nonstate actors.

CHAPTER EIGHT

Toward a Postsecular Communicative Framework

Restoring confidence and building trust with global Islamic communities requires the US Department of State to consider a bold new path that leads to the recruitment of a highly competent Human Communication Specialist Corps to enrich US diplomatic engagement with key religious and cultural players at the grassroots level. This chapter presents the case that while a special corps is vital to enriching US state-nonstate actor relations, particularly in Muslim majority nations, it will be inevitably deficient in the dialogical setting if it is not accompanied by a smart communication approach. This measure is capable of working within a new public diplomacy context to strengthen broad state-nonstate actor relations. In conjunction with US Foreign Service Officer training, consideration of incorporate postsecular approaches will aid in enriching dialogical opportunities between both actors. This chapter will introduce the basis of postsecular communication through an exploration of the Theory of Communicative Action and Coordinated Management of Meaning, two communication theories that when intersected, provide a foundation to commence smart communication as pursued and practiced by this new corps of specialists.

Postsecular Communication

Prominent American-based study groups and think tanks often make the mistake of discounting the importance of dialogue-based engagement, shifting attention toward expediting policy rather than affirming that communication training is a vital resource in dialogical development between state and nonstate actors. For example, the 2006 *Princeton Project on National Security* proposes an alternative public diplomacy strategy with the Muslim world by giving little, if any, attention to how Washington's proposed communication approach might be received by target audiences in the Arab world. While it is correct to assume that greater forms of communication are required to connect with Muslim audiences, the *Princeton* report fell short, proposing that US public diplomacy officers exercise a public relations approach to market US foreign policy and its message to target audiences. Shedding light on this claim, the report reveals that "[America] should shift its public diplomacy efforts from a public relations approach to a sales approach. While public relations involves one-way communication strategies, a sales-based approach requires understanding what motivates the recipient of a message to 'buy' or inhibit the recipient from accepting and embracing the ideas being proffered."[1]

While influential in US public diplomacy circles, the *Princeton* report contributed to a narrow reading of socially constructed societies by affirming it is not cognizant that a "sales" approach inhibits productive relationship making with Muslim audiences. Several private sector post-9/11 studies evade taking seriously the role of dialogue-based public diplomacy that inevitably requires a shift in foreign policymaking. Such a shift challenges a preconstructed set of political norms that are often state-centric in their focus and entrenched in a realist agenda that devalues the perspectives of nonstate actors. In pursuing a new way forward to comprehend whether state and nonstate actors are capable of interlocking in the dialogue setting, it is essential that both accept that a balance in communication is indispensable to ensure a favorable outcome.

As outlined in chapter two, postsecularism as a descriptive term calls attention to the present era, a period where religion is becoming more important in global politics. In addition to this outlook, this term is further represented by the appeal that both sacred and secular actors discern that multiple perspectives are convening presently in the global public sphere demanding that both actors are communicatively astute. Communicating with awareness within this context calls for actors to practice aspects of postsecular communication as a treatment to enhance dialogical relation between sacred and secular players. This will involve both actors (a) embracing creative and diverse styles in the communicative setting, (b) shifting actor behavior by taking a complementary learning approach, and (c) applying both communicative action and the coordinated management of movement to sustain direct two-way dialogical engagement between interlocutors at the grassroots level. Nonetheless, postsecular communication is not the last word on improving communicative relations between sacred and secular actors, but it is a practical starting point for HCS that will supplement Foreign Service Officer training, as it is actor-centered and focused on capitalizing upon shared interest.

Creativity and Complementary Learning

Turning our attention to the advantage of embracing multiple communicative frameworks when practicing postsecular communication, Troy Dostert presents four general qualities that actors might consider if they wish to progressively improve their relations with value-defined socially constructed societies. They include *sincerity, discipline, forbearance* and, above all, *dialogical creativity*. The last of these four qualities, *dialogical creativity* is of great concern in practicing postsecular communication where public and private diplomats might improve communicative relations at home and abroad to formulate effective relationships across sociocultural lines. This entails rethinking how actors must reposition sacred-secular voices to ensure a productive interchange. What is likely to develop when there is dialogical creativity is a conversion of multiple communicative frameworks to create an inclusive context conducive to engagement between religious and secular political actors. "The practice of dialogical creativity presupposes an on going need for scrutinizing our political ideals and adapting them so as to respond to changing social, cultural and political realities."[2] Dostert adds:

> We must always seek to measure the adequacy of our political understandings and use whatever normative resources at our disposal to critique and refashion them when they fall short. This is a process that requires imagination and discovery, as well as flexibility and a desire to experiment with diverse political approaches.[3]

By broadening the communicative framework to ensure multiple discourse opportunities, both sacred and secular actors practicing postsecular communication will discover that new spaces are available to relearn aspects of constructive communication. This dictates that actors should be adept at comprehending both secular and nonsecular visions in order to balance and embrace both the aspirations and perspectives of either the sacred or secular.

> As long as the secular citizens perceive religious traditions and religious communities as archaic relics of pre-modern societies which continue to exist in the present, they will understand freedom of religion as the natural preservation of an endangered species. From their viewpoint, religion no longer has any intrinsic justification to exist in the present, and thus they will understand freedom of religion in this way. From their viewpoint, religion no longer has any intrinsic justification to exist. And the principle of the separation of state and church can for them only have the laicist meaning of sparing indifference. Citizens who adopt such an epistemic stance toward religion can obviously no longer be expected to take religious contributions to contentious political issues seriously or even to help to assess them as a substance which can in any way be expressed in a secular language and justified by secular arguments.[4]

While broadening discourse opportunities in postsecular communication, a behavioral shift must occur between actors. Jürgen Habermas regards this cognitive behavioral shift in a postsecular setting as the *complementary learning process* (CLP), a pre-engagement approach. The aim of the CLP is to establish that a cognitive level of respect is necessary between the sacred and secular in society, by emphasizing that neither should consider itself a social burden to the other. The process emphasizes that differences between the two groups will be apparent, but the good gained by joining them derives from their very diversity. The aim is to ensure that both voices understand that they each have qualities from which other actors can learn. Taking a complementary learning approach to postsecular communication ensures that when making this introductory step, religious actors in particular will not renounce their sacred beliefs when engaging the secular, and state actors, in return, will maintain their traditional secular beliefs when addressing religious actors. However, the focus turns to embracing tolerance, mutual understanding, and a common ground to build communicative relations on. "In view of what an ethic of democratic citizenship requires in terms of mentalities, we come up against the very limits of a normative political theory that can justify only rights and duties. Learning processes can be fostered, but not morally or legally stipulated."[5]

Making this shift toward a more engaged response, the space for discussion will broaden, thereby allow for more direct yet peaceful public debates and deliberations between both worlds. Additionally, a diminution of political apprehensiveness will follow, since both citizens will have an idea of the other's objectives. Even with such aims, it would be naive to assume that the process will not throw up great cognitive challenges. The problem often identified between both mindsets is that each world struggle with considering the other a "complementary equal"—a problem persisting in Western society since the seventeenth century at the nation-state level. With the CLP, a reflexive convocation of learning develops and is imbued with respect in order to encourage the primary adjustment of attitude needed to ensure a more engaged response between sacred and secular actors.

A Theory of Communicative Action

Comprehending how postsecular communication may further accompany the HCS during their dialogical engagement opportunity with key nonstate actors at the grassroots level, let us turn to first establish the role of language in discourse. According to German linguist Karl Buhler, three specific functions are assigned to language with reference given to the first, second and third persons, which includes: "the 'cognitive' function of representing a state of affairs; the 'appeal' function of directing requests to addressees; and the 'expressive' function of disclosing the experiences of the speaker."[6] Hence, James Finalyson of the University of Sussex makes the case that Bühler's argument, though disputable at first glance is rather clear, contending that "any instance of language-use involves a triangle comprising *speaker, hearer,* and *world,* and that the theory of language must do justice to them all."[7] In a real sense, doing justice to language requires that actors promote direct communicative engagement rather than indirect approaches that are often disingenuous. Thus, the HSC in this case is unlikely to convey a substantive (or what she/he perceives as a substantive) message if it is not perceived as direct or coherent during human-to-human engagement. "Habermas argues that the primary function of speech is to coordinate the action of a plurality of individual agents and to provide the indivisible tracks along which interaction can unfold in an orderly and conflict-free manner."[8]

Here, we will gather the function of postsecular communication as will be practiced by the HCS by evaluating Habermas' *Theory of*

Communicative Action. This communication theory consists of four sociological concepts exercised by actors that are *teleological, normatively regulated, dramaturgical,* or *communicative.* "The one-sidedness [in communication] of the first three concepts of language can be seen in the fact that the corresponding types of communication singled out by them prove to be limited cases of communicative action."[9] When placing Habermas's argument in context with post-9/11 US public diplomacy efforts to win hearts and minds, it is clear the first three concepts run counter to the proposed communicative action approach that the HCS must pursue when interlocking with religious actors in the dialogical setting.

Four Sociological Concepts

The first concept, *teleological action,* is a form of indirect encounter displayed by actors and groups. In projecting this action, actors set out to attain "an end or brings about the occurrence of a desired state by choosing means that have promise of being successful in the given situation and applying them in a suitable manner."[10] Interest-based goals are often pursued here through indirect communication toward actors or the target audience. Arriving at this point, Habermas suggests, "Success in action is also dependent on other actors, each of whom is oriented to his own success and behaves cooperatively only to the degree that this fits with his egocentric calculus of utility."[11] In most cases, actors employing teleological actions seek to reach a preestablished ends by controlling target audience member behavior in a given encounter. "It is this model of action that lies behind decision-theoretic and game-theoretic approaches in economics, sociology, and social psychology."[12] Teleological action was taken up months prior to and after 9/11 at the State Department with Charlotte Beers and Karen P. Hughes overlapping nation branding and public diplomacy approaches by pursuing an overarching agenda to win hearts and minds.

Second, *normative* expression refers in part to interactivity where an actor seeks to relate to members of a social group by orientating their actions to the common values shared by members of the target audience. It is within this form of communicative expression that actors "do not have a cognitive sense of an expected event, but the normative sense that members within the target audience are entitled to expect a certain behavior from the actor."[13] In a sense, normatively regulated actions are generally culturally based and ensure that actors enter social settings or societies by either transforming their actions or altering the character of the participants to suit the dominant group. Roger Bolton acknowledges "that often this action is performed almost automatically, in rote fashion, from second nature, out of deeply extended shared habits and regarded as unproblematic by the actors, rather than in a calculated instrumental way."[14] This form of expression is highlighted with US public diplomacy after 9/11 that encouraged audiences in the Muslim world to participate in exchange programs held in settings with a pre-existing set of rules and objectives to be carried out by participants.

Unlike teleological and normatively regulated actions, *dramaturgical* action is slightly different in that it pursues indirect actor relations via communication with mass audiences. It relates "neither to the solitary actor nor to the member of a social group, but to participants in interaction constituting a public for one another, before whom they present themselves."[15] Though often indirect in his/her actions, state actors generally have "privileged access to their personal intentions which may be tailored by mass communication outlets."[16] Habermas adds, "This, the central concept of the presentation of self does not signify spontaneous expressive behaviour but stylising the expression of one's own experiences with a view to the audience."[17] After 9/11, we witnessed high-ranking US state actors presenting a set of rehearsed symbolic gestures to Muslim audiences that easily may be categorized as stereotypical, indirect, or even stylized. During this period, a wave of short-term symbolic gestures in an orchestrated effort to gain legitimacy and attention throughout global Islamic communities by US government officials was paramount to Washington's public relations and public diplomacy campaign. Top ranking US state actors, including Secretary Condoleezza Rice, Karen P. Hughes, Michael Chertoff, David Welch, and numerous ambassadors and diplomats, participated in mass media public diplomacy campaign to market American leadership in conjunction with the promotion of American values by utilizing radio and television appearances, cyber-activity, multimedia programming and social networking to connect with Muslim audiences, after 9/11.

The last, but most important, sociological concept presented by Habermas is *communicative* action. Unlike the above actions, which are generally indirect, the sociological concept of communication action moves beyond symbolic gestures that gear audiences toward a predetermined end: a new way forward beneficial to the agenda of the HCS at the grassroots level. In this last concept, both interpersonal relations and objective expressions are expressed as vital elements to build new and restructure previous relations. In juxtaposition with the previous three concepts, communicative action signifies "the interaction of at least two subjects capable of speech and action who establish interpersonal relations (whether by verbal or by extra-verbal means). In this case, [state/nonstate actors]...seek to reach an understanding about the action situation and their plans of action in order to coordinate their action by way of agreement. The central concept interpretation refers in the first instance to negotiating definitions of the situation which admit of consensus."[18] Hence, in this last concept, the presupposition of the linguistic medium of language reflects the actor's world and is also given a prominent place in discourse.[19] Unlike *teleological, dramaturgical,* and *normatively* regulated actions—which adopt a one-sided and indirect approach to communal relations—*communicative* action ensures directness through actor accountability. Within this specific concept lies an opportunity for the HCS who is the *listener,* to raise, for example validity claims; or fall back on the fact that rules of discourse exist that keep both the *speaker* and *listener* in lock-step while engaged in dialogue at the grassroots level.[20]

As secular state actors are apprehensive about allowing nonsecular customs to permeate through the public sphere to challenge secular traditions, so are socially constructed traditional societies about the attitude of secular actors toward their value system. A *sacred-secular equilibrium* or CLP is imperative in most cases to ensure objective communicative exchange between state and nonstate actors. The State Department's failure to take into account the social terrain of the Muslim world prior to and after 9/11 in part is a reason why US government officials considered it advantageous to project one-way transmission models of communication to Muslim audiences. However, the point, made earlier in chapter one, is that by utilizing this strategy, Washington might pacify Muslim voices with short-term gestures, but these have inevitably created a wider trust deficit between the United States and Muslim world. Jürgen Habermas reminds us that such actions fit into the *instrumental* action model, which is fundamentally success-oriented. In the case of the HCS, it is imperative that she/he comprehends from the outset that success-oriented approaches, when projected at socially constructed worlds will end in failure. "Success is defined as the appearance in the world of a desired state, which can, in a given situation, be causally produced through goal-oriented action or omission."[21] Clearly, it is more beneficial that actors gear their actions toward the strategic action model that is *understanding-over-success* oriented.

By looking to Habermas's fourth concept, the HCS will be able to adopt a progressive way forward that leads to improving the current state of US human-to-human interaction at the grassroots level. In its endeavor, the HCS must apply: (i) constructive engagement with Muslim audiences through language; (ii) communicative relationship building through agreed rules of engagement; (iii) direct communication which allows actors in Muslim audiences to keep the HCS message candid by raising validity claims about the core US foreign policy message; and, (iv) in this case, apply an *understanding-over-success* model for social interaction and dialogical engagement when interaction with Muslim audiences is vital. Thus, the second proposed component to enrich the HCS's communicative development intersecting with the Habermasian theory of communicative action focuses particularly on the medium of language and on how actors must manage language in the discourse setting. In comprehending how the HCS might interject a more direct approach into its communicative engagement at the grassroots level let us turn our attention to surveying W. Barnett Pearce's practical theory of the coordinated management of meaning (CMM) that further complements the concept of postsecular communication.

The Coordinated Management of Meaning

W. Barnett Pearce's communication theory on the CMM complements the practice of postsecular communication suggestion that there are "two concepts" in comprehending the general purpose of communication. The two models that reveal the relevance of communication are the *transmission* and *social construction* models. Pearce asserts that the "transmission model defines the purpose of communication as the transfer of information from one mind or place to another...[which] works best when messages clearly and accurately represent the meaning in the mind of the person who says, writes, draws, or performs them."[22] From a simple but basic form of ordinary communication—human interaction—he maintains that actors in most cases should aspire to exercise a more substantive and detailed form of exchange when at the grassroots level. However, regarding the social construction model, it "is more of a way of making the social world rather than talking about it, and this is always done with other people. Rather than, 'What did [the Muslim clerics] mean by that?' the relevant questions are 'How are we making it?' and 'How can we make better social worlds?'"[23] In this training with CMM, the emphasis is geared now toward communicating one's core message coherently and directly in order that critical religious infrastructures at a grassroots level are comprehended respectfully.

In this context, postsecular communication is neither concerned with replicating talking points or projecting short-term gestures to connect with target audiences. When looking through Pearce's communicative lens, we come to understand here that postsecular communication is centrally focused on ensuring both sacred and secular actors enter into dialogue to make social words better by establishing new worlds by reconstructing old worlds through dialogue-based engagement. Pearce's analysis on the challenges presented in the discourse setting reminds us that the HCS may confront several basic setbacks as she/he attempts to establish new and improve previous relations with value-defined socially constructed societies throughout the Muslim world.[24] For example, upon entering Islamic society, the HCS may initially experience confusion regarding the basic functions of the society and of their role as an interlocutor. In addition this may lead to experiencing direct confrontation if she/he draws upon secular "one-way communication models" when engaging these social societies that center around critical knowledge and function toward one another on the basis of direct engagement and mutual understanding.

Ensuring that the HCS performs evenhandedly in the dialogical setting this postsecular communicative framework further incorporates two additional concepts taken from Pearce's practical theory of CMM. By surveying its two most influential components—a *communication perspective* and the *coordination of language*—it becomes conceivable how postsecular communication will be indispensable to HCS training at the US Foreign Service Institute.

A Communication Perspective

For example, when taking a communication perspective in the dialogical setting, HCS will initially enter by appreciating the communicative roles that both state and nonstate actors may generate together, thus directing both to act wisely in discourse. [25] "The *communication perspective* demonstrates that by looking into the process of communication rather than through it, we treat communication itself as substantial and consequential."[26] Pearce highlights this position in the context of a communication situation of the importance for an actor to identify "bifurcation points" in dialogue. These bifurcation points, which are regarded as the most important episodes in dialogue, are moments within the conversation that may potentially alter the trajectory of the conversation, leading to either a positive or negative end. "In a real sense, we see what we know rather than the other way around, and our ability to discern bifurcation points and to make wise decisions about how to act into them requires some sharper conceptual tool for understanding communication."[27]

In the case of the HCS engaging global Islamic communities at the grassroots level, she/he must be willing to see "organisations, families, persons and nations as deeply textured clusters of persons-in-conversation."[28] Many traditional outlets within predominantly Muslim audiences are part of an entire system that the HCS must recognize as integral to the communication process, and not as an extended entity apart from the political, economic, and social structure of that community (or the *umma*). It is this entire entity that the HCS must initially engage as a whole before relationship building occurs. Pearce points out that societies and organizations must be recognized "as clusters of conversations and managers as orchestrating conversations rather than embodying information or power. Matters of efficiency, morale, productivity, and conflict can be handled by attention to what conversations occur, where, with what participants, in what type of language, and about what topics."[29] Additionally, the HCS must comprehend that communication is substantial, and that its properties have consequences. Drawing attention to Deborah Tannen's study, *The Argument Culture: Moving from Debate to Dialogue*, she suggests that commercial US communication outlets are dominated by adversarial forms of communication.[30]

In fact, this "sell-sell" hostile debate culture has no place in the postsecular communicative framework, as the basis of this framework is built upon recognizing the worth and value of directly engaging socially constructed worlds. In this case, the HCS is required to trust such socially constructed belief systems and ideals as consequential elements to be taken seriously and valued in dialogue.[31] Acknowledging Pearce, this is key to understanding that the HCS will be instrumental in shaping outcomes based on the merit of good communication. Mindful of the social construction model, the HCS will comprehend that good communication leans more toward establishing or rebuilding social worlds in partnership with other agents and actors than unilaterally defining rules and implementing them without acknowledgment from key religious nonstate actors and cultural leadership in parts of the Muslim world.

Taking a communication perspective in dialogue is one of the most substantial actions to enrich state-nonstate actor engagement. When engaging with Muslim audiences at a grassroots level, the specialist is able to change the relationship dynamic by sharing with critical decision makers and opinion formers the same responsibility to produce a progressive body of communication that the public may find acceptable. This means that the body of communication was directly constructed on the basis of mutual understanding rather than on indirect assumptions. Far from being success-oriented, it is aware of "critical moments" at which the conversation may take a negative turn.

Applying Coordination

Pearce's second concept that aids HCS communicative development relates to how actors should be cognizant of the coordination of language while in the dialogical setting. This concept of coordination is a valuable asset to actors when presenting their core message, while interacting communicatively to ensure a balanced dialogue. The concept of coordination is simply that of paying close attention the many "turn-by-turns" or critical moments occurring in conversation.

> Using the term "coordination" as a way of understanding these experiences is part of. . . the 'social construction' approach to communication. It suggests that, instead of a correspondence between mental state and action, we pose questions and look for answers in the flow of actions themselves. That is, we understand what people say and do as taking "turns" in the patterns of communication, not as "signs pointing to something else."[32]

For example, the HCS will need to pay close attention to the communicative actions projected by sacred actors in the dialogical setting to comprehend the direction in which the dialogue is headed. A communicative partnership between the HCS and sacred actors can form only when they are both in sync with each other, and this is a sign of the depth of their engagement. In this case, actors may be able to see the entire conversation and into its changing trajectory that inevitably (after presenting its core message) determines the general outcome and the afterlife of the dialogue.

> The term "coordination" is used in CMM to direct attention to our efforts to align our actions with those of others. Among other things, the necessity to coordinate with others shows that communication is inherently and fundamentally social. No

matter what speech act—whether threat, compliment, instruction, question, insult, or anything else—its successful performance requires not only your action but the complementary actions of others.[33]

When applying this concept, the HCS will be informed on how best to act wisely within these critical moments of conversation. She/he can, within a split second, be capable of mentally reviewing critical episodes from the past that may become vital to the development of social construction within these audiences. As human beings, it is true that "we have trouble recognising and acting wisely into bifurcation points because we are so caught up in the meaning of what is going on that we lose sight of the possibilities of changing the shape of the pattern."[34] Coordinating action and paying attention to the flow of the dialogue emerges as conducive to constructing cohesive communication.

This means that the new diplomatic specialist must take seriously the act of making and managing meaning in the dialogue setting. We may see this point in terms of comparing artificial with authentic human relations. If we recall again the indirect engagement efforts of overlapping public diplomacy and nation-branding approaches to sell American values prior to and after 9/11, we see that such efforts were neither authentic nor perceived as genuine by global Islamic communities, considering Washington's inability to raise U.S. favorability. In this sense, public diplomacy efforts by Beers and Hughes were largely artificial in that they both failed at directly engaging Muslim audiences by initially reading the social terrain of the Muslim world to understand that one-way transmission models of communication would serve as an inadequate resource to win hearts and minds. However Pearce concludes by stating that the essence of "meaning is so important to what it means to be a human being and in the making of social worlds that it has distracted us from the other half of the process of communication."[35] This aggressive position only indicates how important both aspects—communication and meaning—are. In a nutshell, the duty of the HCS will be to ensure that its communicative actions entail a meaningful dialogue, no matter whether the communication process lasts five minutes or five hours—in order to create new and improved social worlds. On the whole, previous actions indicate why a HCS corps must be implemented to engage grassroots audiences to facilitate in restoring US-Muslim world relations.

Assessing the Postsecular Communicative Framework

Herein lies the main reason why this study is not concerned with upgrading public diplomacy but with urging that Washington move beyond the laurels of Cairo and equally successful moments in post-9/11 US public diplomacy, resulting only in short-term symbolic gestures. Extensive forms of engagement will be required at all levels, including US presidential Oval Office diplomacy with global Islamic communities and leadership in Muslim majority nations that consider adjusting aspects of Washington's diplomatic infrastructure. This should begin first with how the US Department of State approaches international religious affairs, how it sets out to assess value-defined traditional societies, and the path it takes to ensure the practice of postsecular communication in conjunction with core Foreign Service Officer training. As this study makes clear, previous State Department initiatives, which were reduced to overlapping nation branding and public diplomacy, were inadequate measures leading to teleological acts employed to win hearts and minds through one-way communicative relations, inviting religious actors and Muslim audiences to participate in programming efforts that lacked promoting dialogue-based engagement from the bottom up, and dramaturgical initiatives toward target audiences in the Muslim world resulting in the presentation of rehearsed/stylized messaging.

Reaching the core of Islamic society and the base of global Islamic communities dictates the need for a more substantive communication approach—grounded in the strategic action model of understanding-over-success, which proves to be reliable in this case. While working within a postsecular communicative framework, actors are able to engage across sacred-secular lines freely from the bottom up. Here the HCS corps will not only be able to employ traditional approaches (along with its diplomatic duties) with civil society and government officials at US embassies, but also practice a new public diplomacy approach that ensures postsecular recognition, acknowledging the legitimacy of nonstate actors in the dialogical setting, and applying aspects of postsecular communication to enrich discourse opportunities.

Three major strengths of this postsecular communicative framework are: First, it ensures that a constructive communication protocol (providing additional padding) in some US public diplomacy efforts in the Muslim world exists. Far from addressing a commercial trend within this community, a structured communicative approach is used when employing direct human-to-human relations at a people-to-people and organizational level to Muslim audiences. Second, this framework provides a legitimate communication approach that allows this new specialist to reach beyond traditional zero-sum diplomatic methods when engaging religious and tribal audiences. Instead of trying to appeal to the Muslim world by marketing foreign policy through secular means, the HCS is able to reach across secular lines in order to meet the religious players on common ground. Lastly, drawing on a complementary approach to engagement, postsecular communication aids HCS development within the new public diplomacy environment by introducing a substantive style of communication into the sociopolitical dialogical setting to enrich engagement opportunities between sacred and secular actors, while ensuring balanced discourse.

Postsecular communication does not stop at being a communication approach in this context; it is a springboard for improving promotion of sacred-secular relations between state and nonstate actors in the twenty-first century. This communicative framework provides a realistic starting point to enhance US state actor engagement through communication training in order to restore trust with global Islamic communities. It is imperative the HCS applies postsecular communication to rechannel the perspectives held by Muslims at the grassroots level back into the foreign policymaking discussion in order to promote both sustainable relations and dialogue-based new public diplomacy measures. Hence, this approach will not only aid in consolidating the aspirations of Muslims into the dialogical setting, but it will serve as a vital instrument that will publicly contribute to shrinking the existing US-Muslim world trust deficit.

Conclusion

Pursuing Understanding-over-Success

The central argument of this book proposes that US post-9/11 public diplomacy measures were shortsighted and failed to reach the core of global Islamic communities. Though its robust and well-funded efforts would include relaunching antiquated Cold War era measures, overlapping public diplomacy and nation-branding practices, or even conducting outreach to Muslim majority nations by increasing foreign aid and exchange programs, none were advantageous at restoring America's ailing image abroad. This book makes the case that it is imperative that both the White House and US Department of State move beyond relying on symbolic gestures and empty political promises to consider a more practicable and realistic response that will reach the core of Islamic society.

Reaching the core requires a threefold shift: in foreign policy, state actor attitude toward postsecularism, and diplomatic renewal that calls for a new type of representative to engage Muslim majority audiences at the grassroots level. The analysis here takes into account that religion-based societies that are socially constructed and value-defined as global Islamic communities require a more strategic form of engagement as considered through the medium of a dialogue-based "new public diplomacy." In order that we might begin down a path that ensures trust with the Muslim world, immediate US diplomatic action is required at the grassroots level that engages the aspirations and perspectives held by nonelite Muslims.

This fundamental measure must function from the bottom up and apply aspects of postsecular communication that sets out to appreciate both sacred and secular voices within the dialogical setting to build sustainable relations. Furthermore, moving forward requires that the US Department of State dismantle the use of one-way communication models (as overlapping nation branding and public diplomacy) to sell America when conducting outreach to religion-based societies such as the Muslim world. A more culturally defined and competent public diplomacy approach that caters directly to engaging key nonstate actors within these communities should be executed in parallel with postsecular communication. Enhancing the dialogical opportunities between state and nonstate actors must become an immediate priority at the State Department, as it is apparent that key global issues between the United States and Muslim world will be a central priority over the next decade.

Overcoming Limitations

Furthermore, it is important to emphasize that a forward thinking project that promotes a structural long-term strategy materialize. In this case, US foreign policy must move in a direction complementary to innovative public diplomacy initiatives that are *understanding-over-success* oriented. This concern is linked to the existing limitation of Washington's traditional bureaucratic maneuvering that reinforces the support of one-way communication attempts directed primarily at elites and state actors. Applying this book's forward thinking project will not occur without consideration of both Washington's foreign policy and bureaucratic limitations that are set.

First, US Middle East foreign policy toward the Jewish state of Israel and the Palestinian territories presents a visible limitation that will continue to impede most public diplomacy efforts with Muslim majority audiences in the Arab world. For example, dithering on whether or not to chastise Tel Aviv publicly on settlement development in East Jerusalem sends the signal that Washington endorses an imbalanced regional foreign policy that particularly favors the Jewish state. In order for Washington to recover from this limitation it should consider promoting an evenhanded foreign policy that stands firm with the Jewish state but incorporates the larger Arab agenda that includes the creation of a separate sovereign Palestinian state.

Second, beyond a set of broad foreign policy issues stands an additional limitation, related to existing bureaucratic maneuvers, which may reinforce the support of one-way communication, directed primarily at state actors and foreign audiences. As the State Department and Pentagon often collaborate on critical projects to ensure international security and postconflict peace building, various limits are set that often hamper prospective State Department communication projects that seek to promote two-way communication in key predominantly Muslim regions. This includes the Pentagon's success oriented agenda to distort information operations, by promoting highly successful propaganda campaigns. The Pentagon's ability to reach Muslim audiences quicker than the State Department in combat zones is linked in part to its increasing budget that contributes to its dominant position in shaping the US foreign policy agenda throughout the Middle East, North Africa, and South Asia.

A striking financial comparison is recorded in the current White House's FY 2011 budget request with $708.2 billion for the Pentagon and $52.8 billion requested for the State Department and the United States Agency for International Development.[1] A mammoth budget coupled by an American foreign policy that works in parallel with one-way communication, either to influence or to coerce foreign public, is a formula that obstructs potential US-Muslim relations. Giles Scott-Smith presents an accurate assessment: "When referring to the dominance of the Pentagon, it is not just a matter of weaponry or the questionable deployment of US Marines. Looking to develop its role in the field of 'strategic influence,' the military has also greatly expanded its activities in communication and media, with questionable consequences."[2] Thus, instead of recognizing the value in applying an *understanding-over-success* posture, the US Department of Defense benefits from maintaining a *success-over-understanding* oriented position to win hearts and minds, especially in South Asia.

Given this, both public diplomacy practitioners and US diplomats should be cognizant at this point that most effective two-way communication models will succeed if consideration is given to a more creative form of US foreign policymaking, the nature of the bureaucracy that implements it in the Muslim world, and the role that competent communication play in the overarching grand strategy. Bureaucratic recognition includes putting a two-way approach in the hands of state actors who are mostly capable of carrying out public diplomacy projects that are *understanding-over success* oriented. A "feedback loop" created by two-way dialogical communication will aid in introducing grassroots perspectives upon US foreign policy. Typically, the policies that state actors pursue should not be separate from this effort, for they are integral to the success or failure of this approach.

Despite gradual troop withdrawals set to take place in Afghanistan, and Washington's recent expansion of its national security interests to the Asia-Pacific region, integral security concerns throughout parts of the Muslim world ensure that American public diplomacy will be required for the foreseeable future to quell international tension. During this period of great transition in global politics, US policymakers and key state actors must be mindful that a bold new strategy that strives to counter Islamophobia in Washington, while embracing a broad range of nonelite Muslim voices at the grassroots level is the essential path to ensure a new way forward in the twenty-first century.

NOTES

Introduction

1. Phyllis d' Hoop, *An Initiative: Strengthening US-Muslim Communications* (Washington, DC: Center for the Study of the Presidency, 2003); Hady Amr, *The Need to Communicate: How to Improve US Public Diplomacy with the Islamic World* (Washington, DC: Saban Center for Middle East Policy at the Brookings Institution, 2004); Peter G. Peterson, et al., *Finding America's Voice: A Strategy for Reinvigorating US Public Diplomacy* [document online]; available from www.cfr.org/content/publications/attachments/public_diplomacy.pdf; US Government Accountability Office (GAO), Report to the Chairman, Subcommittee on Science, the Departments of State, Justice and Commerce and Related Agencies, House Committee on Appropriations, *U.S. Public Diplomacy: State Department Efforts to Engage Muslim Audiences Lack Certain Communication Elements and Face Persistent Challenges*, GAO-06-535 (May 2006); Stephen Johnson and Helle Dale, *How to Reinvigorate US Public Diplomacy* [document online]; available from http://www.heritage.org/Research/PublicDiplomacy/upload/bg_1645.pdf; Richard L. Armitage and Joseph S. Nye, ed. *CSIS Commission on Smart Power: A Smarter, More Secure America* (Washington, DC: The CSIS Press, 2007); Document [available online] http://www.csis.org/media/csis/pubs/071106_csissmartpowerreport.pdf.
2. See Barack Obama, *President Barack Obama's Inaugural Address* [document online] available from http://www.whitehouse.gov/blog/inaugural-address/.
3. Phillip M. Taylor, "Public Diplomacy on Trial?" *The Trials of Engagement: The Future of Public Diplomacy*, Scott Lucas and Ali Fischer, ed. (Boston: Martinus Nijhoff Publishers, 2010) 17–32.

1   Engaging the Muslim World

1. Jon C. Pevenhouse and Joshua S. Goldstein, *International Relations: Brief Sixth Edition* (Boston: Longman Publishing), 37.

2. Hans Morgenthau, *Politics among Nations: The Struggle for Power and Peace*, 5th ed. (New York: Alfred A. Knopf, 1978), 4–15.

3. G. R. Berridge, *Diplomacy: Theory and Practice* 3rd ed. (New York: Palgrave Macmillan, 2002), 1.

4. R. S. Zaharna, *Battles to Bridges: U.S. Strategic Communication and Public Diplomacy* (New York: Palgrave Macmillan, 2011) 84–86.

5. Jan Melissen, "The New Public Diplomacy: Between Theory and Practice," in *The New Public Diplomacy: Soft Power in International Relations*, ed. Jan Melissen (New York: Palgrave Macmillan, 2005), 5.

6. Ibid., 5.

7. Jamie A. Fullerton and Alice G. Kendrick, *Advertising's War on Terrorism: The Story of the U.S. State Department's Shared Values Initiative* (Spokane: Marquette Books, 2006), 50.

8. Nicholas J. Cull, "Public Diplomacy Before Gullion: The Evolution of a Phrase," *CPD Blog* (April 18, 2006) [article online] http://uscpublicdiplomacy.org/index .php/newswire/cpdblog_detail/060418_public_diplomacy_before_gullion _the_evolution_of_a_phrase/.

9. USC Canter on Public Diplomacy, *What is Public Diplomacy?* [article online] http://uscpublicdiplomacy.org/index.php/about/what_is_pd.

10. William A. Rugh, ed. *Engaging the Arab & Islamic Worlds through Public Diplomacy: A Report and Action Recommendations* (Washington, DC: Public Diplomacy Council, 2004), 1.

11. Gyorgy Szondi, "Public Diplomacy and Nation Branding: Conceptual Similarities and Differences," *Netherland Institute of International Relations "Clingendael"* (2008): 2–3.

12. Philip Seib, ed. *Toward a New Public Diplomacy: Redirecting U.S. Foreign Policy* (New York: Palgrave Macmillan, 2009), 1.

13. R. S. Zaharna, "Obama, U.S. Public Diplomacy and the Islamic World" *World Politics Review* (March 16, 2009) [article online] http://www.worldpoliticsreview .com/articles/3450/obama-u-s-public-diplomacy-and-the-islamic-world.

14. USC Canter on Public Diplomacy, *What is Public Diplomacy?* http://uscpublic diplomacy.org/index.php/about/what_is_pd.

15. Juan Cole, *Engaging the Muslim World* (New York: Palgrave, 2009), 7.

16. John Esposito, *Who Speaks for Islam?: What a Billion Muslims Really Think* (New York: Gallup Press, 2007), 65.

17. Jan Melissen, ed. *The New Public Diplomacy: Soft Power in International Relations* (New York: Palgrave Macmillan, 2005), 7.

18. Noam Chomsky, *Hegemony or Survival: America's Quest for Global Dominance* (New York: Metro Politian Books, 2003), 9–10.

19. Jeremy M. Sharp, *U.S. Foreign Aid to Israel* (Washington, DC: Congressional Research Services, 2010), 1.

20. John J Mearsheimer and Stephen M Walt, *The Israel Lobby and U.S. Foreign Policy* (New York: Farrar, Straus, and Giroux Press, 2007), 78–79

21. Ibid., 175–178.

22. See Noam Chomsky, Gilbert Achcar, and Stephen Rosskamm Shalom. *Perilous Power: The Middle East & U.S. Foreign Policy: Dialogues on Terror, Democracy, War, and Justice* (Boulder, CO: Paradigm Publishers, 2007). See also John L Esposito, *Unholy War: Terror in the Name of Islam* (Oxford: Oxford University Press, 2002); Noam Chomsky, *The Fateful Triangle: The United States, Israel and the Palestinians* (London: Pluto Press, 1999).

23. Unger, Craig. *House of Bush House of Saud: The Secret Relationship between the World's Two Most Powerful Dynasties* (London: Gibson Square, 2007).

24. P. W. Singer, M. J. Akbar, and Kurt M. Campbell, "A Strategic Look at US-Muslim World Relations," *Brookings Project on US Relations with the Islamic World* (Washington, DC: Saban Center for Middle East Policy at the Brookings Institution, 2008); Morris Mehrdad Mottale, *The Origins of the Gulf Wars* (Lanham, MD: University Press of America, 2001).

25. Regarding the US-Saudi relationship and the tension present since September 11 see, Rachel Bronson, *Thicker Than Oil: America's Uneasy Partnership with Saudi Arabia* (Oxford: Oxford University Press, 2006).

26. Juan Cole, *Engaging the Muslim World* (New York: Palgrave Macmillan, 2009), 21.

27. Jeremy M. Sharp, *U.S. Foreign Aid to Israel: CRS report for Congress* (Washington, DC: Congressional Research Service, 2006), 1.

28. U.S.–Muslim Engagement Project, Search for Common Ground and the Consensus Building Institute et al., "Changing Course A New Direction for US Relations with the Muslim World" (Washington, DC: U.S. Muslim Engagement Project, 2009).

29. T. G. Fraser and Donette Murray, *America and the World since 1945* (New York: Palgrave Macmillan), 104.

30. See Scott Kaufman, *Plans Unraveled: The Foreign Policy of the Carter Administration* (DeKalb: Northern Illinois University Press, 2008).

31. Based on the social theory that Muslim governments should rule according to Islamic law (*Sharia*), political Islam gained a unique popularity throughout the Middle East, South and Southeast Asia, as a way to express opposition to authoritarian governments and Western influence.

32. See Lawrence Freedman, *A Choice of Enemies: America Confronts the Middle East* (New York: Public Affairs, 2008).

33. Ibrahim Al-Marashi and Katherine Durlacher, *Iraqi Perceptions of UK and American Policy in Post-Saddam Iraq* [document online] available from www.foreignpolicy society.org/iraq.pdf.

34. Examples include the shift in relations with Saddam Hussein after 1992 and the US Gulf War; the US expansion of military bases throughout parts of Saudi Arabia and other Muslim countries; and tension inside such countries as Algeria, Uzbekistan, and Chechnya, all of which claimed to struggle with Western secular influence in the region.

35. U.S.-Muslim Engagement Project, *Changing Course A New Direction for US Relations with the Muslim World* (Washington, DC: US-Muslim Engagement Project, 2008). 108.

36. The overall study between 2001 and 2006 polled more than 110,000 people in 50 countries.

37. Pew Forum, "America's Image in the World: Findings from the Pew Global Attitudes Project Testimony of Andrew Kohut" [document online] available from http://pewglobal.org/commentary/pdf/1019.pdf.

38. Juliana Menasce Horowitz, "Global Unease with Major World Powers," in *The Pew Global Attitudes Project* (document online) http://www.pewglobal .org/2007/06/27/global-unease-with-major-world-powers/.

39. Ibid., 5.

40. Juliana Menasce Horowitz, ed. "Global Unease with Major World Powers," *The Pew Global Attitudes Project* (Washington, DC: Pew Forum, 2006), 5. Note: Some rows will not equal 100 percent because many polled expressed no opinion.

41. Dalia Mogahed, *Some Arab Countries Make U-Turn on U.S. Leadership in 2010 Gallup Center for Muslim Studies* (May 2010) [article online] available from http://www .gallup.com/poll/137759/arab-countries-turn-leadership-2010.aspx; This survey was conducted annually in 2008, biannually in 2009, and the 2010 measure was the first of two this year. Early Iraq 2009 results were not recorded by Gallup.

42. R. S. Zaharna, "American Public Diplomacy and the Islamic and Arab World: A Communication Update & Assessment." Paper presented to the U.S. Senate Committee on Foreign Relations, Washington, DC, February 27, 2003.

43. Liora Danan and Alice Hunt, "Mixed Blessings: US Government Engagement with Religion in Conflict-Prone Settings." *CSIS Report.* (Washington: CSIS Press, 2007).

44. Ibid.

45. W. Barnett Pearce and Stephen Littlejohn, *Moral Conflict: When Social Worlds Collide* (California: Sage Publications, 1997), 51.

46. Ibid., 51.

47. Akbar S. Ahmed, *Islam Today: A Short Introduction to the Muslim World* (New York: I. B. Tauris Publishers, 1999), 8.

2   Calculating the Cost of Manufactured Fear

1. Jürgen Habermas and Joseph Ratzinger, *The Dialectics of Secularization: On Reason and Religion* (San Francisco: Ignatius Press, 2005), 46.

2. Pippa Norris and Ronald Inglehart, *Sacred and Secular: Religion and Politics Worldwide* (New York: Cambridge University Press, 2004), 3. See, C. Wright Mills, *The Sociological Imagination* (Oxford: Oxford University Press, 1959), 32–33. See also Emile Durkheim, *The Elementary Forms of Religious Life: A Study in Religious Sociology* (New York: Macmillan, 1915); August Comte, *The Positive Philosophy* (New York: Calvin Blanchard, 1858); Sigmund Freud, *The Future of an Illusion* (New York: Norton, 1975); Karl Marx and Fredrick Engels, *Manifesto of the Communist Party* (London: International, 1948); Herbert Spencer, *The Principles of Ethics* (1897) (Indianapolis: Liberty Classics, 1978).

3. Max Weber, *The Protestant Ethic and the Spirit of Capitalism* (New York: Penguin Books, 2002).

4. Hans Henirich Gerth and C. Wright Mills, eds. *From Max Weber: Essays in Sociology* (New York: Oxford University Press, 1958), 282.

5. W. S. F. Pickering, *Durkheim's Sociology of Religion* (London: Routledge, 1984), 445; see also Emile Durkheim, *The Elementary Forms of Religious Life* (New York: Free Press, 1965/1915).

6. See Sigmund Freud, *The Future of Illusion* (New York: Norton, 1975).

7. See Pippa Norris and Ronald Inglehart, *Sacred and Secular: Religion and Politics Worldwide* (Cambridge: Cambridge University Press, 2004).

8. William H. Swatos and K. J. Christiano, "Secularization Theory: The Course of a Concept", *Sociology of Religion*, 60 (1999): 209–228.

9. However, the July 2008 Gallup research findings indicate that both faith practices and a belief in God in the western part of the United States are lower than in other regions of the country. See Frank Newman, "Belief in God Far Lower in Western US " *The Gallup Poll Briefing* (July 2008): 103; report available online, http://www.gallup.com/poll/109108/belief-god-far-lower-western-us.aspx.

10. Douglas Jacobsen and Rhonda Jacobsen, eds. *The American University in a Post-secular Age* (Oxford, Oxford University Press, 2008), 10.

11. Pippa Norris and Ronald Inglehart, *Sacred and Secular: Religion and Politics Worldwide* (Cambridge: Cambridge University Press, 2004) 5–24; See Hugh Mcleod and Werner Ustorf, *The Decline of Christendom in Western Europe, 1750–2000* (Cambridge: Cambridge University Press, 2003); Vivian S. Patrick, "Scholars Find Decline of Christianity in the West" (March 6, 2004) [article online]; available from http://www.christianpost.com/article/20040306/scholars -find-decline-of-christianity-in-the-west.htm. Despite signs of religious erosion in several Western countries, the United States, for the last century, has maintained a consistent religious posture in Judeo-Christian practices owed primarily to an outstanding religious market. This concept is regarded as *religious-supply* and is held by Stark and Iannanccone. See also Norris and Inglehart, *Sacred and Secular*, 89–95.

12. George J. Holyoake, *The Principles of Secularism*, 3rd ed. (London: Austin & Co., 1870) 11–12; see also writing from twentieth-century writers such as Peter L. Berger, *The Sacred Canopy: Elements of Sociology Theory of Religion* (New York: Doubleday Publishing, 1967). However, it was in 1999 that Peter Berger shifted his position on the belief in the effectiveness of the secularization thesis, making the claim that "loose assertions were placed on the impact urbanization would have on Western society"; Thomas Luckman, *The Invisible Religion: The Problem of Religion in Modern Society* (New York: Macmillan, 1967); Harvey Cox, *Secular City: Secularization and Urbanization in Theological Perspective* (New York: Macmillan, 1966); Elizabeth Shakman Hurd, *The Politics of Secularism in International Relations* (Princeton, NJ: Princeton University Press, 2008).

13. See C. V. Wedgwood, *The Thirty Years War* (London: Pimlico, 1992); Geoffrey Parker, *The Thirty Years' War* (London: Routledge, 1997).

14. Daniel Philpott, "The Founding of the Sovereign States System at Westphalia," *Revolutions in Sovereignty: How Ideas Shaped Modern International Relations* (New Jersey, NJ: Princeton University Press, 2001), 73–150.

15. Derek Beales, "Religion and Culture," *The Eighteenth Century*, ed. T. C. W. Blanning Publishing (Oxford: Oxford University Press, 2000), 133.

16. Roy Porter, *The Enlightenment*, 2nd ed. (New York: Palgrave, 2001) 29–37; see also Kenneth W. Applegate, *Voltaire on Religion: Selected Writings* (New York: F Ungar Publishing, 1974).

17. See Dennis Diderot and Russell Goulbourne, *The Nun* (Oxford: Oxford University Press, 2005); Paul Henri Thiry Holbach, Baron d' and Jean Meslier, *Superstition in All Ages* (New York: Arno Press, 1972).

18. Immanuel Kant, *An Answer to the Question: What is Enlightenment? (1784)* [article online]; available from http://www.english.upenn.edu/~mgamer/Etexts/kant.html.

19. Joachim Whaley, "Religion," in *A Companion to Eighteenth-Century Europe,* ed. Peter H. Wilson (Oxford: Blackwell, 2008), 176–177.

20. Derek Beales, "Religion and Culture," in *Short Oxford History of Europe: The Eighteenth Century*, ed. T. C. W. Blanning (Oxford, Oxford University Press, 2000), 131–177.

21. Noah Feldman, "The Intellectual Origins of the Establishment Clause," *NYU Law Review* 77, No. 2 (2002): 346–428; see also Noah Feldman, "The Origins," *Divided by God: America's Church-State Problem* (New York: Farrar, Straus and Giroux, 2005), 19–56.

22. See John Marshall, *John Locke, Toleration, and Early Enlightenment Culture* (Cambridge: Cambridge University Press, 2006); Aloysius P. Martinich, ed. *Leviathan* (Ontario: Broadview Press, 2002).

23. Montesquieu's critical perspectives helped to shape the new republic's idea of tolerance. He asserts in *The Spirit of Laws* (1748), "When the legislator has believed it a duty to permit the exercise of many religions, it is necessary that he should enforce also toleration among these religions themselves." Charles de Montesquieu, *The Spirit of Laws* (1748) [article online]; available from http://www.constitution.org/cm/sol-02.htm.

24. Roger Trigg, *Religion in Public Life: Must Faith Be Privatized* (Oxford: Oxford University Press, 2007), 211.

25. Isaac Kramnick, ed. *The Federalist Papers* (Harmondsworth: Penguin Books, 1987), 124.

26. David Wooten, *The Essential Federalist and Anti-Federalist Papers* (Indianapolis: Hackett Publishing, 2003).

27. See Noah Feldman, "The Birth of Secularism", *Divided by God*, 111–134.

28. Erling Jorstad, *The Politics of Moralism: The New Christian Right in American Life* (Minneapolis: Augsburg Pub. House, 1981), 54; Christian Voice (organisation), *Christian Voice Congressional Report Card: How Your Congressman Voted on 14 Key Moral Issues, 96th Congress, 1st Session, January-December, 1979* (Washington, DC: Christian Voice, 1980).

29. Jorstad, *The Politics of Moralism*, 7; see Robert Webber, *The Moral Majority: Right or Wrong?* (Westchester: Cornerstone Books, 1981).

30. Jorstad, *The Politics of Moralism*, 5.

31. Robert Liebman and Robert Wuthnow, *The New Christian Right* (New York: Aldine Publishing, 1983), 16; Steve Bruce, *The Rise and Fall of the New Christian Right: Conservative Protestant Politics in America, 1978–1988* (Oxford: Clarendon Press, 1988).

32. Erling Jorstad, *The Politics of Moralism*, 5.

33. Ibid., 9

34. Ibid., 84.

35. Ibid., 84–85.

36. Ibid., 84.

37. Sharon Linzey Georgianna, *The Moral Majority and Fundamentalism: Plausibility and Dissonance* (Lewiston, NY: E. Mellen Press, 1989).

38. See Fawaz A. Gerges, *America and Political Islam: Clash of Culture Clash of Interests?* (Cambridge, Cambridge University Press, 1999), 20–26.

39. Edward Said, *Orientalism* (London: Penguin, 1977), 20.See also Edward Said, *Orientalism* (London: Penguin Books, 1977).

40. Ibid., 19.

41. Lawrence Pintak, *Reflections in a Bloodshot Lens: America, Islam & the War of Ideas* (Michigan: Pluto Press, 2006), 3.

42. Ibid., 8.

43. John Winthorp, "A Model of Christian Charity" (1630) [sermon online] http://history.hanover.edu/texts/winthmod.html.

44. Tobias Hübinette, *Orientalism Past and Present: An Introduction to a Post-colonial Critique* [article online] http://www.tobiashubinette.se/orientalism.pdf.

45. Gerges, *America and Political Islam*, 24–25.

46. Applying the term "fundamentalism" to Islam often generates criticism in academic circles on whether it is practical to link a nineteenth century term related to Christian revivalism to twentieth century Islamic movements. Its usage in context with both Christianity and Islam refers here to how some of its adherents interpret religious scripture text and the "fundamentals" of the faith as God's literal word on creating a less morally decayed society. The term Islamic fundamentalism gained popularity during the late 1970s amid extensive coverage of the Iranian revolution. The dismay by Iranian religious clerics and the potential consequences of Western secularism penetrating Islamic society sparked an Islamic revivalist movement drawing upon the teaching of Sayyid Qutb and his commentary in *Fi Zial al-Koran* and *Maalim fi al-Tariq for Islamic Puritanism* throughout the *umma* and in political leadership. Thus both Christian and Islamic revivalist movements which are referred to as fundamentalist share two common objectives: their open rejection of modernity and the public call that their religions return to the literal and fundamental state to purge acts leading to moral decay from within society.

47. Fawaz A. Gerges, *America and Political Islam: Clash of Culture Clash of Interests?* (Cambridge, Cambridge University Press, 1999), 24.

48. Ibid., 24.
49. This point is reintroduced in 2003 in Bernard Lewis, *The Crisis of Islam: Holy War and Unholy Terror* (New York: Modern Library, 2003).
50. Bernard Lewis, "The Roots of Muslim Rage," *The Atlantic* (September 1990) [article online]; available from http://www.theatlantic.com/doc/199009/muslim-rage.
51. Ibid.
52. Samuel P. Huntington, "The Clash of Civilizations?" in *Foreign Affairs* (Summer 1993): 22.
53. Fuad S. Naeem, "A Traditional Islamic Response to the Rise of Modernism, in Islam," *Fundamentalism, and the Betrayal of Tradition* by Joseph E. B. Lumbard (Bloomington: World Wisdom 2004), 82.
54. Ibid., 82–83.
55. See Maulana Ashraf 'Ali Thanwi, *Answer to Modernism*, trans. Muhammad Hasan Askari and Karrar Husain (Karachi: Maktaba Darululoom, 1976; reprint, Delhi, 1981).
56. Tobias Hübinette, "Orientalism Past and Present: An Introduction to a Post-colonial Critique" [article online] http://www.tobiashubinette.se/orientalism.pdf.
57. Youssef M Choueiri, *Islamic Fundamentalism* (Boston: Twayne Publishers, 1990).
58. See Lawrence Davidson, *Islamic Fundamentalism: An Introduction* (Connecticut: Greenwood Press, 2003), 10.
59. Noah Feldman, *The Fall and Rise of the Islamic State* (Princeton, NJ: Princeton University Press, 2008), 19.
60. Ibid., 111.
61. Johannes J. G. Jansen G, *The Dual Nature of Islamic Fundamentalism* (Ithaca, NJ: Cornell University Press, 1997), 2.
62. Ibid., 7.
63. Akbar S. Ahmed, *Islam Under Siege* (Cambridge: Polity, 2003), 78.
64. Ibid., 81.
65. Ibid., 14–15.

3 The New Public Diplomacy Argument

1. See Joseph S. Nye Jr., *Soft Power: The Means to Success in World Politics* (New York: Public Affiars Books, 2004), 3.
2. Hans J. Morgenthau, *Politics among Nations: The Struggle for Power and Peace* (New York: Alfred A. Knopf, 1978), 10–11.
3. Ibid., 4–15.
4. Elizabeth Shakman Hurd, *The Politics of Secularism in International Relations* (Princeton, NJ: Princeton University Press, 2007), 1.
5. Ibid., 1.

6. Shaun Riordan, "Dialogue-based Public Diplomacy: a New Foreign Policy Paradigm?" in *The New Public Diplomacy: Soft Power in International Relations*, ed. Jan Melissen (New York: Palgrave Macmillan, 2005), 182.

7. Elizabeth Shakman Hurd, "Theorizing Religious Resurgence," in *International Politics*, 33, (2007): 647–665.

8. Monica Duffy-Toft. "Religion Matters in International Relations," *The Huffington Post*, March 1, 2010.

9. Fox and Sandler, *Bringing Religion into International Relations* (New York: Palgrave Macmillan, 2006), 9–10.

10. Craig Calhoun, "Recognizing Religion," *Immanent Frame SSRC* [article online]; available from http://www.ssrc.org/blogs/immanent_frame/2008/03/24 /recognizing-religion/.

11. Gerard A. Hauser, *Vernacular Voice* (Columbia: South Carolina Press, 1999), 13–36; see also Cornel West, *Democracy Matters: Winning the Fight against Imperialism* (New York: Penguin Press, 2004), 201–218.

12. Roger Trigg, *Religion in Public Life: Must Faith Be Privatized* (Oxford: Oxford University Press, 2007), 236.

13. Charles Taylor, *A Secular Age* (Cambridge: Harvard University Press, 2007), 423.

14. Ibid., 423.

15. Jurgen Habermas, *The Structural Transformation of the Public Sphere: An Inquiry into a Category of Bourgeois-Society* (Cambridge: The MIT Press, 1989), 1.

16. Taylor, *A Secular Age*, 2.

17. Ibid., 2.

18. Jürgen Habermas, "The Public Sphere: An Encyclopedia Article (1964)," *New German Critique*, 3 (Autumn, 1974): 49–55.

19. Jürgen Habermas, *The Structural Transformation of the Public Sphere*, 1–26; see also Frank Bechhofer and Brian Elliot, eds. *The Petite Bourgeoisie: Comparative Studies of the Uneasy Stratum* (London: Macmillan Press, 1981). See James Gordon Finalayson, *Habermas: A Very Short Introduction* (Oxford: Oxford University Press, 2005), 10–13; Michael Schaich, "The Public Sphere," in *A Companion to Eighteenth-Century Europe*, ed. Peter H. Wilson (Oxford: Blackwell Publishing, 2008), 125–140.

20. Habermas writes, "The bourgeois avant-garde of the educated middle class learned the art of critical-rational public debate through its contact with the 'elegant world'. This courtly-noble society, to the extent that the modern state apparatus became independent from the monarch's personal sphere, naturally separated itself, in turn, more and more from the court and became its counterpoise in the town. The 'town' was the life centre of civil society not only economically; in cultural-political contrast to the court, it designated especially an early public sphere in the world of letters whose institutions were the coffee houses, the *salon* and the *Tischgesellschaften* (table societies). The heirs of the humanistic-autocratic society, in their encounter with the bourgeois intellectuals (through sociable discussions that quickly developed into public criticism), built a bridge between the remains of a collapsing form of publicity (the courtly one) and the precursor of a new one: the bourgeois public sphere," Habermas, *The Structural Transformation of the Public Sphere*, 30.

21. See James Gordon Finlayson, *Habermas: A Very Short Introduction* (Oxford: Oxford University Press, 2005), 11.

22. Jurgen Habermas, *The Structural Transformation of the Public Sphere: An Inquiry into a Category of Bourgeois-Society* (Cambridge: The MIT Press, 1989) 27; "According to Habermas the bourgeois public sphere originated in the middle-class concern with protecting its commercial interests through the political regulation of civil society. It mustered little sympathy for proletarian or peasant issues. Nonetheless, its discursive standards were not linked to political or economic ideology but to Enlightenment ideals of reason and rational opinion from which society forged a public understand of matters that were consequential in private relations." Hauser, *Vernacular Voice*, 42.

23. Habermas, "The Public Sphere: An Encyclopaedia Article (1964)," 49–55.

24. Phillip Seib, "The New Arab World Requires New Public Diplomacy," *The Huffington Post* [article online] http://www.huffingtonpost.com/philip-seib /the-new-arab-world-requir_b_838111.html.

25. Hauser, *Vernacular Voice*, 40.

26. See R. S. Zaharna, "Mapping out a Spectrum of Public Diplomacy Initiatives: Information and Relational Communication Frameworks," in *Routledge Handbook of Public Diplomacy*, ed. Phillip Taylor and Nancey Snow (New York: Routledge), 86–100; see also R. S. Zaharna, "Bridging Cultural Differences: American Public Relations Practices & Arab Communication Patterns," *Public Relations Review*, 21 (1995): 241–255.

27. See Jan Melissen, "The New Public Diplomacy between Theory and Practice," in *The New Public Diplomacy: Soft Power in International Relations*, ed. Jan Melissen (New York: Palgrave Macmillan, 2007), 10–11.

28. Phillip Seib, "The New Arab World Requires New Public Diplomacy," *The Huffington Post* [article online] http://www.huffingtonpost.com/philip-seib /the-new-arab-world-requir_b_838111.html.

29. USC Canter on Public Diplomacy, *What is Public Diplomacy?* [article online] http://uscpublicdiplomacy.org/index.php/about/what_is_pdf.

30. Ibid.

31. Melissen, "The New Public Diplomacy: Between Theory and Practice," 11.

32. Amelia Arsenault, "Public Diplomacy 2.0," in *Toward a New Public Diplomacy: Redirecting U.S. Foreign Policy*, ed. Phillip Seib (New York: Palgrave Macmillan, 2009), 142.

33. Joseph S. Nye, "The New Public Diplomacy" [article online] http://www .project-syndicate.org/commentary/the-new-public-diplomacy.

34. Daryl Copeland, *Guerrilla Diplomacy: Rethinking International Relations* (Colorado: Lynne Rienner Publishers, 2009), 205.

35. Ibid., 206.

36. Shaun Riordan, "Dialogue-based Public Diplomacy: a New Foreign Policy Paradigm," in *The New Public Diplomacy: Soft Power in International Relations* ed. Jan Melissen (New York: Palgrave Macmillian, 2007), 182.

37. Ibid.

38. Jennifer A. Marshall and Thomas F. Farr, "Public Diplomacy in an Age of Faith," in *Toward a New Public Diplomacy: Redirecting U.S. Foreign Policy,* ed. Philip Seib (New York: Palgrave Macmillan, 2009), 204.

39. Ibid., 204.

40. Ibid., 210–211.

41. Ibid., 210.

42. Joseph S. Nye Jr., "Making of Great Communicators," in *The Korea Times,* August 12, 2009.

43. James Notter and Louise Diamond, "Building Peace and Transforming Conflict: Multi-track Diplomacy in Practice," *Occasional Paper—The Institute for Multi-track Diplomacy,* 7 (October 1996): 6–8; Louise Diamond and Ambassador John McDonald, *Multi-Track Diplomacy: A Systems Approach to Peace.* 3rd ed. (Connecticut: Kumarian Press, 1996).

44. Notter and Louise Diamond, "Building Peace and Transforming Conflict: Multi-track Diplomacy in Practice," *Occasional Paper—The Institute for Multi-track Diplomacy,* 7 (1996): 14.

45. Ibid, 15.

46. Notter and Diamond, "Building Peace and Transforming Conflict," 16–17.

47. Louise Diamond and Ambassador. John McDonald, *Multi-Track Diplomacy: A Systems Approach to Peace,* 3rd ed. (Connecticut: Kumarian Press, 1996), 33.

48. Madeline Albright and Bill Woodward, *The Mighty & The Almighty: Reflections on Power, God, and World Affairs* (London: Macmillan, 2006), 64.

49. Ibid., 64–65.

50. Ibid., 65.

51. Albright, *The Mighty and the Almighty,* 64–72.

52. Walter A. McDougall "Religion in Diplomatic History," *Orbis,* 6 (1998) [article online]; available from http://www.unc.edu/depts/diplomat/archives_roll/2001_10–12/mcdougall_religion/mcdougall_religion.html.

53. Ibid., 72.

54. Ibid., 73.

55. Ibid., 73.

56. Ibid., 16.

57. See, Albright, *The Mighty and the Almighty,* 76.

58. Johnston and Cox, "Faith-based Diplomacy and Preventive Engagement," 16–18.

59. Scott R. Appleby, "Retrieving the Missing Dimension of Statecraft: Religious Faith in the Service of Peacebuilding," in *Faith-Based Diplomacy: Trumping Realpolitik,* ed. Douglas Johnston (Oxford: University Press, 2003): 231-258.

4 Distorting the Process

1. See Esther Kaplan, *With God on Their Side: George W. Bush and the Christian Right* (New York: New Press, 2005); see also, Mark J. Rozell and Gleaves Whitney ed., *Religion and the Bush presidency* (New York: Palgrave Macmillan, 2007).

2. George W. Bush, "Address to a Joint Session of Congress and the American People (September 20, 2011)" in *Understanding the War on Terror*, ed. James F. Hoge Jr. and Gideon Rose (New York: W. W. Norton & Company, 2005), 185.

3. Fareed Zakaria, "Why Do They Hate Us?" in *Understanding the War on Terror*, ed. *James F. Hoge Jr. and Gideon Rose* (New York: W.W. Norton & Company, 2005), 116.

4. George W. Bush, "Address to a Joint Session of Congress and the American People (September 20, 2011)," 184.

5. Ibid., 184–185.

6. George W. Bush, "Address to a Joint Session of Congress and the American People (September 20, 2011)," 185.

7. See Melvin Gurtov, *Superpower on Crusade: The Bush Doctrine in U.S. Foreign Policy* (Boulder, CO: Lynne Rienner Publishers, 2006), 35.

8. The Project for a New American Century, "Statement of Principles" [document online] http://www.newamericancentury.org/.

9. Charles Krauthammer, "The Unipolar Moment," *Foreign Affairs* no. 1 (1990): 29, 33.

10. Ibid., 30–31; See also Charles Krauthammer, "The Unipolar Moment Revisited," *The National Interest* (Winter 2002/2003): 5–17.

11. William Kristol and Robert Kagan, "Toward a Neo-Reaganite Foreign Policy," *Foreign Affairs*, no. 4: (1996): 18–32; See also Thomas Donnelly, *Rebuilding America's Defenses: Strategy, Forces and Resources for a New Century* (2001) [document online]; available from *www.newamericancentury.org/RebuildingAmericasDefenses.pdf*.

12. Krauthammer, "The Unipolar Moment," 30–31.

13. Gurtov. *Superpower on Crusade: The Bush Doctrine in US Foreign Policy*, 36.

14. Ibid., 36.

15. See, Stephen Mansfield, *The Faith of George W. Bush* (New York: Penguin Books, 2003); Mark J. Rozell and Gleaves Whitney, *Religion and the Bush Presidency* (New York: Palgrave Macmillan, 2007); Esther Kaplan, *With God on Their Side: How Christian Fundamentalists Trampled Science, Policy, and Democracy in George W. Bush's White House* (New York: New Press, 2004).

16. Richard L. Pace, *The Role of Religion in the Life and Presidency of George W. Bush*, USAWC Strategy Research Project (Carlisle Barracks: US Army War College, 2004).

17. See, George W. Bush, *A Charge to Keep: My Journey to the White House* (New York: Perennial, 2001).

18. See, Bruce Lincoln, "Bush's God Talk," in *Political Theologies: Public Religion in a Post-Secular World*, ed. Hent De Vries and Lawrence E. Sullivan (New York: Fordham University Press, 2006), 269.

19. George W. Bush, *A Charge to Keep*, 229–230.

20. See, George W. Bush, "Compassionate Conservatism," *Vital Speeches of the Day*, 66 (2000): 642–646; Marvin N. Olasky *Compassionate Conservatism: What It Is, What It Does, and How It Can Transform America* (New York: Free Press, 2000).

21. George W. Bush, "Remarks on Compassionate Conservatism in San Jose, California" [speech online] http://www.presidency.ucsb.edu/ws/index.php?pid=62868#axzz1uKytXmjl.

22. Naomi Schaefer Riley, "Mr. Compassionate Conservatism," *Wall Street Journal*, October 21, 2006.

23. Bruce Lincoln, "Bush's God Talk," 272.

24. Ibid., 275

25. Manuel Perez-Rivas, *Bush Vows to Rid the World of Evil Doers* (CNN September 16, 2001) [article online]; available from http://archives.cnn.com/2001/US/09/16/gen.bush.terrorism/ accessed August 20, 2009.

26. James Carroll, *The Bush Crusade* [article online]; available from http://www.thenation.com/doc/20040920/carroll.

27. See, Charles Babington, *Bush: US Must Rid the World of Evil* (September 14, 2001) Washington Post [article online]; available from http://www.washingtonpost.com/ac2/wp-dyn?pagename=article&node=&contentId=A30485-2001Sep14.

28. See Mark Jurgensmeyer, *Terror in the Mind of God* (Berkeley: University of California Press, 2003), 148–166.

29. Ewen MacAskill, *George Bush: God Told Me to End the Tyranny in Iraq* [article online]; available from http://www.guardian.co.uk/world/2005/oct/07/iraq.usa.

30. Bruce Lincoln, "Bush's God Talk," 273.

31. See The Project for a New American Century, "Statement of Principles" [document online] http://www.newamericancentury.org/.

32. Ibid.

33. Ibid.

34. Melvin Gurtov, *Superpower on Crusade: The Bush Doctrine in US Foreign Policy* (Boulder, CO: Lynne Rienner Publishers, 2006); 37.

35. Charles Krauthammer, "The Unipolar Moment," *Foreign Affairs* 1 (1990): 23–33, Charles Krauthammer, "The Unipolar Moment Revisited," *The National Interest* (Winter 2002/2003): 5–17; William Kristol and Robert Kagan, "Toward a Neo-Reaganite Foreign Policy," *Foreign Affairs*, no. 4: (1996):18–32.

36. George W. Bush, *The National Security Strategy of the United States of America September 2002* (New York: Morgan James Pub, 2009). See Brad Roberts, *American Primacy and Major Power Concert: A Critique of the 2002 National Security Strategy* (Alexandria: Institute for Defense Analyses, 2002).

37. George Bush, *The 2002 National Security Strategy* [document online] available from http://georgewbush-whitehouse.archives.gov/nsc/nss/2006/print/sectionV.html.

38. Irwin Stelzer, *The Necon Reader* (New York: Grove Press, 2004), 81.

39. *The National Strategy to Combat Weapons of Mass Destruction* [document online] available from http://www.fas.org/irp/offdocs/nspd/nspd-wmd.pdf.

40. Ibid.

41. The 2002 CIA and National Intelligence Estimate reports concluded that neither country, Iraq or Iran, posed a nuclear threat; and nor did Iraq have WMDs, as implied by US President George W. Bush in his January 29, 2002 State of the Union Address; see Central Intelligence Agency, *The Comprehensive Revised Report with Addendums on Iraq's Weapons of Mass Destruction: Duelfer Report*, (September,

2004); National Intelligence Estimate, *"Iran: Nuclear Intentions and Capabilities"* (November 2007).

42. *The National Strategy to Combat Weapons of Mass Destruction*, 4.

43. Ibid., 5.

44. George W. Bush, *The National Security Strategy 2006* [document online] available from http://www.strategicstudiesinstitute.army.mil/pdffiles/nss.pdf accessed August 20, 2009.

45. See Jonathan Monten, "The Roots of the Bush Doctrine: Power, Nationalism, and Democracy Promotion in US Strategy," *International Security*, 29 (2005): 112–156.

46. Ibid., 112–156.

47. Ibid., 112.

48. Joshua Micha Marshall, "Remaking the World: Bush and the Neoconservatives," *Foreign Affairs*, 82 (November/December 2003): 142.

49. Liora Danan and Alice Hunt, *Mixed Blessings: US Government Engagement with Religion in Conflict-Prone Settings* (Washington: CSIS Press, 2007), 39.

50. Ibid., 41.

51. Ibid., 41.

52. Ibid, 44.

53. Bryan Hehir, "Religion, Realism and Just Intervention," in *Liberty and Power: A Dialogue on Religion & US Foreign Policy*, ed. E. J. Dionne, Jean Bethke Elshtain and Kayla Drogosz (Washington: Brooking Institute Press, 2004), 13.

54. Barry Rubin, "Religion and International Affairs," in *Religion the Missing Dimension of Statecraft*, ed. Douglas Johnston and Cynthia Sampson (Oxford: Oxford Press, 1994), 20.

5 Marketing the American Brand

1. Office of International Religious Freedom [online website]; available from www.state.gov/g/drl/irf/.

2. Liora Danan and Alice Hunt, *Mixed Blessings: US Government Engagement with Religion in Conflict-Prone Settings* (Washington: CSIS Press, 2007), 12.

3. H. R. 808—110th Congress (2007): Department of Peace and Nonviolence Act, *GovTrack.us (database of federal legislation)* [article online]; available from http://www.govtrack.us/congress/billtext.xpd?bill=h110–808.

4. Colin L. Powell, *Secretary Colin Powell's State Department: An Independent Assessment* (Washington, DC: Foreign Affairs Council, 2004), v.

5. Ibid., 1–2.

6. R. S. Zaharna offers an early analysis of this problem years before 9/11. See R. S. Zaharna, "Bridging Cultural Differences: American Public Relations Practices & Arab Communication Patterns," *Public Relations Review*, 21 (1995): 241–255.

7. U. S. Government Accountability Office (GAO), Report to the Chairman, Subcommittee on Science, the Departments of State, Justice and Commerce and Related Agencies, House Committee on Appropriations, U.S. *Public Diplomacy:*

State Department Efforts to Engage Muslim Audiences Lack Certain Communication Elements and Face Persistent Challenges, GAO-06–535 (May 2006), 11.

8. Liam Kennedy and Scott Lucas, "Enduring Freedom: Public Diplomacy and U.S. Foreign Policy," *American Quarterly*. 2 (2005):320; Scott Lucas and Ali Fisher, *Trials of Engagement: The Future of U.S. Public Diplomacy* (Leiden: Martinus Nijhoff Publishers, 2011).

9. GAO, Report to the Chairman, US *Public Diplomacy: State Department Efforts to Engage Muslim Audiences Lack Certain Communication Elements and Face Persistent Challenges*, 11.

10. Ibid., 12.

11. Liora Danan and Alice Hunt, *Mixed Blessings*, 16; see also, Elliott Colla and Chris Toensing, "Never Too Soon to Say Goodbye," *Middle East Report Online*, (September 2003), [online article]; available from http://www.merip.org/mero/interventions/colla_interv.html.

12. GAO, Report to the Chairman, US *Public Diplomacy: State Department Efforts to Engage Muslim Audiences Lack Certain Communication Elements and Face Persistent Challenges*, 4.

13. Simon Anholt and Jeremy Hildreth, *Brand America: The Making, Unmaking and Remaking of the Greatest National Image of All Time* (London: Marshall Cavendish Business, 2010), 24–25.

14. Jan Melissen, "The New Public Diplomacy between Theory and Practice," in *The New Public Diplomacy: Soft Power in International Relations*, ed. Jan Melissen (New York: Palgrave Macmillian, 2007), 20.

15. Ibid., 20.

16. Gyorgy Szondi, "Public Diplomacy and Nation Branding: Conceptual Similarities and Differences," *Clingendael* (2008): 16.

17. Charlotte L. Beers, "American Public Diplomacy and Islam" (speech presented at the hearing before the US Committee on Foreign Relations, Washington, DC, February 27, 2003), 3.

18. Ibid., 4.

19. See R. S. Zaharna, *Battle to Bridges*, 73–91,115–133.

20. Giles Scott-Smith, "Exchange Programs and Public Diplomacy," *The Routledge Handbook of Public Diplomacy*, ed. Nancy Snow and Phillip M. Taylor (New York: Routledge, 2009), 50.

21. U. S. Department of State, "Major Accomplishments 2005–2007," *Office of Public Diplomacy & Public Affairs*, (Washington, DC: July 2008),14.

22. Ali S. Wyne, "Public Opinion and Power," *The Routledge Handbook of Public Diplomacy*, ed. Nancy Snow and Phillip M. Taylor (New York: Routledge, 2009), 39.

23. Karen Hughes, "Foreign Press Center Briefing: Outreach to the Muslim World," *U.S. Department of State* (June 27, 2007).

24. Ibid.

25. The US Government Accountability Office Report to Congressional Requesters, *Middle East Partnership Initiative Offers Tools for Supporting Reform, but Project Monitoring Needs Improvement*, GAO-05–711 (August 2005), 6.

26. Ibid., 14.
27. Steven R. Weisman *Saudi Women Have Message for US Envoy* [article online] available from http://www.nytimes.com/2005/09/28/international/middleeast /28hughes.html?ex=1187409600&en=253f58b29eb5383f&ei=5070.
28. Ibid.
29. Steven R. Weisman *Turkish Women, Too, Have Words with US Envoy (On Iraq War)* [article online]; available from http://www.nytimes.com/2005/09/29/inter national/europe/29hughes.html.
30. The US Department of State, "Major Accomplishments 2005–2007," 21.
31. Karen P. Hughes, "Encouraging Inter-faith Dialogues and Conversations between Cultures," *Presentation to the UN High Level Dialogue on Inter-religious and Intercultural and Cooperation for Peace* (October 4, 2007) [article online]; available from http://2001–2009.state.gov/r/us/2007/93259.htm.
32. Ibid.

6   Shifting the Tide

1. See, Tim J. Wise, *Between Barack and a Hard Place: Racism and White Denial in the Age of Obama* (San Francisco: City Light Books, 2009); see also, Richard Wolffe, *Renegade: The Making of a President* (New York: Crown Publishing, 2009).
2. Barack Obama, *The Blueprint for Change: Barack Obama's Plan for America* [online document]; available from www.barackobama.com/pdf/ObamaBlueprintForChange. pdf.
3. Ibid.; see also Scott Lucas, (April 15, 2009) *US-Iran Engagement: Washington to Drop Nuclear Precondition on Talks?* [article online] available from http://enduringamerica .squarespace.com/april-2009/2009/4/15/us-iran-engagement-washington-to -drop-nuclear-precondition-o.html.
4. Deborah P. Atwater, "Senator Barack Obama: The Rhetoric of Hope and the American Dream," *Journal of Black Studies*, 38, No. 2 (2007): 121–129; Barack Obama, "The World Beyond our Borders," *The Audacity of Hope: Thoughts on Reclaiming the American Dream* (New York: Vintage Books, 2006), 320–382.
5. Report of the Leadership Group on U.S.-Muslim Engagement, *Changing Course: A New Direction for US Relations with the Muslim World* [online document] available from http://www.sfcg.org/programmes/us/pdf/Changing%20Course.pdf.
6. See US Government Accountability Office, "U.S. public diplomacy interagency coordination efforts hampered by the lack of a national communication strategy : report to the Chairman, Subcommittee on Science, State, Justice, and Commerce, and Related Agencies, Committee on Appropriations, House of Representatives," (2005) [document online]. www.gao.gov/new.items/d05323. pdfv.
7. US Government Accountability Office, "U.S. Public Diplomacy: State Department Efforts to Engage Muslim Audiences Lack Certain Communication Elements and Face Significant Challenges" (May 2006) [document online] available from www.gao.gov/new.items/d06535.pdf.

8. U.S.-Muslim Engagement Project, Search for Common Ground (Organization); Consensus Building Institute et al., *Changing Course A New Direction for US Relations with the Muslim World* (Washington, DC: US-Muslim Engagement Project, 2008), 4–6.

9. Barack Obama, *President Barack Obama's Inaugural Address* [transcript online] available from http://www.whitehouse.gov/blog/inaugural-address/.

10. Hisham Melhem (January 27, 2009) *President Gives First Interview since Taking Office to Arab TV: "Obama Tells Al Arabiya Peace Talks Should Resume"* [online transcript] available from http://www.alarabiya.net/articles/2009/01/27/65087.html.

11. See, John Esposito, (January 28, 2008) *Obama and the Muslim World: Building a New Way Forward* [article online] available from www.huffingtonpost.com/ . . . /obama-and-the-muslim-worl_b_160392.

12. See, Hillary Rodham Clinton, *Nomination Hearing to be Secretary of State* (January 13, 2009) [online transcript] available from http://www.state.gov/secretary /rm/2009a/01/115196.htm.

13. Joseph S. Nye, *The Power to Lead* (Oxford: Oxford University Press, 2008); Joseph S. Nye, *Soft Power: The Means to Success in World Politics* (New York: Public Affairs Press, 2004).

14. Richard L. Armitage and Joseph S. Nye, eds. *CSIS Commission on Smart Power: A Smarter, More Secure America* (Washington, The CSIS Press, 2007); Document [available online] http://www.csis.org/files/media/csis/pubs/071106_csissmart powerreport.pdf.

15. Ibid., 5.

16. Ibid., 5.

17. US Department of Homeland Security, (January 2008) *Terminology to Define the Terrorist: Recommendations from American Muslims* (Washington, D.C., DHS) [Document online] www.investigativeproject.org/documents/misc/126.pdf.

18. United States, "The National Security Strategy of the United States of America 2010" http://www.whitehouse.gov/sites/default/files/rss_viewer/national_security _strategy.pdf.

19. Ibid., 11–12.

20. Appleby, R. Scott, Richard Cizik, and Thomas Wright. *Engaging Religious Communities Abroad A New Imperative for U.S. Foreign Policy* (Chicago: Chicago Council on Global Affairs, 2010), 55–78.

21. United States, *Swearing-in Ceremony for Frarah Pandith Special Representative to Muslim Communities* (September 15, 2009) [article online] available from http:// www.state.gov/secretary/rm/2009a/09/129209.htm.

22. Michael G. Mullen, "Strategic Communication: Getting Back to Basics" (August 28, 2009) [article online] available from http://www.foreignpolicy.com /articles/2009/08/28/strategic_communication_getting_back_to_basics.

23. Jenifer Logan, "Muslim Engagement: The Obama Administration's Approach" (July 27, 2009) [audio online] available from www.washingtoninstitute.org /templateC05.php?CID=3096.

24. Rami G. Khouri, "Sensible US Courage and Hapless US Imbecility," *Agence Global* (August 31, 2009).

25. Heather E. Harris, Kimberly R. Moffitt, and Catherine R. Squires, et al. *The Obama Effect: Multidisciplinary Renderings of the 2008 Campaign* (Albany: State University of New York Press, 2010).

26. National Public Radio, "Transcript: Barack Obama's Speech on Race" (May 18, 2008) [transcript online] available from http://www.npr.org/templates/story /story.php?storyId=88478467.

27. Nancy Snow, "The Death of Public Diplomacy Has Been Greatly Exaggerated," in *Perspectives,* (November 2009), 1.

28. See Nancy Snow, *Persuader-in-chief: Global Opinion and Public Diplomacy in the Age of Obama* (Michigan: Nimble Books).

29. Scott Wilson, "Saudi king Greets Obama on eve of President's Address" (June 4, 2009) [article online] available from http://www.boston.com/news/world/middleeast /articles/2009/06/04/king_abdullah_welcomes_obama_in_saudI_arabia/

30. Stephen R. Grand, "Obama's Four Challenges" (May 29, 2009) [article online] available from http://www.brookings.edu/opinions/2009/0529_cairo_speech _grand.aspx.

31. The White House, "Remarks by the President on a New Beginning" (June 4, 2009) [transcript online] available from http://www.whitehouse.gov/blog /NewBeginning.

32. Ibid.

33. Ibid.

34. Ibid.

35. Greg Carlstrom, "Scorecard: Obama since Cairo" (November 10, 2010) available from http://www.aljazeera.com/news/middleeast/2010/11/2010119947466214. html.

36. Jayshree Bajoria, "The Taliban in Afghanistan" (October 6, 2011) available from http://www.cfr.org/afghanistan/taliban-afghanistan/p10551.

37. See, Ahmed Rashid, *Taliban: Militant Islam, Oil, and Fundamentalism in Central Asia* (New Haven, CT: Yale University Press, 2000).

38. Jayshree Bajoria and Greg Bruno, "Al-Qaeda" (August 29, 2011) available from http://www.cfr.org/terrorist-organizations/al-qaeda-k-al-qaida-al-qaida /p9126; see also, Bruce O Riedel, *The Search for Al Qaeda: Its Leadership, Ideology, and Future* (Washington, DC: Brookings Institution Press, 2008).

39. Missy Ryan, "Exclusive: Secret U.S., Taliban Talks Reach Turning Point" (December 19, 2011) available from http://www.reuters.com/article/2011/12/19 /us-usa-afghanistan-idUSTRE7BI03I20111219.

40. Josh Rogin, "Taliban Gitmo Deal is Swap for Westerner" (March 12, 2012) available from http://thecable.foreignpolicy.com/posts/2012/03/13 /exclusive_taliban_gitmo_deal_is_swap_for_a_westerner

41. United States, "The National Security Strategy of the United States of America 2010" http://www.whitehouse.gov/sites/default/files/rss_viewer/national_security _strategy.pdf.

42. U.S. Interagency Policy Group, "White Paper of the Interagency Policy Group's Report on U.S. Policy toward Afghanistan and Pakistan" (March 2009) available

from http://www.whitehouse.gov/assets/documents/Afghanistan-Pakistan _White_Paper.pdf.

43. Ashley J. Tellis, *Reconciling With the Taliban?: Toward an Alternative Grand Strategy in Afghanistan* (Washington, DC: Carnegie Endowment, 2009), v.

44. Ibid., 2.

45. Giles Dorronsoro, *Fixing A Failed Strategy in Afghanistan* (Washington, DC: Carnegie Endowment, 2009), 7.

46. Ashley Tellis, "2014 and Beyond: U.S. Policy Towards Afghanistan and Pakistan Part 1" (November 3, 2011) available from http://www.carnegieendowment.org /files/1103_testimony_tellis.pdf.

47. Ashley Tellis, "Negotiations Cannot Solve Afghanistan's Problems" (November 3, 2011) available from carnegieendowment.org/2011/11/03/negotiations-canno t.../8khk.

48. Christopher Clary, *The United States and India: A Shared Strategic Future* (Washington, DC: Council on Foreign Relations Publishing, 2011), 3.

7 Considering a Corps of Specialists

1. See University of Southern California Faith Diplomacy Initiative, [definition online] http://uscpublicdiplomacy.org/index.php/research/project_detail/faith _diplomacy_religion_and_global_publics/.

2. Ibid.

3. See Kenneth M. Pollack, *The Arab awakening: America and the Transformation of the Middle East* (Washington, DC: Brookings Institution, 2011); see also John R. Bradley, *After the Arab Spring: How the Islamists Hijacked the Middle East Revolts* (New York: Palgrave Macmillan, 2012).

4. Clay Shirky,, "The Political Power of Social Media: Technology, the Public Sphere, and Political Change" [article online] http://www.gpia.info/files/u1392 /Shirky_Political_Poewr_of_Social_Media.pdf.

5. "Twitter, Facebook and YouTube's role in Arab Spring (Middle East uprisings)" [article online] http://socialcapital.wordpress.com/2011/01/26/twitter-facebook -and-youtubes-role-in-tunisia-uprising/.

6. Greg Miller, "Senators Question Intelligence Agencies' Anticipation of Egypt Uprising," *Washington Post*, February 4, 2011.

7. Philip M. Seib, *Real-time Diplomacy: Politics and Power in the Social Media Era* (New York: Palgrave Macmillan, 2012).

8. Ibid., 41.

9. Ibid., 42

10. Michele Penner Angrist, "Morning in Tunisia: The Frustrations of the Arab World Boil Over", in *The New Arab Revolt: What Happened, What it Means, and What Comes Next,* ed. Council on Foreign Relations (New York: Council on Foreign Relations, 2011), 76–77.

11. Steven A. Cook, "The U.S.-Egyptian Breakup Washington," in *The New Arab Revolt: What Happened, What it Means, and What Comes Next*, ed. Council on Foreign Relations (New York: Council on Foreign Relations, 2011), 87.

12. Philip M. Seib, *Real-time Diplomacy*, 43

13. Tariq Ramadan makes a unique case on the many voices that shape the principles that define the Arab Spring. This is a defining argument that deserves consideration as US policymakers move forward to engage the Islamic Street. See Tariq Ramadan, *Islam and the Arab Awakening* (Oxford: Oxford University Press, 2012).

14. Edward N. Luttwak, "The Missing Dimension," in *Religion: The Missing Dimension of Statecraft*, ed. Douglas Johnston and Cynthia Sampson (Oxford: Oxford University Press: 1994).

15. Douglas Johnston, *Faith-based Diplomacy: Trumping Realpolitik* (Oxford: Oxford University Press, 2004), 24–25; See Douglas M. Johnston, "The Case for a Religion Attaché," *Foreign Service Journal* (February 2002).

16. Douglas Johnston, *Religion, Terror, and Error: U.S. Foreign Policy and the Challenge of Spiritual Engagement* (Santa Barbara: Praeger, 2011), 88.

17. Ibid., 85.

18. Ibid., 88.

19. Amy Belasco, ed. "Congressional Research Service: The Cost of the Iraq, Afghanistan, and Other Global War on Terror Operations Since 9/11," *CRS Report for Congress* (June 23, 2008).

20. Douglas M. Johnston, *Faith-based Diplomacy: Trumpeting Realpolitik* (Oxford, Oxford University Press, 2002), 24–25.

21. Douglas M. Johnston, "The Case for a Religion Attaché," *Foreign Service Journal* (February 2002), 36.

22. Johnston, *Religion, Terror and Error*, 88.

23. Arguably, Johnston's "Religion Attaché" proposal to improve US relations with predominantly religious audiences is the most undervalued post-9/11 recommendation. In working toward restoring relations with these audiences, he recommends that the State Department's bureaucratic framework might be upgraded in size to accommodate the activity of this new actor via four structural alternatives. *Option one* "Under this option, a Deputy Assistant Secretary for Religion (DASR) would be assigned to each of the six regional assistant secretaries serving under the Under Secretary for Political Affairs (whose title would be changed to 'Under Secretary for Political and Religious Affairs')." *Option two* "Another alternative, one that would further enhance the consideration of religious imperatives in State Department calculations, would e to establish an Assistant Secretary for Religious Affairs (ASRA) under the Under Secretary for Political and Religious Affairs." *Option three* "A third alternative for incorporating religious consideration in DOS decision-making would be to tie them specifically to the public diplomacy function." *Option four* "Yet another structural arrangement that might have merit would be to elevate and expand the scope of the existing Office of International Religious Freedom (OIRF) within the Bureau of Democracy,

Human Rights, and Labor to a stand alone bureau responsible for the oversight of all aspects of religious influence in the conduct of U.S. foreign policy." Douglas M. Johnston, Jr., *Religion, Terror, and Error: U.S. Foreign Policy and the Challenge of Spiritual Engagement* (Colorado: Praeger Publishing, 2011), 219–225.

24. See Liora Danan and Alice Hunt et al. *Mixed Blessings: U.S. Government Engagement with Religion*, 12.

8 Toward a Postsecular Communicative Framework

1. G. John Ikenberry and Anne-Marie Slaughter, eds., *Forging a New World of Liberty Under Law: US National Security in the 21st Century (Final Report of the Princeton Project on National Security)* [online document]; available from http://www.princeton.edu/~ppns/report/FinalReport.pdf.
2. Troy Dostert, *Beyond Political Liberalism: Toward a Post-Secular Ethics of Public Life* (Notre Dame: Notre Dame University Press, 2006), 180.
3. Ibid., 180.
4. Jürgen Habermas, "Religion in the Public Sphere," *European Journal of Philosophy*. 14 (2006): 15.
5. Jürgen Habermas, "Notes on a post-secular society," *Sign and Sight* [article online]; available from www.signandsight.com/features/1714.html/.
6. James Gordon Finalyson, *Habermas: A Very Short Introduction* (Oxford: Oxford University Press, 2005), 32. See Karl Bühler, *Theory of Language: The Representational Function of Language* (Amsterdam: J. Benjamin's Publishing, 1990).
7. Ibid., 33.
8. Ibid., 34.
9. Ibid., 94.
10. Habermas, *Reason and the Rationalization of Society*, 85.
11. Ibid., 87–88.
12. Ibid., 87. "With regard to ontological presuppositions, we can classify *teleological* action as a concept that presupposes *one* world, namely the objective world. The same holds for the concept of *strategic action*. Here we start with at least two goal-directed acting subjects who achieve their ends by way of an orientation to, and influence on, the decisions of other actors."
13. Ibid., 85.
14. Roger Bolton, "Habermas' Theory of Communicative Action and the Theory of Social Capital" [article online] available from http://www.williams.edu/Economics/papers/Habermas.pdf.
15. Habermas, *Reason and the Rationalization of Society*, 85.
16. Roger Bolton, "Habermas' Theory of Communicative Action and the Theory of Social Capital" (available from) www.williams.edu/Economics/papers/Habermas.pdf.
17. Habermas, 86.
18. Ibid.

19. Ibid., 94.
20. James Gordon Finlayson, *Habermas: A Very Short Introduction*, 34–39.
21. Habermas, *Reason and the Rationalization of Society*, 285.
22. W. Barnett Pearce, *Making Social Worlds: A Communication Perspective* (Oxford: Blackwell Publishing, 2007), 30.
23. Ibid., 30–31.
24. Ibid., 40–41.
25. Ibid., x–xvi.
26. W. Barnett Pearce, *Claiming Our Birthright: Social Constructionism and the Discipline of Communication*. Essay presented in conjunction with The National Communication Association and The Crooked Timbers Project (Albuquerque, New Mexico, August 1–4, 2006), 7.
27. W. Barnett Pearce, *Communication and the Making of Social Worlds* (Santa Barbara: Field Graduate University, date unknown), 2.
28. W. Barnett Pearce and Kimberly A. Pearce "Taking a Communication Perspective on Dialogue," in *Theorizing Difference in Communication Studies,* ed., R. Anderson and L.A. Baxter et. al. (Thousand Oaks: Sage Publications, 2003), 39–56.
29. Ibid., 39–56.
30. W. Barnett Pearce, *A Brief Introduction to "The Coordinated Managed of Meaning (CMM)"* [article online] available from http://www.russcomm.ru/eng/rca_biblio/p/pearce.shtml; see also Deborah Tannen, *The Argument Culture: Moving from Debate to Dialogue* (New York: Random House, 1998).
31. W. Barnett Pearce, *Making Social Worlds*, 40.
32. Ibid., 89.
33. Ibid., 46.
34. Ibid., 93.
35. W. Barnett Pearce, *Making Social Worlds*, 95.

Conclusion

1. United States Department of Defense Fiscal Year 2011 Budget Request, "Overview-FY2011 Request" [document online] available from http://comptroller.defense.gov/budget.html. "$548.9 billion for the [Pentagon's] base budget excludes costs related to overseas contingency operations [totalling 159.3 billion]. This is $18.2 billion higher than $530.7 billion enacted for FY 2010—an increase of about 3.4 percent." Considering the State Department's fiscal allocation, Deputy Secretary for Management and Resources, Jacob J. Lew, indicates State and USAID's, "total $52.8 billion is a $4.9 billion increase, $3.6 billion for programs in Afghanistan, Pakistan, and Iraq. War-related spending represents a 7.5 percent increase in overall spending, and funding that is not war-related grows by $1.3 billion, which is 2.7 percent above 2010 total spending." Jacob J. Lew, "President's Proposal for the FY 2011 State Department Budget" [document

online] available from http://www.state.gov/s/dmr/remarks/2010/136358 .htm.

2. Giles Scott-Smith, "Obama's Challenge: Curbing the Pentagon" (November 29, 2008) [article online] available from http://enduringamerica.com/2008/11/29/o bamas-challenge-curbing-the-pentagon/; See also Giles Scott-Smith, "There is No More Outside" (September 24, 2009) [article online] available from http://www.neoamericanist.org/there-no-more-outside; He insists, "The consistent under-funding of the State Department has led to a desperate shortage of trained embassy personnel, especially in languages, and a serious lack of morale. Meanwhile, under Bush the military establishment [took a lead role] in US diplomatic, public diplomacy, and assistance task across North Africa, the Middle East, Central and South Asia, and the Far East. In many regions the Pentagon is at the forefront in engaging with foreign public opinion, even though this remains, officially, the job of the State Department."

INDEX

CPSIA information can be obtained at www.ICGtesting.com
Printed in the USA
LVOW10*0728100614

389377LV00013B/326/P